D0204374

OLDER
FASTER
STRONGER

Also by Margaret Webb

Apples to Oysters: A Food Lover's Tour of Canadian Farms

OLDER FASTER STRONGER

What Women Runners Can Teach Us All
about Living Younger, Longer

Margaret Webb

RODALE.

Rodale books may be purchased for business or promotional use or for special sales.
For information, please write to:
Special Markets Department, Rodale, Inc., 733 Third Avenue, New York, NY 10017

Printed in the United States of America

Rodale Inc. makes every effort to use acid-free ♾, recycled paper ♻.

Book design by Elizabeth Neal

Library of Congress Cataloging-in-Publication Data is on file with the publisher

ISBN: 978-1-62336-169-3 paperback

Distributed to the trade by Macmillan

4 6 8 10 9 7 5 3   paperback

We inspire and enable people to improve their lives and the world around them.
rodalebooks.com

For those who showed me the way:

My mom,

my Ironman sister,

and the running sisterhood

CONTENTS

CHAPTER 1

SUPER-FIT ME

A YEAR AGO, at age 50, I set out on a journey to run my way into a younger self. Just as Henry David Thoreau set off for the wilds of Walden Pond to enter a solitary relationship with nature and understand how to live well, I wanted to enter a deeper relationship with my body and understand how to train it well. I wanted to see if I could run faster and stronger after 50, but more than that, I wanted to enter the second act of my life in the best shape of my life, even fitter than I was as a 20-year-old varsity athlete.

Being somewhat more compulsive than contemplative, I threw myself into this project as I would a race. I immersed myself in studies, picked the brains of leading researchers, and cajoled a team of experts into helping me reach peak conditioning. I also sought out mentors, athletes who have found ways to run strong and long into their 70s, 80s, and even 90s but are quite likely the least studied on the planet: the pioneers of the women's running boom. I tried to apply all that I learned to my own training and then, as the finale to my super-fit year, I tested myself on the world stage by competing in the half-marathon at the World Masters

Games in Turin, Italy, to see where I stood amongst some of the fittest 50-year-old women in the world.

I was not the same person at the start of that race as I was at the finish. When we run hard, we live fully in our bodies and often push ourselves beyond what we thought possible. We finish knowing more about ourselves and what we are capable of—in body, mind, spirit. And in fulfilling our potential in this world.

A race expands us.

In writing this book, I have been in a yearlong race with myself, and now I hardly recognize the runner or even the writer I was at the start. To borrow a line from Bob Dylan: "Ah, but I was so much older then. I'm younger than that now."

But let me take you back to the beginning of my super-fit year, when I was older, at least physiologically, and invite you to join me on this yearlong journey toward a younger, fitter self. It matters not whether you are a runner or do some other physical activity, whether you are older or younger, male or female. For it is my greatest hope that some of the lessons I have learned, the inspiration I have taken from the pioneers of the women's running boom, will help and inspire you to chart your own individual path to greater wellness. Because at the end of my super-fit year, having crossed over the threshold to age 51, I can tell you that the finish line opens to a glorious beginning: the possibility of an entire second act of life.

○　　●　　○　　●　　○　　●　　○

I CAN'T CLAIM that I awoke one morning in September 2013, halfway through my 50th year, suddenly charged up with the bright shiny goal of getting in the best shape of my life. My appetite for this challenge, for more fitness, *for more life,* has been building since I took up serious running.

I can remember *that* day—indeed, the exact moment I made that decision. My sister, Carol, planted that initial challenge in my head, and I can still feel, nearly a decade later, how it electrified and terrified me with about equal jolts.

She was 55 at the time, me a mere 42. With 13 years between us, we were not close growing up and had developed very different personalities and interests. Sports, for instance, weren't exactly Carol's thing, while I liked to think I was the athlete. We have two brothers, born between us, and at every opportunity, I teamed up with them to play hockey, football, and soccer—and to tease our older sister about being a former beauty queen, having won third place in a local contest at age 18. She was the beauty, and I was the brawn, the jock, the tomboy. As a teenager, she was a good enough swimmer to be a lifeguard and complete a 2-mile endurance swim at a summer festival but, after that, her daily workout amounted to little more than a brisk walk with the dogs and some cross-country skiing or cycling on weekends. Then Carol had something of her own fitness awakening at age 50 and started going to the gym, determined, finally, to shed the weight she had gained during two pregnancies. A few years later, she saw an advertisement for a mini-triathlon encouraging people to "try a tri"—and gave it a try. She finished second in her age group and was hooked.

Later that year, over lunch just before Christmas, she asked me if I wanted to run a half-marathon with her.

My impulse was to say no. But how could I say no? My sister is *13 years older* than I. *And the beauty queen was honing in on my territory.*

Yet the thought of running a half-marathon—I didn't even know how far one was at the time—seemed inconceivable, overwhelming, impossible. To explain how it boggled my mind, I'll start with my feet. They are flatter than two planks. Back then, I could not even stand on them for longer than 10 minutes without arch supports. Moving up to my head, I had no confidence that I could accomplish such a feat of endurance, even though I had stayed fairly active as an adult, at various times sailing and playing ice hockey, softball, and golf. Since the invention of orthotics (or rather my discovery of them in my late 20s), I even did a little jogging a couple of times a week, for 15 or 20 minutes at a gait I called my old lady's shuffle—fittingly, through a local graveyard; I was terrified of lifting my knees too high, going too far, or running too fast for fear the pounding on my plank feet would ruin my knees and somehow cripple me for life.

There was every reason to worry, for in the scant 5 feet and 1 inch between the top of my head and the bottoms of my fallen arches, I weighed, at various times in my life, as much as 140 pounds, which is about 20 pounds heavier than female Olympic weight lifters of my height and a full 40 pounds heavier than the first female Olympic gold medalist in the marathon, the 5-foot-2 Joan Benoit Samuelson. Suffice it to say, mine was not a runner's body. And horror of all horrors, I had developed a social smoking habit my sister didn't even know about (or perhaps she did), which was getting more social by the day. Oh, and I liked a drink now and again, preferably *now* and *again*.

My instinctive response to my sister's challenge was to admit defeat before even trying, to declare that I was well beyond my athletic prime and saw no chance of redemption.

But there was a third set of legs under the restaurant table on that fateful day, those of my 80-year-old mother. As my sister and I contemplated our first steps toward the half-marathon, my thoughts leapt to the last steps Mom had taken on "normal" legs, before she was struck with polio at age 25, when my sister was just 6 months old. Mom spent the next 9 months in a rehabilitation hospital, determined to prove wrong the doctors who said she would never walk again. She did walk, though with braces, then a fused ankle and a cane, and always with extreme effort and a terrible limp. She had a good leg and a bad leg, though when I was a kid I never knew which was which, as both were so horribly twisted, one from muscle wasting, one from overuse. Yet the sheer exertion that it took her just to put one foot in front of her, then heft the other one up to join it, did not stop her from having three more children, or from keeping a massive vegetable garden and several flower beds, all while carrying out the hard work of a farmwife: cooking and taking meals to men working in the fields, canning and preserving vegetables, cleaning the house, and hauling herself out to the car to drive us kids to sports and school events and music and swimming lessons while Dad was busy with the farm (which seemed like almost all of the time).

To compensate for her withered left leg, my mother resolved to keep the rest of her body strong. She rode a stationary bike, pushing forward on her good leg in an effort to work her heart and keep her weight in check. Winters, she swam laps at the community pool; summers, lengths of the pond on our farm. She kept up exercises she had learned in rehab, "working out" long before it became fashionable in the city, let alone among rural housewives. She rehabbed herself back from two breaks of her bad leg and a broken hip (after falling in the church parking lot, she dragged herself into the car and drove herself to the hospital).

When my father developed Parkinson's disease and dementia at age 50 and struggled to keep the black dogs of depression at bay, keep his balance when he walked, keep even the thoughts in his head, Mom kept him home and looked after him for 2 decades. A few years after Dad passed away, I took Mom on vacation to a health spa in Canada's Rocky Mountains, where she astonished me anew. In a water aerobics class, with women a decade or two younger than my mother's 80 years, Mom was easily the fittest.

She was the only one who could hoist herself up and out of the pool without using stairs or a ladder or even her legs to kick. She had a life force, a vitality, a vigor the rest could only marvel at. The other women suffered poor health and seemed deeply unhappy. Their knees and hips were bent or ruined from carrying too much weight. I saw them taking stock of my mother: her huge smile, the thrill she experienced in every physical moment of that exercise class in the water—the one medium in which she could move freely without use of her legs. And they looked embarrassed, as if just realizing that it was their inactivity, their neglect of their health, that had invited disability and even depression as inevitably as they aged.

As I write this, Mom is 88, still strong in will, still going to exercise classes, albeit in a wheelchair now, as her bad leg finally gave out. But she was right all those years ago—keeping her body functionally strong enables her now to lift herself from wheelchair to bed to bathtub to toilet and, therefore, to live somewhat independently in her own apartment at a retirement complex.

The example Mom set has inspired my sister and me our whole lives, to exercise enough to maintain at least some level of fitness—though neither of us could begin to comprehend our mother's tenacity, her determination, her sheer courage, until we took up serious training ourselves. Only when we had pushed ourselves beyond what we thought our bodies capable of and begged for the finish line could we begin to feel the gumption Mom must have mustered up every single day, pushing herself to just put one leg in front of her and pull the other one up beside it.

On the fateful day 8 years ago, with Mom sitting beside me and my beauty queen sister peering across the table at me, my sister's challenge translated in my mind in a way that could not have been more poignant: Could I not use my two perfectly good legs to train for a half-marathon? Of course I could. *Of course I would.*

Joining us on the challenge was Carol's daughter, Cindy, 29 at the time and an experienced runner, but also 2½ months pregnant with her second child. During the next 5 months, we ran through a particularly stormy, cold Canadian winter, each of us in a different city, each of us seeking the support of a running clinic and never missing a single mile in our training programs because we were terrified we would never complete the distance if we did. Then my sister, the 55-year-old phenom; I, the flat-footed wonder; and Cindy, my knocked-up niece, as I nicknamed us all, travelled to Canada's capital and ran the Ottawa half-marathon. We crossed the finish line together in a "pregnancy-adjusted" 2:23, as Cindy was 7½ months pregnant by then. But that effort neither dislodged her uterus nor sucked the oxygen from her baby's brain, as medical authorities had long threatened would happen if women ran. A month and a half later, Cindy gave birth to a very healthy baby boy, 2 ounces shy of 8 pounds. In the 2 years of training after, Cindy got faster and stronger, as often happens after a pregnancy, and ran a 3:43 marathon, coming within minutes of meeting her age group's qualifying standard for the Boston Marathon at that time.

What came next for my sister and me, what we would accomplish after that first half-marathon, was beyond anything either of us could ever have imagined.

Over the next 2 years, Carol trained her way into the body of a super-fit 19-year-old—or at least the biological equivalent of one, according to the health scales at her gym—and the beauty queen became an Ironman, completing that monster, full-length triathlon at age 57, in the same year she retired from teaching and took up a second career she could never have fathomed before, as a personal trainer.

I completed a second half-marathon that fall, not quite cracking the 2-hour mark as I had hoped, then relegated my running to

3-days-a-week maintenance mileage while I ate my way across Canada researching a book on local foods. I gained back a few pounds and reacquired a few habits, one of them that social smoking thing. I don't know how that happened—maybe the stress of my first national book tour, or the emptiness after that hoopla. Then, at age 48, staring down 50 and suddenly feeling time running out on all that I yet wanted to do and all the things I wanted to write, and fending off a depression that first arose in my teens with my father's dementia and still slithered back into my life during times of high anxiety, the idea of training for a marathon popped into my mind. I had never dreamed of doing a marathon. In fact, I had emphatically told my running friends that I would never run one. But suddenly the idea was there, and the challenge beckoned with such fierceness that I figured the marathon must have something to teach me about writing, about pushing back that dark mood, about life.

As I trained, some lessons that came to me were shocking: one, that a person can run a lot of miles while still smoking cigarettes. The few friends I did not hide my habit from teased relentlessly that I could finish my first marathon, spark up a butt on the finish line, and become the new poster girl for Marlboro. But later, that habit finally fell away for good, as did a good deal of weight, both physical and metaphysical. As my spirits lifted, then soared, I felt myself literally running my way out of a midlife malaise and into this realization: The more I ran, the younger I felt; running could keep me younger, longer.

My first marathon, the Washington, DC, Marine Corps Marathon, was glorious—well, glorious now that some years have passed since it left me in such wretched condition at the end, nausea pouring from both ends of me for nearly 12 hours after. The glory came in knowing that my suffering was the result of a rookie's mistakes—and I surely made them all. But my fitness level had brought me to the brink, oh so tantalizingly close to knowing that I had it in me to qualify for the most prestigious race that recreational runners can aspire to, the historic Boston Marathon. That drove me to train for a second attempt, and this time, wiser and stronger from 6 more months of training and even more determined, I did not simply qualify, I did so by running 16 minutes under the standard for my age group. Then a year later, a week after turning 50, I crossed that finish line in Boston, my hand raised triumphantly in the firm grasp of my close running pal Mary, who had also turned 50 that year.

Yes, what my sister and I have accomplished is extraordinary, yet the really extraordinary thing is that we do not consider *ourselves* extraordinary. We are but two sisters among tens of millions of women worldwide who have taken up running in the past 3 decades and accomplished amazing things.

It is important to ponder that for a moment, to marvel at all that we have achieved, given that the organized sport of running has been open to women for only a scant few decades. Men have been enjoying support and accolades for attempting marathons since at least 490 BC, when the messenger Pheidippides ran from a battlefield in Marathon to Athens to report a Greek triumph over the Persians, whereupon, according to legend, he promptly dropped dead. The first modern Olympic Games, held in Athens in 1896, celebrated the Pheidippides legend by making the marathon, considered the most challenging event in all of track and field, a marquee event—while barring women from competing in anything. However, one female athlete, Melpomene (and possibly another, Stamata Revithi, though they may have been one and the same person), completed the distance after being barred from the Olympic race. The International Women's Sports Federation rose up in defiance of the Olympics' exclusion of women and finally pressured the Games' organizers to include five women's events in 1928. The 800-meter race was the longest one women were allowed to run, though we were already proving we had the stuff to be superb distance athletes: Two years earlier, Gertrude Ederle had become the first woman to swim nearly 20 miles across the English Channel, breaking the men's record by 2 hours. In 1926, Violet Percy posted the first recorded time by a woman marathoner, 3:40:22, which would have placed her 21 minutes behind the last-place finisher in the men's Olympic marathon in 1928— though ahead of the 12 men who did not finish at all. But in 1928, after horrified spectators watched women competing to the edge of exhaustion in the 800, the Olympic committee promptly cut that middling distance event, a move pioneering marathoner and historian Nina Kuscsik says set women's running back 50 years.

While men gave themselves a considerable head start in the marathon, women have been quick to close the gap. In the early years of the sport, between 1908 and 1948, men lowered the world record by 29 minutes and 39 seconds, or 16.9 percent. In the 40 years after the official inclusion of women, starting with the New York Marathon in 1971, women improved their world-record time by 46 minutes and 17 seconds, or 25.5 percent. Now, across all running distances, the differential between men's world-record times and women's is about 10 percent. Can women close that gap? Does it matter? We bring other strengths to the sport, yet it's difficult to discuss women's performance without constantly comparing ourselves to men. But as the first woman to officially race the Boston Marathon so wisely put it, women are not better or worse but *different* athletes. "Men have been running the marathon for 2,500 years, women for only 40. We're just beginning to explore women's capability in the sport."

That astute observation came from Kathrine Switzer, who in 1967 pulled something of the same trick as Melpomene. At the time, women were banned from road races. Switzer defied convention and ran the Boston Marathon after registering for it under the name K. V. Switzer. She completed that marathon in 4 hours and 20 minutes, which includes the time she spent fighting off an enraged race director who tried to drag her off the course. After Boston, Switzer continued her trailblazing ways, running and volunteering with New York Road Runners to help open the New York City Marathon to women in 1971. Then, in 1978, she took a marketing position with cosmetics giant Avon with a determined focus to ignite a women's running boom around the world. Over the next decade, Switzer worked feverishly with Avon to launch, organize, and galvanize public support for some 400 women's events in 27 countries, generating the global participation needed to establish the women's marathon as an event at the Los Angeles Olympics in 1984.

In the short time since Joan Benoit Samuelson won that first Olympic gold, women have flocked to running, not only fueling a second massive running boom, but also turning the once solely male sport into a thing women do, and do pretty darn well. In 2012, there were a record 15.5 million road-race finishes in the United States (an increase of 80 percent since 2000), according to the nonprofit industry organization Running USA and 56 percent were posted by women. In every distance from the half-marathon down, women competitors now outnumber men, and women dominate the half-marathon, at 60 percent of all participants.

Judging by participation in major road races (few countries keep Running USA's meticulous statistics), the women's running boom continues to build around the world. In my country of Canada, women typically outnumber men in every road-race event from the half marathon down. Ditto for Australia. In the past few decades, women from Kenya and Ethiopia have, like their male counterparts, come to dominate elite distance running. Massive women-only races are common in Europe: About 40,000 women raise money for numerous charities by running the 10-K Flora Women's Mini Marathon, making it the largest single-day fundraising event in Ireland; the Austrian Women's Run in Vienna boasts 30,000 participants; La Parisienne has 28,000; and 18,500 start Berlin's Avon Women's 10-K run. Running is even catching on with women in Asia and the Middle East; Taipei's women's 10-K boasts 10,000 runners; the Dubai Women's 10-K attracts both a field of international elites and local recreational runners. Across the United States, women-only races are also surging in popularity. The Nike Women's Half Marathon in Washington, DC, attracts more than 15,000 runners. In 2011, there were 18 women's running events in the United States; by 2012, there were some 200. These are typically boisterous, hug-happy gatherings of the tribal sisterhood of runners, and moving celebrations of all the ways running has transformed women.

Yet women are also transforming the sport of running. George Sheehan, MD, philosopher king of the first running boom in the 1970s, when men hit the roads in cotton T-shirts and tube socks, wrote eloquent if often melancholic essays for *Runner's World* magazine and his seminal book *Running and Being,* in which he explored the lessons about self and life that come from pounding out solitary painful miles. Thankfully, one of those lessons was that the few women who were gutsy enough to run back then actually ran rather well; the men admired their grit and welcomed them, as men in few other male-dominated sports did. That support helped open the floodgates to women, and men have gained from our participation: Women have injected the loneliest of sports with a joyful and playful exuberance, a no-person-shall-be-left-behind camaraderie, and also a healthy dose of self-doubt that has served the sport rather well. Women like me who didn't believe we could run fast enough to race, didn't know how to train, and certainly did not believe we could run endless miles alone sought out support and knowledge, fueling a boom in running clubs, coaching, and clinics. And we invited our friends along on the journey. And in that way, we made running *fun*.

Take the five women I run with, ranging in age from 30 to 62. While training to run the Boston Marathon, we dubbed ourselves the Beaners, as in Boston baked beans. When I broached the idea of flying to Italy to compete in the half-marathon at the World Masters Games, they immediately rebranded themselves the Fagioli ("Beans" in Italian), offered themselves up as guinea pigs for my research, and immersed themselves in planning the vacation we would take after.

Always pressed for time, always multitasking, women like us have discovered that it is as easy to socialize during runs as it is over martinis. Women who felt they could not take time for their own health away from family and a multitude of other responsibilities found inspiration to do so by teaming up with friends and entering charity runs. Women's zeal to run for something greater than ourselves spurred races to develop charity fund-raising as a major component and establish clinics that have trained millions of new runners—men and women—to take up the challenge of tackling half- and full marathons for a cause.

The women's running boom in the United States was certainly aided by policy changes and, in 1972, by Title IX of the Education Amendments to the 1964 Civil Rights Act, which prohibits sex discrimination in educational programs at any school receiving federal funding. Although it doesn't require schools to allocate equal funding for boys' and girls' athletics, it does force them to support girls' programs to a similar degree, which ushered in a slew of opportunities for girls and women to pursue sports. Women also flocked to running after inspirational TV talk show host Oprah shed more than 70 pounds and ran the Washington,

DC, Marine Corps Marathon in 1994, proving to women that any shape of body can become a running body. And day by day, women have been inspired to take up the sport with a vengeance, as I was, by sisters and friends.

One of my running pals, Phyllis Berck, calls that incitement to run "the cubicle effect." A sports activist, organizer for the 1988 Calgary Winter Olympics, and now director of partnerships for the City of Toronto, Phyllis ran track as a teen and has been athletic all her life, but took up distance running—the half-marathon and marathon—in her mid-50s. At 61, she ran personal bests in both events in times that rank her among the fastest in her age group in the country. She is married to Bruce Kidd, a former Olympic middle-distance runner whose 18 national championship wins in the United States, Britain, and home country of Canada still incite awe. But Phyllis says that her finish times and string of first-place finishes hardly mattered to the co-workers, friends, and family members she has inspired to take up running over the years. Rather, they looked at her—fit, strong, and looking a decade younger than her years—and thought, *Maybe I should try this running thing. If she can run at her age, surely I can.* And that's all right by Phyllis.

In fact, we older women runners are thrilled by the effect we have on family and friends, even on complete strangers who see us streaking past them on city streets or in races, kicking the butts of less-trained 20- and 30-year-olds. The impact we have is not the same as that caused by young men and women running vigorously—people expect them to be strong. Even middle-aged and older men are assumed to have been doing sports since they were young pups, thereby explaining their power. Too often, people look at them in awe and think, *I can't do that.* But women 50, 60, 70, and beyond—supposedly the weakest adults—we feel eyes widen in astonishment, can almost hear the thoughts banging around in people's heads: *Wow, if they can do it. . . . If these old women can run, and with such speed and power and grace, then surely I can try.*

I don't mind that their thoughts shift immediately to their own fitness rather than celebrating ours, earned with the years of training we have put into strengthening our bodies. It is surely one of the greatest of the many legacies of the women's running movement that we would rather inspire people to join us than remain fans on the sidelines of fitness. Older women runners, in particular, understand this: We have all been there, unhappy with our bodies, depressed by our place in life, and wondering how on earth to take that first momentous, transformative step to wellness.

I always tell people who marvel at my running marathons that the marathon is easy compared to the challenge of starting training. By the time we reach that starting line, we have prepared our bodies and minds for the challenge, developed a hunger for it. For those who have been inactive for many years or are carrying more weight than they should or battling self-doubt, running the first mile is hard. That first mile is the true marathon. I say be patient and gentle with yourself, for that is what the body needs to continue from the first step to the even more important second step: keeping at it. When people seek my advice, I tell them to try walking as far as they can; when you find you can complete a mile, walk it as briskly as you can. When that becomes easy, jog for a few yards to the next streetlight, then for a city block. Take a break and walk awhile. Enjoy yourself. Celebrate your achievement! Then jog again, to gradually, very gradually, build up to running a mile. And when that becomes easy, add another. It is essentially the same formula experienced runners follow: Whatever limit you encounter, keep pushing against it. By doing this, you will have found, like many masters athletes have, a way to reach deep inside yourself, grasp the hands of your biological clock, and slow its forward rush.

It is a most wonderful paradox that I am learning during my brief running career as an adult that by moving faster, we slow aging. Masters athletes are proving that as much as 50 percent of age-related decline, maybe even 70 percent, is due to decon-ditioning—losing physical fitness by doing nothing or very little—rather than aging. When scientists probe the bodies of endurance athletes, they discover 80-year-olds with muscles and cardiac capacities akin to those of 20-year-olds.

And elite women masters runners (over the age of 35), especially, are turning in performances that elite runners decades younger are challenged to beat, forcing us to redefine not only aging, but also how long our so-called athletic prime can last. Consider the world record for my 50-plus age group in the marathon, the 2:31:05 set by the Ukraine's Tatyana Poz-dniakova. That time would have easily put her in the top half of women finishers in the London 2012 Olympics. Leading up to those games, 21 masters women qualified for the US Olympic Trials, compared to just one man of masters age. Some are seasoned marathoners, but many are women who took up run-ning later in life and discovered they had a talent for it. Training on fresher legs, these late starters may get even faster after 50.

Greg Wells, PhD, author of *Superbodies: Peak Performance Secrets from the World's Best Athletes* and a professor at the University of Toronto, believes that we can extend our athletic prime much longer than previously thought. "These are exciting times," he tells me. "We're just learning what the human body is capable of. Forty years ago, women weren't supposed to run mar-athons, and look what they have accomplished. Much of what we know is being rewritten. We have to throw out our preconceived notions about aging."

For women like me who came to running later and will never know what we might have achieved in our athletic prime, will never come close to Olympic glory, training so intensely may seem silly, yet an improved finish time matters as a measure of fitness, as a new limit that we can then push hard against. Because whether we run, walk, cycle, or do some other physical endeavor, it seems to be in pushing against that personal best, in trying to go faster and stronger, that we slow the biological ticking. Scientific dogma used to say that at 60, our bodies lost the ability to adapt to exercise. According to Wendy Kohrt, PhD—founder of IMAGE, Investigations in Metabolism, Aging, Gender, and Exercise, a research group at the University of Colorado—older adults figured there really wasn't any point to exercising. Now, says Kohrt, research as well as the performances of masters athletes show "that older people can adapt with the same relative improvements as healthy young adults—in bone density, aerobic capacity, muscle strength, and cardiovascular fitness in general."

Now I am about to test that hypothesis in the most dramatic way I can think of: by training to see just how much fitter, stronger, and faster I can get after 50.

CHAPTER 2

TRAINING SMARTER

A TEAM OF doctoral and master's students swarms about me in a shockingly bright lab, strapping my face into a ventilator contraption and then stuffing me into a vest packed with various thingamajigs that will feed my bodily statistics through some half-dozen wires and tubes to a nearby computer screen. Catching a glimpse of my masked face in a mirror, I can't decide if I look more like Hannibal Lecter or a futuristic Medusa with plastic snakes streaming down my back.

Standing at my right hand is Jason Vescovi, PhD, who holds aloft a gleaming silver needle and informs me that he will jab it into my index finger every 2 minutes while I run. I can hardly run away from him because the high-tech gadgetry tethers me to a treadmill. And, well, I did ask for this treatment.

The team is about to measure my life force, my vitality, my internal candle burning brightly (hopefully), or, in their scientific terminology, my max VO2 (the maximum amount of oxygen my body can use to make fuel), max HR (maximum heart rate), and lactate thresholds. To offer a translation somewhere between art and science, they are about to gauge the working capacity of my internal engine—lungs, heart, muscles—and tell me, with some

19

numerical precision, on which side of the precipice I stand, fitness-wise, at the age of 50.

To determine that, Vescovi, a leading expert in assessing the performance of elite female athletes, will run me on the treadmill, cranking up the speed every 2 minutes, until my heart maxes out and I can't run anymore.

I ask Vescovi if anyone has ever dropped dead during the test. Usually a rather serious guy, he flashes a somewhat maniacal grin and suggests that I not be the first.

On this glorious fall day, I have returned to the very building where I had my first extensive fitness test, conducted during my freshman year at the University of Toronto in 1981, when I was 19 years old and oblivious to just how quickly time was about to fly by. Back then I was no slouch fitness-wise, a good enough athlete to make the varsity ice hockey team as a rookie even though I was probably about 25 pounds overweight and had no idea how to train or eat properly. Still, I remember the tester telling me that my lungs and heart were small but highly efficient, and she pronounced me fitter than 90 percent of my peers.

For this latest, considerably more sophisticated test of my aerobic capacity, considered the key biomarker of physiological age, Greg Wells (the University of Toronto professor mentioned in Chapter 1) has offered up the use of his human physiology research lab, as well as advice as I attempt to become fitter after 50 than I was in my 20s as a varsity athlete. Wells, a leading authority on health and exercise, has advised Olympic athletes and coaches on training regimes and regularly appears on Olympic TV broadcasts to explain how elite athletes achieve exceptional performances.

Wells's particular specialty is studying human performance under extreme conditions, such as the cardiovascular systems of children suffering from cystic fibrosis (CF) and ultramarathoners running across South America and the Andes. He can get absolutely giddy talking about the power of exercise to improve the human body at any age and in almost any circumstance. In the case of kids with CF, a disease that attacks the lungs and severely compromises breathing to the point where some patients require lung transplants, he says parents often try to protect them from activities that make them breathe harder. But research shows that exercise can actually slow the decline in lung function by 37 percent compared to the decline in children with CF who do not exercise. As for the ultramarathoners, Wells has seen their bodies not only rapidly adapt to extreme conditions—from running through searing desert heat to the cold, thin air of 12,000-foot altitudes—but also, in one case, heal a sprained ankle while the ultramarathoner continued to run.

After hearing these stories, I feel a bit sheepish presenting myself to Wells with my particular challenge of running personal bests and getting fitter after 50. Yet, from the research I am gathering, it seems that aging also qualifies as an extreme condition that puts me up against quite a lot. Consider this sampling of obstacles.

- **MORE INJURIES:** According to a study of some 2,500 older athletes by researcher Vonda Wright, MD, the director of the Performance and Research Initiative for Masters Athletes and author of *Fitness after 40*, some 89 percent had experienced at least one sports-related injury since turning 50, and more than 50 percent had suffered more than one. Major problems occur where tendons connect with bones, which makes me all too average in this regard, as I have developed chronic bilateral hamstring enthesopathy and some lumbar neural tension. Translation of that medical mouthful: I have a major pain in the butt (both cheeks) resulting from repeatedly straining the tendons that connect my hamstrings and glutes. And apparently I am no ultramarathoner capable of healing myself on the run, as both my running coach and my sports physiotherapist have advised against intensifying my training until after my butt heals, making it rather difficult to ramp up my super-fit training.

- **DECLINING CARDIAC OUTPUT:** On average, the greatest amount of oxygen we can take in and pump to muscles declines at a rate of about 1 percent a year between ages 35 and 70. This decrease correlates roughly to the slowing finishing times of masters runners, whose performances typically drop off by 1 percent a year between ages 30 and 50 and by 2 percent between 50 and 75, and after that can fall off dramatically, by 6 to 8 percent a year. Not surprisingly, that decline in performance can zap motivation—if you can't get faster, what's the point of training so hard?

- **LOSS OF LUNG CAPACITY:** Maximum breathing capacity—the most air the lungs can take in over 1 minute—can decline by up to 40 percent between the ages of 20 to 70. For seniors, this capacity, or lack thereof, closely corresponds with what researchers call physiological functional capacity, which is the ability to carry out everyday tasks—say, whether you can walk, breathe, and carry a bag of groceries at the same time, and therefore live somewhat independently.

- **LOSS OF BALANCE:** From as early as age 25, our ability to balance begins to decline; after 65, the peripheral senses, brain signals, and vision functions that keep us balanced and generally upright become so impaired that one in three people will topple over just doing normal activities, like walking with a bag of groceries.

- **LOSS OF DEXTERITY AND FLEXIBILITY:** Muscles, ligaments, and tendons all become stiffer, turning into, as Wright describes them, something akin to dried-out rubber bands (contributing to the increased risks of injury and falling). Flexibility can decline by 6 percent in every decade after age 50, even if you're exercising regularly, as your connective tissue degrades; in addition, muscles lose contractile function and power, possibly more so in women than in men, according to muscle researcher Mark Miller, PhD, of the University of Vermont.

- **LOSS OF BONE DENSITY:** We achieve peak bone mass at age 30; after that, the quantity of bone cells can decline at a rate of 0.3 to 2 percent per year until the 40s. Menopause can accelerate this loss of density to more than 3 percent yearly in the 2 to 3 years before and 10 years after.

- **LOSS OF LEAN MUSCLE MASS:** Between ages 50 and 70, we can lose about 15 percent of our muscle mass each decade; after 70, it's more like 30 percent. What rushes in to replace lost lean mass is fat.

- **INCREASE IN FAT:** This gelatinous replacement for muscle can hit women particularly hard at menopause, as it did me. In the 4 months after turning 50, I somehow managed to pack on 8 pounds, putting me at 126 pounds—a tad beefy for a 5-foot-1 marathoner. What's even more astonishing is that those 8 pounds larded on while I was logging between 31 and 44 miles (50 to 72 kilometers) a week on a half-marathon training schedule and consistently following a healthy eating plan. As men lose muscle mass in middle age, they gain fat as well, but typically, men start out with 12 to 16 percent body fat at age 20, while women have 23 to 28 percent (which is a fantastic evolutionary trick that enables us to hole up in a cave and pump out children or withstand famine while simultaneously breastfeeding). By age 60, when a man's body fat reaches 19 to 26 percent—the range of a young woman's—a woman's body fat can soar to 28 to 38 percent, which is not so great when the reproductive need for that protective stockpile disappears. Worse, where we pack that fat becomes a big problem. Before menopause, we store it under the skin, in our thighs, hips, and arms. This makes it a great insulator, and perhaps even a protector of health, as demonstrated by younger women's lower risk of heart disease compared to men's. In contrast, men store their fat in the worst possible place: in their guts, between and around their organs. But after menopause, women tend to pack their greater stores of fat in that same dangerous place. And according to Robert Ross, PhD, of Queen's University in Kingston, Ontario, that "visceral" fat doesn't just sit in the gut benignly minding its own business. Oh, no, it makes its presence menacingly felt, spitting out hormones that may cause high triglycerides (types of fat in the blood), high blood sugar, high blood pressure, low HDL (the good cholesterol), and high LDL (the bad cholesterol), and possibly triggering metabolic syndrome, which significantly

increases the likelihood of developing type 2 diabetes, having a heart attack, and dying of that heart attack.

- **LOSS OF ESTROGEN:** Oh, and this is the biggie. I had no idea what an extraordinary, superheroine hormone I possessed until I began sweating it out in the human equivalent of tropical downpours every night. Male athletes looking for a competitive edge might do well to consider doping with estrogen. This wonder steroid not only regulates body temperature (when it's at adequate levels, that is) and helps our bodies retain more fluids in extreme conditions by sweating less, but also diminishes inflammation, stimulates muscle repair and regeneration, stores fat in good rather than bad places, offers pain protection during grueling marathons (or childbirth), preserves fitness for longer after a period of inactivity (such as childbirth), increases growth hormone and insulin responses to a single bout of sprinting, and even provides superior endurance by enabling us to burn a longer-lasting, more energy-dense, and readily available source of fuel—the fat that is packed under the skin rather than the dollop of carbohydrates that men store in muscles. Evidence: When Canadian researchers convinced a group of gutsy young men to be injected with estrogen before a bout of strenuous cycling, they burned fuel differently (becoming fat burners more than carb burners), sweated less, and had fewer postrace markers of muscle damage. Presumably, the experiment was too focused on the physical to measure if the young men also became more complex thinkers, which some researchers argue is yet another virtue of estrogen.

Now, just as I am realizing how great a role my precious estrogen played in getting me through more than 3,700 training miles (6,000 kilometers) for three marathons in the past 2 years, my superheroine hormone, my strength, my steel, my stamina, my everything, is almost drained from my system. As a postmenopausal woman, I now have about the same amount of the hormone circulating in my system as mere mortal men.

So I put this question to University of Toronto professor Wells (roughly in these words): "Do you think my attempt to become the fittest I have ever been in my life *after 50* is impossible, even insane?" I laugh as I say it, having convinced myself that it is certifiably so.

But he will utter no such thing. Rather, he argues that exercise can improve our bodies at any age, hailing it as the most powerful tool we have to forestall aging and extend the prime years of our lives as well as prevent and even treat just about every chronic disease that exists today. "If we had a drug that did what exercise did, it would be the biggest revolution ever and would be promoted all over the world and be hailed as the greatest achievement of humankind, when all you have to do is go out for a run or a walk."

Wells cites a raft of recent research proving that exercise can counteract just about every negative thing about aging that I dredged up. Indeed, tests of masters athletes in their 70s have revealed that their max VO2, muscle mass, muscle condition, and athletic performance can be similar to those of people in their 20s. "A lot of research now shows that training—aerobic, anaerobic, and strength—has effects on the human body at any age," he says. "At any age, you can improve the human body. Exercise can literally keep you young."

Wells contends that one of the most interesting developments in sports in the last 20 years has been the competitive performances

of older athletes, such as swimmer Dara Torres, who at 41 became the oldest swimmer ever to compete in the Olympics and still took home three silver medals from those 2008 Games. "Now we're seeing a 100-year-old man run marathons and an 80-plus-year-old woman complete an Ironman," says Wells. "The limits of human capabilities are being pushed. We can learn from these athletes. It's a really exciting time."

He then rattles off a half-dozen things I can do to improve my fitness and the quality of my life, if not extend it indefinitely. "We don't know how long we can prolong life, but we know absolutely how to improve the quality of life through exercise and nutritional strategies. For example, if you die at 85, why not have 84.9 great years and 1 bad week before dying? I believe we're going to look back on this time in 20 or 30 years and ask, 'Why did we not prescribe exercise to deal with the effects of aging?'"

I'm keen to take that medicine—and a goodly dose of it—because my end point is more likely to be 95 years or even older, given that my two grandmothers lived into their late 80s and early 90s and one great-grandmother came within days of celebrating her 101st birthday. If I can stay fit and robust into my 90s, I will be able to enjoy an entire second act of my adult life and writing career—a wonderful thought. If not, that's a whole lot of decades to put up with chronic pain and miserable health.

As for what dose I should take in order to stay fit into old age—to live younger, longer—Wells says that more exercise is almost always better than less, and that I should not be afraid of the stresses that marathon training puts on my body, which is something not all medical professionals agree with. "I believe training for a marathon is absolutely good for your health," contends Wells, "because it stresses the oxygen transport pathway; it puts pressure on your lungs, your heart, your blood, your muscles, inside your muscles, your brain, your nervous system. The stress stimulates your body to adapt and improve. Your body adapts as long as it has time to recover and you don't overtrain, get injured, lose sleep; as long as you're incorporating recovery, you'll improve."

"Recovery" is becoming my favorite training buzzword, as it refers to delicious things like sleep, rest days, massages, and a whole lot more that I will talk about later. Essentially, recovery is a major plank in a new approach to exercise that is especially appropriate for masters athletes: It's about training smarter rather than harder.

When Jason Vescovi measures my aerobic fitness at the University of Toronto lab, he, too, will help me master that smarter approach, by gathering numbers to pinpoint the three training zones I should be working out in to maximize the benefits of exercise and minimize the potential for overtraining and injury. Or, in other words, to get the most bang for my effort.

In Vescovi's current project, the Female Athletes in Motion study, the single largest of its kind, he uses GPS technology to measure the speeds and distances that soccer players travel during games and practices, from top youth leagues right up to professional women's soccer and international elites. With the information he collects, Vescovi can then recommend training protocols that will improve players' development and ultimately the performance of female athletes. His study has recently been extended to other team sports in which running is key—lacrosse, field hockey, and rugby.

That his research focuses on female athletes is rarer than you might think. Back when exercise physiologists could get away with being blatantly sexist (and it seems they still can), they deliberately left female athletes out of studies, claiming that hormonal fluctuations over a menstrual cycle threw in too many variables or that there were too few female athletes to draw from. It's true that a man's hormone levels remain constant through the prime years of his life, and that the amount of estrogen (and other sex hormones) coursing through a woman's system can swing wildly during each month, from lows during the early follicular phase to highs during ovulation and the luteal phase after. And the hormone does affect the cardiovascular system and hence performance: Generally, faster runs may seem easier during the low-estrogen (pre-ovulation) phase, when the body tends to burn carbs (or glycogen, as it's called when packed into muscle), while long, slower runs may seem easier during high-estrogen phases, when the body shifts to sparing glycogen and tends to burn fat. Yet, as Vescovi points out, estrogen fluctuates in a "predictable way" each month that researchers can certainly account for.

As for the argument that there are too few female subjects for studies, that really hasn't held true in the United States since 1972, with the passage of the Title IX legislation that leveled the playing field in school-sports funding and made female participation in sports soar. Nevertheless, many researchers still get away with saying that female athletes are just too complicated for their studies, though I would argue that it's far more likely they still consider us unworthy of their attention. Indeed, major journals still publish studies that include only male subjects, and their findings are widely reported in mainstream media. Yet, we can't just extrapolate results from studies of men and attribute them to women, whose body composition, hormones, metabolism, and socialization are all different. So in exercise science, what holds true for men can be wildly off for women (and even more so for older women) when it comes to everything from nutrition, training, recovery, coaching, and psychological approaches to competing, which, of course, all impact performance. This might be something to contemplate: World records show that male runners are about 10 percent faster across all distances; what impact might gender-neutral exercise science have on closing that gap?

Vescovi is that special type of researcher who enjoys what he calls the "complexity of issues" inherent in working with female athletes. He also appreciates our more "cognitive approach" to sports. As he explains, "You point to a brick wall and tell a team of guys to run into it and they'll do it, without question. Women will ask why. They want to understand why they're doing something. They'll say, 'Give me a good enough explanation, and we'll do it.'"

I may be the lame exception to that more cognitive approach. After a day of bending my brain around writing and research, running is my mind's escape. I love its simplicity, although that's by virtue of having a coach who keeps it simple for me by doing all the hard thinking in designing my training program. I belong to a club coached by Elaine McCrea, who once ranked among the top 10 female marathoners in Canada and still races at age 55. She has vast experience in coaching masters runners, and I rarely question what she tells me to do, though I must say, she's never asked me to run into a wall. As long as I've followed her plan, my finish times have always improved.

But I concede that supercharging my performance will require me to get a whole lot more intellectually engaged with my training, and I'm about to learn how to do that, in the most physical way possible.

○   ●   ○   ●   ○   ●   ○

I HAVE BROUGHT ALONG a couple of filmmaker friends to record my fitness assessment. This is not to capture evidence should something go horribly wrong (though dying on a treadmill while trying to outperform my 19-year-old self *would* make for a great YouTube video). Rather, without their footage to refer to, my description of the three training zones Vescovi and his team work me through might be "I ran, then I ran harder, and then I ran even harder, until—spoiler alert!—I pooped out, but did not die."

Now I can look at the footage and explain, with the help of Vescovi's analysis, what I was experiencing as well as how I can train more efficiently in each zone to improve my fitness, as I want to train smarter, not necessarily longer.

Before cranking up the treadmill, Vescovi plunges that gleaming silver needle into my right index finger and swabs out a drop of blood and inserts it into a lactate analyzer to take a baseline measurement of my lactic acid. He will jab my finger every 2 minutes throughout the test to monitor the buildup of this by-product of working muscles. It offers another measure of fitness—the less I produce at increased speeds, the fitter I am.

The minutes I spend in the first training zone are like a jog in the park, starting at a slow pace and peaking at a relaxed pace of 10 minutes a mile (6.2 minutes per kilometer). With every increase in speed, my heart rate ticks up on the computer monitor, from 112 beats per minute (bpm) to 130, then to 142 and 147. This rate might put some people in the third and toughest training zone, but for others with a naturally higher heart rate or one boosted by endurance exercise—as mine is—running with the heart thumping away at 153 beats per minute is working the heart in pretty relaxed fashion. And working out in this first training zone *should* be fairly relaxed; indeed, that's why training plans refer to them as "easy runs," "recovery runs," or "base building."

I feel as if I could hold this pace for a very long time, and I probably could because up until now, though my heart rate has increased with the increases in speed, the amount of lactic acid in my blood has not increased. Lactic acid is a metabolic by-product of working muscles burning fuel. It's always being produced, but at rest and during low-intensity running, it doesn't accumulate because the body can perform a neat trick of recycling it into a secondary fuel to feed to working muscles. The body's primary fuel in this low-speed zone, I am thrilled to learn, is fat, which requires oxygen to burn—hence the first zone often being called "aerobic."

Vescovi tells me that I should spend the majority of my training time—up to 75 percent of it—running in this first zone. One of the more appealing aspects of endurance training is that getting fitter and stronger requires spending the bulk of my time running slower and easier. All that easy running gently stresses the body into making a whole myriad of amazing adaptations: Tendons and muscles strengthen; heart and lungs get stronger so they can pump more oxygen; the number of red blood cells increases so they can carry more oxygen; blood vessels sprout ever more capillaries (proliferating by as much as 40 percent!) to carry more oxygen to working muscles; and mitochondria, the microscopic power-generating parts of cells that convert food into fuel, both multiply and get up to 35 percent larger so they can burn even more fat and produce even more energy to power running.

A primary aim of slow running is to build these fat-munching, energy-producing mitochondria in muscle cells. For fat loss, conditioning the body to burn it is a very good thing, but it's also great for building endurance, because fat delivers twice as much energy per calorie as carbohydrates. Energy from fat is available in greater quantities (particularly in me, but even in skinny runners) than from carbohydrates, which are stored as glycogen in limited quantities in the liver and muscles.

Amazingly, all these internal adaptations occur while you run at a moderate pace, chatting away with pals. And a key marker showing that you're training properly in this first aerobic zone is whether you can hold a conversation. It's just a wild guess, but I'm thinking women are particularly good at building endurance because so many of us enjoy putting in lots of these fat-burning miles while we're yakking up storms in our running groups.

Ah, but if I start to gasp for air between sentences, that's an indication I've crossed into the second training zone, a slightly less aerobic one often called the tempo zone. And that's what happens when Vescovi notches up the treadmill again. A chart tracking my lactic acid level on the computer screen pinpoints the demarcation; it's starting to accumulate in my blood, though not exactly flooding it. It's more like a slow leak. I have been running for too short a time to feel its searing effects, but my muscles are starting to work somewhat anaerobically, so they're producing lactic acid at a rate slightly faster than my body can convert it back into fuel.

I enter this training zone running at a pace of 9:39 minutes per mile (6 minutes per kilometer), with my heart rate hitting 155 beats per minute. Again, these numbers are entirely individual, being determined by your fitness level. Joan Benoit Samuelson, who ran a 2:50:59 at the 2013 Boston Marathon at age 55, within 30 minutes of her world-record time of 30 years earlier, may well click off 7:47-minute miles (4:50-minute kilometers) without accumulating two licks of lactic acid.

From my own training, I know this second zone oh so well. I'm breathing harder, my heart is working a lot harder—160, 163, 169 beats per minute—and I hit paces toward the faster end of the zone that I race at: my marathon pace, then my half-marathon pace, and finally, my 10-K pace. Indeed, without this elaborate and expensive test, I could find this zone by calculating the paces of my recent finish times at those distances. Racing regularly is also helpful to understanding this training zone and how it changes, as it's far from static. As my fitness improves and I become stronger and my body becomes more proficient at burning fat and converting lactic acid into fuel, I will be able to hold faster and faster paces in this zone. To hit these paces during training, a GPS watch is helpful, as it automatically calculates your pace for you. Or, using the talk test, as your tempo pace quickens, your conversation capability may go from being able to utter a sentence or two before having to haul in air to being able to grunt a phrase between gasps. To train—or race—in this zone, I have learned to forgo chatting and direct all that precious oxygen to my hardworking muscles.

Although this second training zone corresponds to the paces I race at, Vescovi recommends spending the least amount of time running in it—as little as 5 to 10 percent, or perhaps one run a week. And that's because most bodily adaptations occur in that first aerobic zone or in the third zone and above. "This is about training smarter," he says. "It's about training as elite endurance athletes do, and they spend very little time in this zone."

But training smarter, I realize, is also about being aware of how my body feels in each zone versus how it *should* feel. When my coach gives me target race paces she wants me to hit while I'm training, I too often run them stupidly when I should be asking myself a few questions: How am I breathing? How are my legs moving and feeling? How long can I hold the pace? Toward the end of a 16-week training course, holding a target race pace should feel a lot easier. If not, it's time to readjust that target or risk blowing a race with a too-fast start that will leave you sputtering to a staggering jog at the end, as happened to me in my first marathon. So training smarter also leads to racing smarter.

As my treadmill gets cranked up yet again, I cross over the next threshold—sometimes called the anaerobic or lactate threshold— into the third and toughest training zone. On the computer screen, the demarcation is dramatic: The line showing my lactate level was flat in the first zone and rose gently in the second; now it curves up sharply as my body, pressing for about a 10-K race pace, rapidly accumulates lactic acid. Typically, most runners can maintain a 10-K to 5-K race speed at their anaerobic threshold for about an hour. Once you cross over the threshold into the third and faster training zone, the distance you'll be able to go will progressively fall, from a 5-K down to a lung-busting mile and then to a sprint distance as your heart rate rises because your muscles simply can't get enough oxygen or recycle the lactic acid fast enough. Using the talk test, when I'm running in the third training zone, my conversation sounds more like single-word guttural outbursts, many of them profane.

At the threshold to this third training zone, my pace rises to 8 minutes per mile (5 minutes per kilometer), and my heart rate hits 170 beats a minute. Again, these numbers are all relative to a runner's fitness level and very individual cardiopulmonary system. What matters is finding your threshold so you can train at it and above it, because these high-intensity workouts pay big, big dividends, boosting power, speed, overall fitness, and also psychological well-being. Yes, these fast runs are huge mood boosters, though it might not feel like that at the time—running in this third zone is not easy.

On the treadmill, as I push ever closer to my max HR, sweat pours off me. I'm hauling in air, but my heart and lungs are still unable to supply enough oxygen to my working muscles, tipping them into oxygen debt. Lactic acid floods my bloodstream as my body shifts to anaerobic metabolism, away from burning energy-rich fat—which requires oxygen—to burning a thinner (less productive and plentiful) energy source, carbohydrates, which are stored in the muscles and liver as glycogen. Most people can store only limited amounts of glycogen—well-trained athletes, maybe 2 hours' worth—which is why the end of a marathon can be so painful, especially if you're not taking in enough energy gels or sports drinks to add electrolytes and carbs along the way. When all the glycogen in the muscles is used, the body will suck glucose from the blood, which will run out even faster. When that happens during a half- or full marathon, it's called hitting the wall, though a more apt metaphor might be running out of gas, because the body has run out of fuel. If you slow down to an aerobic pace, your body can get enough oxygen to revert to burning fat for fuel. Slowing down will also enable your body to clear the accumulated lactic acid by recycling it into fuel. You can then press on, though you might be staggering painfully, as draining the fuel tank zaps your energy, leaves you fatigued, and can also unhinge the mind a bit. When it happened to me during my first marathon, my quads felt like pork roasts tied up tight with butcher's string and slapped on a hot grill to sear. When I bonked (another word for depleting the body's glycogen stores) trying to summit the 19,340-foot peak of Kilimanjaro, I longed to curl up at the side of the trail and sleep, which is not a great idea when the temperature plunges below freezing. But runners can avoid this nasty fate by refueling with energy gels and sports drinks during hard workouts lasting more than an hour (something I failed to do on Killy because the altitude had killed my appetite) and also by racing within their fitness level (something I spectacularly failed to do in my first marathon).

Training in the third zone simulates, to a far less painful degree, the hard going at the end of a race. My coach puts us through it at Thursday night training clinics, when we run hills and speed intervals. We curse her for it, though always with a smile, because without this intense work stressing our bodies, our fitness levels and finish times would plateau. Too often, people miss out on the fitness benefits of this third zone when all it really requires is picking up the pace in circuit training, riding a bike at about your maximum speed, or even speedwalking as if you're late for an appointment. It's the work that spikes the heart rate and brings on a sweat and some labored breathing. Uncomfortable as it may be, this intense training delivers massive rewards, boosting max VO2, increasing the body's ability to convert lactic acid to fuel, and improving overall cardiovascular capacity. Or, in my less scientific jargon, this is the training that will spark up that internal candle, that life force, and make it roar.

This training also injects the body with youthful vitality by stressing it just enough to make it release human growth hormone—often called the "youth hormone" by life-extension types—which rushes in to repair, rebuild, and renew muscles. According to John Ratey, MD, and Eric Hagerman, the authors of *Spark: The Revolutionary New Science of Exercise and the Brain,* our production of growth hormone slows to a trickle at middle age unless we are subjected to something akin to a full state of emergency. Starting to exercise or, in my case, stepping up my exercise intensity simulates that crisis. One session of sprinting, as our ancestors might have done fleeing a predator, can elevate production of growth hormone for up to 4 hours, rejuvenating cells in both the body and the brain. This intense work will also go a long way toward restoring our youthful figures, as it brings on an intense calorie burn by depleting the glycogen in our muscles, forcing the body to repack them in a process that can last for hours. As for improving running performance, the lactic acid flooding the bloodstream also forces the body to increase its capacity to recycle more lactic acid, and at a faster rate. Indeed, training in this zone will turn me into a lactic acid–burning machine, allowing me to push up my anaerobic threshold and hold ever-faster race paces before lactic acid rapidly accumulates.

This intense training also forces crucial psychological adaptations. Once the mind gets used to doing this hard work, running fast will feel more like it did when we were kids, like playing, and soon your body will want more of it. I used to hate hill workouts and loathed speed sessions even more. I was so slow during sprint intervals at the track that I used to cut across the field at the turns just to keep up with the back-of-the-pack runners in our club. Often, I skipped these training nights. The result? I stayed slow. Then, when I was training for my first marathon and the prospect of running that monster distance scared me into attending every single workout, I began to get faster and faster. As my fitness improved, I began looking forward to these hard workouts, even craving them, because it's in this zone, I discovered with delight, that the brain pumps out those feel-good endorphins. While I always feel better after a run, after speedwork, I feel downright giddy and can cruise on a runner's high for hours. I'm not alone. According to a study in the *Journal of Sports Sciences,* recreational runners reported enjoying a higher-intensity session more than a steady 50-minute run. Boosting my bright mood even higher is the fact that a little bit of hard work in this third zone has a slingshot effect: On my very next run, I almost always feel like I can run faster and hold that faster pace for longer.

All these great effects come with spending just 15 to 20 percent of your total training time in the third zone. That might represent one run and a portion of another run a week. Vescovi recommends that it be no more than that, because it can lead to overtraining, fatigue, burnout, and injuries. Plus, more is not really helpful since the bulk of the adaptations increasing your endurance and thus your speed occurs way back in that first training zone, under that first training threshold. So training smart, training effectively, involves cycling through the three zones in any given week or training block: 75 percent easy running, 5 to 10 percent running at target race paces, and 15 to 20 percent fast running or hill training in the third zone to spike the heart and breathing rates.

In my 5-days-a-week running schedule, that cycle looks like this: On Monday, I cross-train. Tuesday, I do an easy run in zone one, then speed up to a target race pace for a mile or two of zone-two work. On Wednesday, it's an easy zone-one run. Thursday is an intense third-zone workout with hills, speed intervals, or a combination of the two. Friday is a recovery day to give my body time to adapt. On Saturday, I do a relaxed run with perhaps another mile or two of zone-two race pace or zone-three speed. Sunday is a long, slow run. That constant cycling through the three zones—a hard day followed by an easy or rest day—gradually improves my performance in each zone and my overall fitness.

But today is not about training. It's about cranking up that treadmill yet again, pushing me to run ever faster in the third zone, so Vescovi can measure my max HR and my max VO2, the greatest amount of oxygen my heart and lungs can pump to muscles working at their peak. When I pass into this third zone, Vescovi and his team start cheering: "Great job!" "Awesome!" "Nice work." They sound impressed. And when I am in the moment of running rather than watching myself later on film, I really think I am impressing them, that I am lighting up the computer screen with numbers they have rarely seen from a middle-aged marathoner, maybe even from an Olympian in her prime. It's not impossible: A test of male endurance athletes in Sweden, all over the age of 80 and having 50 years of consistent training for cross-country skiing, found they had relative max VO2 values ("relative" because the person's weight was included in the calculation) comparable to those of men half their age and 80 percent higher than their sedentary cohorts. And I am going for a high max VO2. I am hauling in air. I am running well over what should be my max HR of 170 (according to that oft-used mathematical formula, 220 − age) and way over the 162 calculated using the Gulati formula, which is considered to be more accurate for women (0.88 × age, the result of which is then subtracted from 206). Those mathematical formulas simply can't account for individual variables and fitness levels. A more accurate way to measure max HR, other than the test I'm in the middle of, is to strap on a heart rate monitor and run four laps at a 400-meter track, starting out at a moderate pace and running faster on each lap, then running the last one full out. That should spike your heart into its maximum range. My high max HR is not surprising, since endurance runners usually develop both a higher maximum rate at peak effort and a lower rate at rest than unconditioned people. What is surprising is that as the treadmill gets cranked up again, I find yet more speed to keep up with it.

In my oxygen-deprived delirium, my endorphin-charged giddiness, I hear the cheers coming ever louder. Vescovi's voice blasts over the others: "Drive, drive, drive." And I am driving hard to score a high VO2. That measure of cardiovascular capacity, that gold standard of fitness, is pretty essential to being an elite marathoner. Genetics is a huge contributing factor in your max VO2, so I'm channeling Mom here. But so is an active childhood, featuring plenty of running games like tag that mimic the three training zones of slow running, faster running, and sprinting, as well as spending hours a day *moving,* as I did when I was growing up on a farm. In fact, a physically active childhood happens to be a common denominator in Kenyan and Ethiopian elite athletes as well as in many other world-class masters athletes. And that is what children should have—physical activity that will get them to adulthood with as high a max VO2 as possible, because that is the life flame. And, as we age and become less active, that flame burns down a little more each year. Shockingly, many college-age women in these couch-potato times have a relative max VO2 in the range of 25 milliliters per minute per kilogram of body weight, which is not so far off a 15, which is considered the lowest value required to live independently. If people fall below that, they have to struggle with disability. But as Vescovi says, it is always possible to spark up that VO2 capacity with training, even by as much as 10 to 15 percent in just 4 months according to one study of healthy men and women over the age of 60.

After a few minutes of running in this third training zone, I think of my VO2 as a bonfire built in childhood and stoked by marathon training as an adult. As the team roars ever louder—"Hard!" "Stay on it!" "All the way now!" "Keep pushing!"—I actually wonder if I am going to hit a max VO2 rivaling first Olympic gold medalist Joan Benoit Samuelson's chest-thumping 78.6, or nine-time New York Marathon champ Grete Waitz's 73.5, which stack up impressively against the legendary middle-distance runner Steve Prefontaine's 84.4, one of the highest ever measured. Or maybe I'll just nip into the vicinity of Frank Shorter's rather pedestrian 71.3 VO2, which he maximized with fantastic running efficiency to win a marathon gold medal for the United States in 1972 and set off that first great running boom in North America.

I have long suspected that there must be some freak-of-biology reason to explain how I, a latecomer to running, short, flat-footed, stocky, and so slow in other running sports that coaches usually stuck me in the goal or on defense, could hit my age-group qualifying standard for Boston on just my second marathon, and with 16 minutes to spare! With everyone in the lab cheering me on, I imagine that the numbers soaring across the computer screen reveal that I possess some cardiovascular superpower that compensates for all of my physical shortcomings, that I have magical lungs or a piston for a heart or muscles that can feed on lactic acid. I can't run fast, but I can hold a brisk pace for a pretty long time, and even at this murderous pace on the treadmill, I feel like I can run forever, even as I am suddenly staggering like a drunk at last call.

Looking back at the footage, there is a lot of excitement around the computer at this point because the line tracing the once gradual accumulation of my lactic acid has spiked upward in nearly a straight line. My running gait is breaking down because I am breaking down, unable to get enough oxygen to my muscles to keep them working, which is when Vescovi pats me on the back to stop, and my fitness test is suddenly over.

The buzz dies down just as suddenly. Turns out all that wild cheering was simply to push me to run hard to hit my max VO2, which turns out to be more ordinary than I had imagined. I reach a relative max VO2 of 39 milliliters per minute per kilogram of body weight, a far cry from those marathon heroes' rates and lower than the 60 to 65 relative max VO2 female elite endurance runners typically have. It's even on the low side for female endurance runners in my age group of 50 to 59, who typically have a relative max VO2 of between 40 and 46.

I must look like I need consoling. "You're right there in terms of the maximum values of endurance masters athletes," Vescovi tells me. He points out that my absolute max VO2 (which doesn't include my weight in the equation) of 2.05 is in the 2-to-2.5-liters-per-minute range for female masters marathoners in my age cohort (though relative max VO2 is a better measure of fitness). Still, Vescovi says my 39 is significantly higher than the 28 to 29 more typical of sedentary menopausal women, and even higher than the 30 to 35 range for untrained women in their 20s. And it's just shy of the 40 to 45 range for active, athletic, trained college-age women—likely where I would have fallen as a varsity athlete back in my 20s.

After some discussion with Vescovi, I get over the crushing disappointment of not possessing a supersonic max VO2 and come around to seeing that my measurement puts me within striking distance—oh, just 1 milliliter per minute per kilogram of body weight—of regaining the cardiovascular glory of my youth, and that yes, losing a few of my lard-handle pounds will almost instantly get me closer.

Yet improving max VO2 at my age and training level is akin to a battle pitting aging against training. Yes, training can improve max VO2, perhaps by as much as 10 percent, but Vescovi points out that the bigger improvements tend to be achieved by untrained adults. My gains as a trained endurance runner will be more difficult to reach because my max VO2 is already relatively high for my age. And aging is a tough opponent. Max VO2 tends to decline as we get older, by 1 percent a year in untrained adults and as much as 2.5 percent in female masters athletes, according to some research (compared to just 1.5 percent for male masters athletes), though even that greater rate of loss will likely leave the athletes' max VO2 values much higher, given how much we've stoked it up. That slightly faster reduction in VO2 for women compared to men may be the result of the loss of that superheroine estrogen at menopause or of reducing our training intensity and volume, as often happens with masters athletes over 50. Christine Wells of Arizona State University found in a 1992 study that menopause did not affect cardiovascular fitness in highly trained runners and, in another study, that running is one of the best ways to retain cardiorespiratory efficiency because female masters runners tended to score higher than their cohorts in other sports. Vescovi says there's little literature on how menopause affects performance, but he agrees that training volume and intensity may have more impact: "Research shows that a reduction in VO2 is tightly associated with a reduction in training volume," he says, and points out that masters women in the 50-to-59 age range who have absolute VO2 values of between 2 and 2.5 typically run 31 to 37 miles per week (50 to 60 kilometers), while younger elites put in 62 to 93 miles (100 to 150 kilometers). When I'm training for a marathon, I increase my distance from 31 to 55 miles (50 to 90 kilometers) a week. "If your training stays up, maybe your max VO2 stays up," Vescovi tells me. "And your weekly running volumes are right up there, so you should be able to maintain [your] VO2."

Maintain? In the battle of training versus aging, there's a draw? This is a shock. I'm looking for a max VO2 improvement, a *win* for training, maybe even a *knockout* for training. This may be the tough reality of turning 50: I may be running hard just to maintain the cardiovascular fitness I have, running in one place like a rat on a treadmill to improve my max VO2 by 2.5 percent a year just to stay ahead of the 2.5 percent age-related decline.

I put that theory to Vescovi. "If we anticipate a 2.5 percent reduction a year," he says, "if you don't decline, that would be an improvement because you would have improved 2.5 percent not to decline." In other words, the rat hypothesis holds.

But, as Vescovi points out, max VO2 is only one predictor of marathon performance. In fact, it can be a poor predictor, more a measurement of *potential*. A better indicator is my second training threshold, that anaerobic threshold into zone three. Recreational marathoners tend to race at somewhere between 80 and 85 percent of their max HR, which falls under that anaerobic threshold, in the second training zone. Good racers can run smack up against their thresholds. Great racers are superior lactic-acid burners, and through training, they can push that second threshold outward, enabling them to run at closer to 90 or 95 percent of their max HR in a marathon.

And still another key factor in performance is running economy. An athlete with a low max VO2 may run more efficiently on a liter of oxygen, allowing her to run faster than a runner with a much higher max VO2 who clomps along, all elbows and splaying feet, sucking up oxygen like a Hummer does gasoline.

Suddenly, Vescovi's numbers are challenging my entire perception of myself as a talentless plodder. Clearly, I didn't get to the start line of the Boston Marathon with the genetic luck of having a high max VO2. Thanks to very good training, I have become an efficient runner who can squeeze more miles out of my smaller VO2 gas tank. Plus, I can race half-marathons at closer to 90 percent of my max HR, indicating that I'm a pretty good lactic-acid burner to boot, which is also an effect of good training. In just 2 years of marathon training, I have been able to push out that anaerobic threshold to my third training zone considerably: My previous 5-K pace is now my half-marathon pace, an improvement that still astounds me. In those 2 years of dedicated training, I have morphed from being one of the slowest women in my club to being among the fastest. And I suppose I do possess some of my mother's grit. I still remember the very first night I trained with my club and ran farther than I ever had before, and it was on a Canadian winter night so cold that sweat dripping into my eyelashes froze into icicles. I returned home exhilarated, exclaiming to my partner, "I ran 10 kilometers! And with hunks of ice hanging off my face!"

Like so many of my sisters in this running boom, I have discovered not only joy in running, but also that I have some aptitude for it.

But sadly, it appears that I have no vast reservoir of undeveloped genetic potential to tap into in my quest to achieve superior fitness after 50. My rapid improvement in the 2 years since I started marathon training is precisely because of training. I have been running, more or less, aware of it or not, in the three zones Vescovi put me through, thanks to the training plans my coach writes for me and my own discipline in following them.

Which leaves me with this question: How can I possibly train smarter to eke out more gains? Because now my goals for the year seem rather daunting.

My first goal—to get myself into that 40 to 46 max VO2 range with trained college-age women—may not require a huge leap. It will almost certainly entail trimming off the pounds I have packed on since hitting menopause, and I had already made some progress on that before this test.

The second goal will be considerably more difficult: To prove

I can attain the fitness of well-trained women in their 20s, I will attempt to meet the toughest Boston qualifying standard for women, the 18-to-34-year-old age cohort, which will require lowering my personal best marathon time from 3:49 to 3:35, a whopping 14-minute improvement.

And the third goal will be even tougher: At the World Masters Games in Italy, I want to do something I have never done in a race before, which is to challenge the elite front-runners in my age group. That will require lowering my time in the half-marathon from my previous best of 1:46 to the vicinity of 1:36, a 10-minute improvement that I must trim from a much shorter distance.

I float these goals out to Vescovi, and I will give him credit for not laughing. Rather, he suggests that I keep my mileage up, focus on training in the three zones, and also look to improve in a number of key areas—cross-training, recovery, nutrition, hydration, race strategy, sports psychology. Squeezing out small gains in a number of these could add up to big gains in performance.

Then Vescovi offers this reality check: Elite athletes train for years to achieve an improvement of 2 or 3 percent. And I'm gunning for something like a 10 percent improvement *in 1 year,* and that's not taking into account any age-related decline. "It's an uphill climb to get there, for sure," he says. "I'm not sure you expected anything less."

When I get home and ponder my calendar, the challenge seems even more monumental, as it's already the end of September. And the finale to my year, my race in Italy, is just 10 months off.

CHAPTER 3

EATING SMARTER

FOR A FEW WEEKS after my super-fit tests, I flounder like a hooked fish, wondering exactly what to do next. Compounding my inertia is my injury. Given my weak and sore hamstrings and glutes, I can't just go out and run harder and longer, as I might have in the past. I can't even run in the three training zones that Jason Vescovi pinpointed in my max VO2 test because my running coach has cautioned against fast runs and long runs until I can run pain free.

So the pain in my butt is really forcing me to use my head, to figure out how to train smarter and seek out small gains in all those areas that Vescovi and Greg Wells pointed out. According to multiple experts, this is something older women runners do particularly well. Apparently we listen to and care for our bodies better and have the patience to back off training when we need to. We also tend to work on training-smarter techniques such as getting proper nutrition, rest, and recovery and also cross-training to build strength and flexibility.

I use the term "we" pretty loosely here, as I was late to join this sisterhood of older runners, at least cognitively. For up until

47

now, my brain has been about as engaged in my training as my lazy glutes. But that will have to change if I am to give myself any hope of improving my running performance by 10 percent over the next year.

Which is when this training-smarter brainstorm comes to me: Why not seek guidance from older runners in the running sister-hood who have lived all my questions about how to train smarter? And why not start with perhaps the most durable elite marathoner in the world?

○　　●　　○　　●　　○　　●　　○

LINDA SOMERS SMITH, a year older than I, has been running at an elite level through an incredible 3 decades, since her first marathon in 1984 at age 23. Eight years of dedicated training later, she ran into her glory years, winning the Chicago Marathon in 1992 and the California International in 1993, capturing the United States national marathon championship twice, and competing in the 1996 Olympics. Perhaps more impressively, she has qualified for the US Olympic marathon trials *a record seven times,* more than any other athlete. Her last qualification was in 2012, at the age of 50. In that trial, she ran a 2:37:36, a mere 7:30 slower than her personal best of 2:30:06, set at age 34. In those intervening 16 years, she lost just 17 seconds per mile off her best race pace—less than 1 second per year. And she has managed to maintain that speed and endurance while completing law school, having a family, running a busy law practice, and, as Linda puts it, not cannibalizing her body to become super thin in order to squeeze out every second of speed.

Linda tells me that she is considering trying to qualify for an eighth trial—she will be 55 if she runs it in 2015—and the only way to keep in shape for that will be to *moderate* her running and train smart. "I can't stay in tip-top shape year-round. You get too torn up, and it's not necessarily the best idea. I stay relatively fit; then, when I have a goal, I'm good to go. I take a 12-week window to get in race shape for the marathon."

The key to her durability, she says, is this: "I'm a really good cross-trainer. You can become a weakling by just running. I believe you should be overall strong." To maintain strength, she cycles and swims several times a week. When she ramps up for marathon training, she adds circuit training to build core, leg, and upper-body strength. She also does plyometrics, explosive jumping movements that rapidly move muscles from extension to contraction to build strength and power. She wants to be strong not only for running, but also to enhance the quality of her life and do the activities she loves. "It's fun to be strong," she says. "Swimming builds back strength, which is important for me when I'm sitting all day." To save her body from high-mileage pounding, she does a 35-mile (56-kilometer) bike ride before a 10-mile (16-kilometer) tempo run to simulate a long run. Using her body in different ways, she believes, is key to maintaining her overall fitness, strength, and flexibility.

Eating healthy is also part of her fitness plan: "lots of salads, vegetables, chicken, and fish," though she admits she has cut back, as her metabolism has also slowed down from menopause—or, depending on how you think about it, become super efficient. To train hard, she needs adequate sleep to let her muscles repair themselves and grow stronger after hard workouts. "I don't operate on 6 hours," she says. "I need 7 hours to do anything well. If I go without sleep, I'll get injured."

She also strives for mental fitness, and running is key to that. "If I don't run, I'm miserable. It's my antidepressant. It relaxes me, keeps me calm, keeps me confident. It's a form of meditation. I can be processing information through a run, not consciously, but I'll come back and say, 'Now I understand.'"

Keeping the fun in the run has been critical to keeping running through all these years. Linda lives on the coast of California, near Montaña de Oro State Park, a running mecca. She went there to train for the 1996 Olympics and never left. It offers fantastic year-round weather as well as a variety of terrains to train on—hills, beach, trails, quiet country roads. As we chat by phone—she in her law office, I at my writing desk—I imagine scampering after her on her favorite ocean-side trail. My fantasy isn't totally delusional. She tells me she'll run with anyone. Plus she takes her long runs really slow. When logging maintenance mileage, she tries to run anywhere from 7 to 12 miles (11 to 19 kilometers) on each of 6 days a week, often with friends. "A lot of my social life is running. My friends keep me going."

Linda says she's coming to terms with having her personal bests behind her. "In the last year, training has not been giving me [improved] results. So I am now training to stay where I am. I don't like that, but it's better than declining. It's easy to use age as an excuse [to stop]. I focus on just doing what I can do. I like to challenge myself."

Still, she admits she's nervous about taking a run at qualifying for an eighth Olympic trial, fearing that old injuries might flare up. She doesn't want running to negatively impact the rest of her life. She doesn't want to run with pain. "I don't feel exhausted or hurt right now. I don't want it to hurt to walk up stairs." She grapples with the same questions I do as I try to attain super fitness after 50: How much training is enough and how much is too much? "I need role models too," she tells me. "People look up to me for blazing a trail in my 50s. I'm looking to women in their 70s and 80s."

After speaking with Linda, the challenge that lies ahead of me doesn't paralyze me quite so much. As she points out, having mentors will be helpful. Also, I can't do everything at once, but I can break my year into training segments and start doing *something*. Apparently, "periodization" is the buzzword for chunking a year out into different training segments that each have an end goal—such as a race—to measure progress.

The final third of my year is easy enough to figure out: During the spring and summer leading up to my half-marathon at the World Masters Games in Italy, I will work on increasing speed. In the second training block, the winter months leading up to a spring marathon in May, I can build strength and endurance. And in this first third of the year, what I can work on becomes suddenly, stunningly obvious: healing me—the injured me, the weakling me, the stressed-out me, and, most obviously, the pudgy me.

Funny, but that's exactly what I would recommend to anyone contemplating a marathon: Work up to that distance gradually, getting your body in shape first so it can handle the high mileage.

o   •   o   •   o   •   o

SPORTS PSYCHOLOGIST PETER JENSEN, PhD, who helps Olympic athletes and business executives develop high-performance strategies, is fond of saying that when we are ready for the lesson, the teacher will appear. Clearly, I'm ready, because as soon as I articulate my plan, teachers come flying at me from every direction.

I initially don't recognize one of the first who comes to my aid, as she appears in the guise of a student wanting *me* to be *her* teacher. Kirsten Bedard read my first book, *Apples to Oysters,* about eating my way across Canada in search of fantastic local and sustainable foods, and e-mailed me to ask if I would be her writing mentor as she writes about her passion: helping people lose weight with sensible eating and exercise rather than dieting. Her request strikes me as pretty cheeky, and I refer her to the writing course I teach at Ryerson University in Toronto. Then I look up her Web site and discover her business moniker is Ladylean, and that she is a nutritionist and personal trainer, the two professionals I need and struggle to afford. That's when this cheeky training-smarter idea comes to me: If we trade services, I will get two teachers to her one.

I am in dire need of what she might teach me. After celebrating my 50th birthday by running the Boston Marathon, my body rewarded me by going into full-blown menopause and slowing my metabolism to a snail's crawl. Over the summer months, while following a half-marathon training schedule *and* what I thought was a pretty healthy eating plan, I somehow larded on 8 pounds. With my running injury curtailing my mileage, my super-fit-me year is threatening to look more like super-size-me redux.

In the past, I would try to run off my excess poundage with marathon training. Now, this training-smarter idea strikes me: Why not start that training already at race weight or close to it? How much easier would logging all those miles be on my body? How much more effective could that training be if I start out in better shape?

I tell Kirsten that, like many women, I have gained and lost the same 20 pounds about five times over in my life, and I want to lose those pounds once and for all. But I warn her that I detest the very thought of dieting. I hate counting calories, controlling portions, obsessing about food, and constantly thinking in terms of what I can and can't have, especially if wine is on the "can't" list. I want to eat in a way that will make it so I don't have to diet or worry about what I eat ever again, if such a thing is possible.

Kirsten tells me that it is.

I'm immediately interested. I suggest we go for a run and get to know each other better.

When we meet up, we fall right into the thick of conversation, as women runners often do, gliding through a leafy uptown neighborhood—or rather, Kirsten glides while I chug along beside her. We both love good food and wine, cooking, and great restaurants, yet within a couple of blocks, we also become fast soul mates over our mutual disgust for Big Food.

In their drive for market control, giant food corporations are remaking the global food system to feed their appetites for profit at the cost of our health. They're squeezing the quality and nutrition out of food, dumbing down both eaters and farming, and addicting us to cheap and deadly ingredients like overly processed grains and starches, chemical additives, high-fructose corn syrup, sugar, and salt. We are paying dearly for that cheap food with our health and also with the soaring monetary costs associated with obesity and diet-related diseases such as some cancers, heart disease, stroke, and type 2 diabetes. It's almost as if the health care and food sectors are teaming up to make big bucks by first making us fat and sick and then trying to cure us. Governments are in on this sick fix too, arranging subsidies, trade agreements, and market infrastructure to support industrial agriculture so it can supply cheap ingredients—corn, soy, wheat—to Big Food. Meanwhile, farmers growing healthy foods such as vegetables, fruits, and grass-fed animals struggle to stay in business.

Just a mile into our run, I'm on a rant, with Kirsten easily keeping up with me in pace and ranting. Her goal as a nutritionist, she says, is not to tell people what to eat, but to help them understand how food affects our bodies so we can choose to eat smarter, for optimal health. She wants to empower people to resist the misinformation spewed by the food industry—and to put the blame where it belongs. Oh, yes, Big Food companies love to place the responsibility on us for making poor food choices; meanwhile, they're flooding the market with poor but cheap food choices. An international team of researchers recently concluded that unhealthy food producers, benefiting from aggressive marketing and undue influence on government policy, are now major drivers of the worldwide explosion of obesity and diet-related chronic diseases. Yes, we have to take personal responsibility in this epidemic. That means not just improving the way we eat, but also trying to improve our entire food system so healthy foods are the predominant and most affordable options.

Currently our food system is awash in cheap simple carbohydrates of the most overly processed, nutritionally empty, and dangerous kind. Negotiating this high-carb food system is particularly treacherous for women because our metabolism differs from men's in significant ways. Evolution has given us more efficient bodies that require fewer calories, even during exercise. In addition, men burn more carbohydrates during a run. Given that women of reproductive age are constantly ready for pregnancy, childbirth, or breastfeeding, their bodies try to maintain fat and conserve carbs. In the absence of carbs to use, women will burn excess fat just fine; as described in Chapter 2, fat is our preferred fuel source for running until we push ourselves over the anaerobic threshold, when muscles, lacking the oxygen needed to burn fat, must burn carbohydrates. But if we take in too many simple carbs, our bodies will burn those and store the excess as fat. That not only increases our fat stores, but also prevents us from reaching into them to burn fat for energy—making it difficult to lose weight.

The challenge of matching energy intake to expenditure doesn't necessarily get easier as female athletes become fitter, because our metabolisms adjust more readily than men's and we become like fuel-efficient cars, able to squeeze ever more distance from every calorie. In a food system awash with cheap, convenient, but nutritionally empty carbohydrates, it can be hugely challenging for female athletes to get enough nutrition from the calories we consume without packing on weight, which is a big drag on performance. The battle some female runners do with food even has a name: "the female athlete triad." It sounds like a car. It's more like a car crash happening in slow motion.

In an effort to control their weight while having to eat in a food system infested with fattening carbs, many female athletes develop disordered eating patterns. We might eat fewer calories than are required to fuel our training, or eat too many nutritionally empty calories and then restrict our intake of good calories, or practically starve ourselves to bring our weight down before a competition. And there are countless other creatively destructive things we can get up to with our diets. Whatever the form, disordered eating can lead to having too little body fat, which suppresses estrogen levels and results in irregular or even no menstruation. And that can play havoc with fertility and result in early-onset osteoporosis—bone mineral loss that leaves bones frail and susceptible to multiple fractures. Studies suggest that 25 percent—possibly as many as 65 percent—of female runners struggle with some aspect of disordered eating, and even older women are not immune.

This is shocking, yet not. Given that the mainstream food supply is chock-full of bad food, it's easy to see how eating from that trough can become disordered.

My run with Kirsten turns into a therapy session as I tell her about my own battles with the bulge. When I arrived at university and bellied up to the cafeteria feed trough, my weight soared to 140 pounds—obese, considering my 5-foot-1-inch frame—and I packed on those pounds while playing varsity ice hockey four times a week. When I popped the buttons off my latest pair of yet-larger jeans, I started restricting calories, primarily by cutting my servings of grains in half, eliminating soda and beer (not so easy in university), and eating according to government food guidelines. I lost 40 pounds in 4 months—and also my period. Everyone told me I looked great, except my father. Though he was struggling so profoundly with dementia by then that he had started signing his name with an *X*, he recognized a human coat hanger when he saw one: "You're too skinny," he told me bluntly one day. That shocked me off my rigid calorie restriction, and I let my weight drift back up, to about 115 pounds. Over the next 2 decades, however, the pounds kept drifting on, even though I stayed relatively active by walking, swimming, sailing, golfing, and playing hockey and squash. By my 40s, I was back up to 135 pounds, nearly as much as the most I had ever weighed. My bad cholesterol and blood sugar levels were high enough to concern my doctor.

When I added a huge dose of exercise by training for my first half-marathon at age 42, I lost 10 pounds without changing my diet. But I also developed an attitude that Kirsten believes is all too common in runners. You see the slogans on headbands and T-shirts: "I run to eat" and the like. It's odd, really, to put so much into training our bodies and then reward ourselves by filling up on junk calories. It's akin to fueling a Ferrari with the cheapest grade of gas. A running body simply can't overcome all the effects of a poor diet, or perform well on one.

I could maintain my weight while doing high mileage, but as soon as I scaled back to running three times a week when I was researching my food book, those 10 pounds starched right back on even though my partner and I had adopted an ethical diet that had us eating super-healthy "real" foods: local and organic vegetables and fruits, which have more nutrients because they are grown in healthier soils, as well as meat from grass-fed animals, which has fewer calories, less fat, and none of the growth hormones or antibiotics that are fed to feedlot animals to fatten them up faster and enable them to survive their unhealthy diets and living conditions. Medical professionals have been warning us for years that feeding antibiotics to livestock undermines the effectiveness of antibiotics for humans by helping to create antibiotic-resistant superbugs that kill tens of thousands of people every year in North America alone. The World Health Organization has called it an urgent problem. During my research on sustainable foods, I saw firsthand how closely our health is connected to the health of the plants and animals we eat and, in turn, to the health of the soil, water, and plants those plants and animals feed on. My partner and I also came to realize that a diversified food system is more responsive to our health, so rather than eating at Big Food's feedlot, we switched to eating "Small Food," buying as much of our food as possible directly from farmers and small retailers, cooking most of our meals from scratch, and avoiding junk and processed foods like the plague they are.

Our Small Food diet is pretty healthy and tasty, yet both my partner and I continued to struggle with a slow, steady, seemingly unstoppable weight gain. We are far from alone. At 2010 study published in *JAMA: The Journal of the American Medical Association* followed 34,000 middle-aged women for 13 years, monitoring their diet, exercise, and weight. Only 13 percent managed to avoid significant weight gain—and that group averaged 1 hour of exercise a day.

I was getting far more than that when I returned to running with a vengeance at age 48 to train for a marathon, but this time, I had to change my approach to food to lose weight. Before eating those pancakes or that slice of pizza, I considered whether I really wanted to carry it over the length of a marathon. The answer was almost always no. I also cut out drinking wine during the week—for me, the biggest hardship—but I dropped to 118 pounds. Carrying a lighter load, I was able to slash 34 minutes off my first marathon time to qualify for Boston on my second attempt. And that's when my body rewarded me with menopause, which slowed my metabolism even more.

"Seriously," I tell Kirsten toward the end of our run, "If I can't lose weight while running marathons and eating a pretty healthy diet, how can anyone maintain a healthy weight?"

Well, clearly Kirsten can. At 36, she's lean, yet so strong she looks like she could hold a plank for half a day. Still, she admits that before she happened upon the way she eats now, she was continually chasing her tail at the gym, trying to control her weight.

At the end of our run, I suggest an exchange: my editing help for her nutrition and personal-training guidance. She agrees, but she resists talking about weight loss, dieting, or reaching some kind of ideal body weight. Rather, she wants me to think about exchanging fat for muscle, which strikes me as exactly what I need—a performance eating plan!

But when Kirsten delivers my new eating plan, I freak out.

It cuts out all grains—pasta, bread, wheat, cereals, and rice— as well as legumes, most dairy products (except for yogurt and cottage cheese and small quantities of cheese), and definitely all processed foods, junk foods, and sugar. Her eating plan is about as anti–Big Food as she can throw at my ranting big mouth. Yet I balk, because it goes against the high-carb, pasta-loading mantra that sports nutritionists have been preaching to runners since at least the start of the first running boom back in the 1970s. Ironically, I did not eat much pasta or bread until I took up distance running, and with it, the marathon diet—porridge or cereal for breakfast, whole grain sandwiches or wraps for lunch, and pasta or rice a few times a week.

"Just try it," Kirsten urges me, "for 2 weeks and see how you feel."

Kirsten writes a blog under the moniker Ladylean, but she resists any buzzy name for her eating plan, insisting it's just sensible eating. It resembles many low-carb diets, such as the new Atkins (which includes more fruits and vegetables than the earlier, protein-heavy prescription), the Wheat Belly (which recommends cutting gluten and wheat), the Paleo (dubbed the "caveman diet," it advocates eating more like our preagricultural ancestors did—grass-fed meats, fish, fruits and vegetables, nuts—and cutting out all processed foods, including agricultural commodities such as grains, dairy, and legumes), and the Paleo Diet for Athletes (which concedes that athletes need some simple carbs to fuel hard runs).

For lack of a name for Kirsten's eating plan, I dub it the "Cavemam," though that name's more quirky than descriptive, because virtually everything in our food supply has been touched by agriculture. Still, thinking like a Paleo woman—tuning in to what my body craves for optimal health rather than what our modern food system wants me to crave—should help me make healthier food choices that are, inevitably, less processed and closer to nature.

The eating plan certainly appeals to my desire to starve Big Food rather than myself, and also to eat simply. There is no calorie counting or prescribed meal plan, and portion control is idiot-proof enough even for me.

Kirsten tells me to think of every meal in "thirds," in terms of the body's three fuel sources—one-third protein, one-third healthy fats, and the rest good complex carbohydrates such as fruits and vegetables, which are low in sugar and calories, yet packed with fiber and nutrition. We need all three at each meal, as they all work together and perform specific functions: Protein helps repair and build muscles; complex carbohydrates provide quick energy; and fat is a long-lasting fuel that protects cell membranes, benefits brain and nervous system functioning, and is required to metabolize protein, minerals, and vitamins.

As for serving size, the protein at each meal should be about 15 to 25 grams—2 eggs, a cup of yogurt or cottage cheese, or a piece of meat or fish about the size of a deck of cards. Our bodies can't use more protein than that in a single meal to build muscle (any extra is burned for energy or stored as fat), so that expensive grass-fed steak will be better used if it's divided among three meals. A healthy fat serving can be 2 tablespoons of ground flax-seeds at breakfast, one-quarter of an avocado (delicious on salads), a tablespoon of olive oil, or 2 ounces of cheese. As for complex carbs, as long as the vegetables I eat are low in starch, my appetite is the only limit.

Kirsten recommends a midmorning and midafternoon snack of ¼ cup of nuts (except peanuts), because the fat they contain staves off hunger and helps keep blood sugar levels even throughout the day, which in turn keeps our energy level even—the primary goal of this eating style. Eliminating simple carbs also keeps our blood sugar even, which keeps our energy level even and liberates us from frequent hunger pangs and constant cravings, usually for bad simple carbs.

Eating those simple carbs, in contrast, puts us on a dangerous roller coaster, sharply elevating our blood sugar (called "glucose," which is burned by cells for energy). High blood sugar provokes a massive insulin response to rush that sugar into cells. Our cells can use only so much at once, however, and any extra is packed away into fat cells. After that cleanup, blood sugar is then too low, bringing on a wave of fatigue and triggering a craving for more simple carbs—which cranks up the whole nasty cycle again.

Once we get off the carbs roller coaster, we stop craving them and obsessing about food, and the body can get back to work burning off the energy stored in fat.

There are two caveats.

The first: While I can eat all the vegetables I want, I should limit fruits and starchy vegetables—corn and white potatoes, which are relatively high in sugar—while I am trying to lose weight, or rather, as Kirsten puts it, freeing up the energy stored in fat to build muscle.

The second caveat: Rather than carb loading with pasta for races or intense runs longer than an hour (when the body needs the energy from simple carbohydrates), Kirsten recommends taking in what she calls "timed carbs" just before and right after the workout. These can be carbs that deliver a punch of sugar—a sports gel, bar, or drink, or something more natural, such as a couple of dates filled with almond butter or a smoothie (a cup of fruit blended with whey or vegan protein powder and almond milk or coconut milk). When our bodies are working hard, we will use the glucose from these carefully timed carbs as fuel rather than packing it into fat cells. The carbs eaten postrun will repack muscles depleted of glycogen.

It's the flip side of a "run to eat" approach. It's more like "eat well to run well." Or as Kirsten puts it, "Don't think about working off your weight. Your eating style should maintain your weight without running. Then fuel your exercise with timed carbs."

I must admit that my body, since heading into menopause, has been screaming for more vegetables, even though we were already eating a lot. And the science makes a ton of sense. Yet, I still resist Kirsten's eating plan, citing all the preaching by sports nutritionists, food guides, and experts to eat grains and beans because we need these carbs not only for performance, but also for our brain function!

Kirsten assures me that I will get all the good complex carbs I need from fruits and vegetables, plus a whack of nutrition in the forms of vitamins, minerals, phytonutrients, antioxidants, fiber, and water. She reminds me of the crashing fatigue

I complained about after eating my "healthy" lunch of grass-fed chicken on two slices of multigrain bread. Those two slices are the culprit, as they have as many carbs as a can of Coke, and even more calories. Instead, I could gorge on a massive bowl of broccoli, peppers, zucchini, kale, brussels sprouts, asparagus, celery, mushrooms, tomatoes, cauliflower, fennel, watercress, eggplant, and spinach—a nutritional smorgasbord—and still take in fewer calories than in those two slices of bread. As for pasta, if I substitute spaghetti squash for a cup of cooked pasta (which I can never limit myself to), I will save 140 calories, yet double the fiber, as well as get a host of other good stuff, such as potassium; beta-carotene (which lowers the risk of chronic disease); vitamins C, A, and B_6; calcium; iron; and omega-3 fatty acids.

Then Kirsten pitches me yet another argument for cutting out all grains and legumes and eating far less cheese: They are all acidic foods. Exercising as well as aging tend to make our body fluids more acidic, which leads to inflammation, perhaps another contributor to my postrun achy, cranky stiffness. The majority of vegetables and fruits, on the other hand, are alkaline and may help the body maintain a more alkaline state—and ease inflammation. The effect of diet on metabolic acidosis is controversial and requires more research. A review of studies on the alkaline diet in the *Journal of Environmental and Public Health* suggests that a more alkaline diet may not have much impact on pH in the blood, as the body is amazingly adept at maintaining the proper levels, but there is evidence of a number of health benefits. Two major ones are improving the ratio of potassium to sodium (hunter–gatherer diets had a 10-to-1 ratio while the modern agricultural diet reverses that to 1 to 3), which may benefit bone and muscle health and mitigate some chronic diseases such as stroke and hypertension; and increasing growth hormone, which stimulates cell reproduction and regeneration, pretty critical to maintaining overall good health.

"Just try it," Kirsten urges, "for 2 weeks and then see how you feel."

On Kirsten's recommendation—and because menopausal women may absorb fewer nutrients from food—I also start supplementing with a vitamin B complex (to help convert food into energy), magnesium and calcium (for muscle contraction and bone health), and vitamin D (older women are often low, and it helps with calcium absorption).

I should introduce my partner here, because she commits to going along with me on this food journey. Yes, my partner is a she and we have been together for 18 years, 6 of those happily married, thanks to Canada's equal marriage laws. Nancy is the steady rock to my adventure-gal-goes-sailing-in-stormy-seas-for-the-thrill-of-it personality. Here's how we get along: I occasionally crash and scramble to her rock for safety. And she only gloats for a short time.

Initially, Nancy thinks my Cavemam plan is wing-nutty and extreme, but then she thinks running marathons is extreme. If that's the case, I say, then an extreme sport requires extremely good fueling, and what if this is it? She puts up her own resistance, grunting out teasing quips such as "Me tired, you kill dinner." Yet she quickly joins me around the fat-burning fire when she sees me lose 2 pounds in the first week.

The meals are easy enough to make (especially for Nancy, given that I make most of them) and delicious, especially in the fall when the farmers' markets are bursting with autumn-ripe flavors.

Breakfast is a bowl of local berries and half a banana topped with cottage cheese and Greek yogurt and 2 tablespoons of ground flaxseeds. I swap out my latte for a caffe Americano and come to prefer it. Lunch is big enough for a hungry marathoner and maybe even a horse, like it was dumped from a wheelbarrow:

a massive salad of romaine or kale or spinach or all three as well as raw vegetables, avocado, whatever cooked vegetables are left over from the night before, and topped with a serving of meat, fish, or eggs. Dinner is meat or fish with three or four grilled and steamed vegetables, often anchored with sweet potato fries or parsnip fries baked in olive oil. I make extra of everything so that pulling together a salad for the next day's lunch is a cinch.

Fueling runs proves a little trickier. One night, I forget to take that "timed carb" before a particularly hard hill-running session, as Kirsten had warned me not to do. On the cooldown jog back to our club, the world begins to spin around me, and I feel very close to passing out. This is a brain too low on glucose. It is a tough reminder that it's critical to fuel workouts at tempo threshold or above as well as long runs. On slower runs, it's better to forgo that fuel and train our bodies to dig into the energy stored in fat and burn it so that we become fat-burning machines, which is why I don't take sports gels, bars, or sugary sports drinks on training runs of less than 16 miles (25 kilometers). Fueling requirements during a training run depend very much on an individual's fitness level and metabolism, but if we're constantly fueling with easy energy sources such as gels, we're not training the body to dig into fat stores for energy. Still, my near-fainting spell makes me anxious all over again about whether this low-carb eating can provide enough fuel for the really long runs that will come during marathon training and especially racing.

So I put in a call to a senior sports nutritionist for Canada's national track-and-field athletes, Trent Stellingwerff, PhD. He has conducted a number of studies on nutrition for marathon athletes. I expect him to tell me the eating plan is wacky. Instead, he says that our ancestors existed on fruits, vegetables, nuts, and meat— this is what we are meant to eat. But he cautions that our ancestors did not do high-intensity marathon training or racing. They likely travelled about 20 miles a day at a walk or slow jog, well below the intensity at which runners train and run marathons. That our muscles can pack, at most, 2 hours' worth of glycogen to fuel high-intensity runs suggests that the modern human body has not adapted to racing marathons. So he also says that it's critical to fuel hard workouts with more energy-dense carbs and glucose in the forms of sports bars, sports drinks, energy gels, or the poor man's version of gels—honey, water, and salt. Some athletes, he says, burn so many calories that they require energy from grain carbs. Get to know your own body, he suggests, figure out what it needs for fuel, and pay attention to how it responds.

I put in another call to Mark Tarnopolsky, MD, a neuromuscular and neurometabolic disorders researcher at McMaster University in Hamilton, Ontario, who also conducts studies on nutrition and sports performance. Based on studies he's led—ones that actually include women—he says that this timed-carbs, low-carb approach may be highly effective for women. Too often in the past, researchers included only male participants in studies and extrapolated dietary advice for women by simply scaling their findings down to a smaller size, as if size were our only difference. But our metabolisms work quite differently and, consequently, we have different energy needs. For instance, exercising women preferentially burn the energy stored in fat rather than the glycogen from carbohydrates that's stored in muscle—we burn about 75 percent more fat than men when exercising at 65 to 70 percent of VO2 (which is below the anaerobic threshold). Given that fat delivers twice the energy of carbohydrates, this may give us an edge in the slow-running endurance events such as ultramarathons.

Another major difference, he tells me, is that women don't carbohydrate load as effectively as men. Indeed, that long-recommended practice of carb loading before a marathon or half-marathon may even be detrimental to our performance. In one study of male and female cyclists, carb loading (increasing carbohydrate intake from 55 percent to 75 percent of calories on the 3 days prior to an event) increased glycogen in the men's muscles by 43 percent, which resulted in corresponding improvements in performance. But for women, pasta bingeing had virtually no effect in either increased muscle glycogen or performance. The researchers deduced that the women, due to their overall lower calorie intake, were not taking in enough carbohydrates (5.7 grams per kilogram versus 8 for the men) to increase their muscle glycogen levels, so in a follow-up study, the researchers boosted the carb intakes of women to 8 grams per kilogram of body weight. To get that much, men merely had to shift a percentage of their calories away from protein and fats to carbohydrates, while women had to eat 30 percent more calories overall. (A 120-pound woman exercising for 30 minutes a day requires only about 1,900 calories, but she would have to eat nearly 1,800 calories in carbohydrates alone. That would make it impossible to meet fat and protein requirements without taking in extra calories.) Yet, even when the women cyclists managed to take in as many carbohydrates as the men, they were only able to increase their muscle glycogen by half the magnitude that the men were. The follow-up study did not look at whether the slight increase in muscle glycogen improved performance. Tarnopolsky believes it would, at least for a cyclist riding on flat ground when weight was not an issue. But he concedes that weight gained from increasing calories when tapering (reducing training close to a race) could slow down a runner. He believes that women would be better off taking in carbs during a race rather than trying to carb load before. "Males and females are at least equivalent in terms of their ability to oxidize it, if not a slight advantage going to females," he tells me. "They were burning a substantial amount of carbs from gels and sports drinks. If I were a female, I would be less worried about trying to carb load and be much more aggressive with consuming carbs during a run or a race."

Since Tarnopolsky's earliest research days, he has been poking holes in the conventional high-carb marathon diet for both men and women. His studies show that male runners doing high mileage require more protein—1.4 to 1.6 grams per kilogram of body weight versus the recommended daily intake of 0.8 or 0.9— which is more than a high-carb diet can deliver, especially for women. "Women who exercise have more efficient bodies, so they have a lower calorie intake," says Tarnopolsky. "They can't eat the same calories per kilogram of body weight. If they are trying to take in a lot of carbs to maintain glycogen stores, then protein intake is going to suffer. Another problem with eating a high-carb diet in our society is that it can be a pretty barren diet. The food is so processed we end up with few other nutrients or nutrients we haven't even identified yet. You end up with a lot of empty calories. A Paleo-style diet increases that protein intake. Eating close to nature means eating better food, lots of fruits and vegetables, which increases the intake of nutrients that we need, and that probably contributes to the sense of well-being that people feel on the diet." Overall, he says, reducing carbs and increasing protein intake is "probably a reasonable strategy" to improve my running performance.

Still, I want to know how other women fuel their health and running. Linda Somers Smith says she never carb loads leading up to a race. She just eats her regular healthy meals, which include rice and beans (virtually a staple of the Cal-Mex California diet) along with vegetables, fish, and white meats. One of Canada's top-ranked female marathoners, Krista DuChene, 36, a mother of three and also a registered dietitian, recently cut down on grains (barley, wheat, rye) and avoids refined, processed, high-sugar, high-sodium, and high-calorie foods. She went on to run personal bests at nearly every race distance that year. She tells me that she opts for maximum nutrition, going for nutrient-dense, low-calorie complex carbs such as fruits and vegetables and unprocessed foods. Eliminating gluten, she says, has helped reduce inflammation and speed up recovery. Most of the older runners I write about in the chapters to come don't follow any particular diet other than eating "real food" made from scratch, with plenty of fruits and vegetables and a moderate amount of fish and meat for protein (though not much red meat). Many include whole grains in their diets, and enjoy a glass of wine and the odd treat. But they eat much like their mothers and grandmothers, limiting their exposure to packaged, processed foods chock-full of unpronounceable ingredients. Thanks to a lifetime of exercise and good eating, none has had any difficulty maintaining her weight.

When my partner and I start Cavemam eating, Kirsten warns that we might feel a bit wonky during the second week as our brains adjust to life off the carb roller coaster. On this point, she is dead wrong. Nancy and I both feel fantastic. Given the Small Food eating plan we were already following, the only big change we have to make is cutting out grains and milk in our lattes. But what a difference that makes. My running pals tease me about gorging on meat, but we don't eat more. Instead, we spread our protein over three meals, which helps repair muscles and speeds recovery. To replace grain and rice carbs, we eat far more than the 5 to 10 fruit and vegetable servings a day that national food guidelines recommend to reduce the risks of developing some cancers, obesity, heart disease, stroke, and type 2 diabetes. Only one-quarter of North Americans eat even those recommended servings. We're eating closer to 15 a day. Every week, it seems, researchers report that fruits and vegetables contain some newly identified disease-fighting antioxidant or all-powerful phytonutrient. It feels as though the bushel baskets of the stuff we're eating are supercharging our diet with nutrition. These complex carbs are low in sugar and slower to break down, so they deliver a steady release of energy without spiking our blood sugar and causing a huge insulin response. I no longer want to nap after lunch. My energy remains high throughout the day, and my moods are steadier, too. I feel lighter in weight and spirit.

Perhaps most incredibly, my recovery from runs is vastly improved. Almost immediately, my postrun stiffness is significantly reduced, and it all but disappears by the next day.

I talk about giving up wine, but talking is as far as I get. There seems to be no compelling need to. I still lose weight, and I sleep better if I have a glass or two with dinner. Sleep, given my menopausal hot flashes, remains the one thing Cavemam eating can't fix. So, over a glass of wine, I remind myself that proper rest and recovery are part of training smarter too!

Nancy and I still enjoy cheese during our weekend happy hour and will "break Cavemam," as we call eating off the plan, if we're out for dinner with friends. It's not a 100 percent or nothing thing. But we prefer eating Cavemam style and do so more than 90 percent of the week. We both feel better, our digestive systems work better, and, truly, the food tastes better. Our taste buds, liberated from deadening chemicals, fats, heavy oils, sugar, and salt, prefer the clean, tongue-popping flavors of juicy heirloom tomatoes, sugary grilled beets, golden butternut squash, woodsy kale, grass-fed meats. The first time I share a pizza while out with friends, my stomach bloats and cramps, and I'm hit with a wave of fatigue right after. This, I realize, is my body on grains.

By cutting them, we both lose weight, me steadily, Nancy more gradually, which makes sense given that she hits the gym for 45 minutes four times a week compared to my 10 to 12 hours of training each week. In 9 weeks on the diet, I drop from 126 to 118, then 115. Through the winter, after ramping up my mileage for my marathon training, my weight comes down to 113 just before race day. As I train through the final third of my super-fit-me year, my speed session in the summer, my weight will finally level out at 110 as I head to Italy. At any time, I can stabilize my weight by eating more dense vegetables—sweet potatoes, squash—and simply upping the quantities of everything.

Instead of carb loading on pasta before a race, I now complex carb load with spaghetti squash (slice one in half, scoop out the seeds, bake cut-side down at 350°F in a pan with about an inch of water for 20 minutes, then cut-side up for another 20 minutes; then, pull out the flesh into long, spaghetti-like strands and top with a favorite sauce). To boost endurance, I also juice about 20 beets and drink a 6-ounce glass a day in the 5 days leading up to a race. Research has shown that runners who ate baked beets before a 5-K time trial were able to run faster, with the last 1.8 kilometers speeded up by 5 percent. Cyclists who drank beet juice as a regular part of their diets could ride 16 percent longer in endurance tests. And trained divers who downed beet juice before a dive could hold their breath a half-minute longer. Researchers aren't sure why consuming beets works, but believe our bodies convert the nitrates in beets into nitric oxide, which improves blood-flow, getting more oxygen to working muscles. (Practice drinking beet juice in training first, as some digestive systems may not react well.)

My directly prerace eating routine becomes this: Two hours or so before a race, I drink a caffe Americano (espresso diluted with hot water), because research shows that caffeine boosts performance; I also have a protein smoothie (a small banana, ½ cup of frozen fruit, 1 cup of almond milk, 2 tablespoons of ground flax-seeds, and a scoop of protein powder). To get a quick burst of carb energy about 45 to 60 minutes before a marathon, I eat a PowerBar, sometimes washing it down with another cup of coffee.

Before shorter races, I eat two Medjool dates stuffed with almond butter. And *during* races longer than a 10-K, I do as Tarnopolsky advises and hit the carbs hard, taking a gel every half hour instead of every hour, as I did before.

With superior nutrition and steady weight loss, my running speed picks up dramatically, and running feels much, much easier. This makes sense given that every running step places about five times your body weight on your knees and feet. Losing 10 pounds reduces the force of each footfall by about 50 pounds. With about 10,000 steps in a 5-mile (8-kilometer) run, that translates into some 500,000 fewer pounds of me hitting the pavement during that short run. Instead of a thud, my foot now lands with a soft tap and has a spring in it.

Despite all our initial resistance to Kirsten's challenge to "just try it for 2 weeks," both Nancy and I agree that Cavemam eating is not a diet or a quick fix for losing 10 pounds. This is a style of eating we will follow for life.

CHAPTER 4

SMART THINGS
TO WORK ON

MY MISSION TO seek out mentors to guide me through my super-fit year takes me on a road trip with two of my greatest fitness heroes—my Ironman sister and my 88-year-old mom—as we go in search of the world's oldest yoga instructor, so proclaimed by Guinness World Records. Conveniently, Ida Herbert is not hard to find, as she lives in the northern part of the county where I grew up and, at age 97, is still teaching at the local community center. My beauty-queen-turned-Ironman-turned-personal-trainer sister recently added "yoga instructor" to her fitness résumé, which is how she heard about the legend of Ida, who started running long before the women's running boom and then took up yoga at age 50, well before that boom, too. From the moment Carol told me about this exercise pioneer, I wanted to meet her, first to see what a super-fit 97-year-old looks like, but also to ask Ida her thoughts on achieving the enduring fitness that has kept her strong and healthy through a very long lifetime.

Because as much as I want to run the fastest marathon of my

life and compete with the front-runners at the World Masters, what I really want out of this super-fit year is to attain the fitness of a 20-year-old athlete *and* maintain that superior fitness for, oh, the next 3 or 4 decades, if that's possible. But almost as soon as I set that lofty goal, I realize that I don't really understand what superior fitness is, let alone how to achieve it.

That became abundantly clear when I called Mark Tarnopolsky to talk about my performance eating plan. He also studies the power of exercise to prevent and heal disease as well as stall aging. An elite masters athlete himself, he's fascinated by how running can give us what Ida enjoys: not just a longer life, but a compressed period of aging that has enabled her to live with the fitness of a much younger person well into her advanced years. In a rapid-fire monologue, Tarnopolsky told me about numerous studies that show runners have a lower risk of all-cause mortality and also experience a far lower rate of aging-related diseases, such as cancers, heart disease, type 2 diabetes, and dementia.

When I put my super-fit goals to Tarnopolsky, he said there was no doubt that a 50-year-old could turn back the biological clock and achieve the fitness of someone in her 20s, but he cautioned that my benchmarks—such as running the fastest marathon of my life—could actually be incompatible with my larger goal. Superior performance, like that Olympians strive for, requires specificity of training, but that singular focus can undermine overall fitness. Or as Tarnopolsky put it to me, running can make us strong, but it can also make us weak in all the places that it does not make us strong. My current condition is ample proof. Two years of focused marathon training has made me aerobically fit and much faster, but also left me with frail arms, little grip strength, and even some weak muscles in my legs, which is what created the imbalance that resulted in my strained hams and glutes.

I like to think that my reaction to Tarnopolsky's warning is an indication that I'm at least starting to think smarter, if not yet train-ing smarter: Achieving enduring fitness for the long haul—such as Ida appears to have—is more important to me than racing faster, although hopefully I won't have to sacrifice too much time in my quest for overall fitness.

As for exactly how I should train to help myself live younger longer, science is beginning to offer some quantifiable proof. While fitness encompasses far more than cardiovascular health, until recently the only ways we had to measure the impact of fitness on health were aerobic exercise tests like my max VO2 test, with a low score being the clearest predictor of disease and early mortality. Running speed, which is closely linked to VO2, is another indicator. Indeed, researchers at the Cooper Institute in Dallas concluded that the speed at which we can run a mile in our 40s and 50s is a "spooky prediction" of heart disease 30 or 40 years later. For men, a study suggested 8 minutes is good; for women, it's 9. Women who struggle to complete a mile in 12 minutes (10 for men) have a 30 percent greater risk of developing and dying from heart dis-ease. For walkers, the Rockport walk test offers another measure of cardiorespiratory fitness: Strap on a heart rate monitor and walk briskly for 1 mile (1,609 meters) and then enter your peak heart rate, your weight, and your walking time into an online calculator like the one at exrx.net/Calculators/Rockport.html. That calcula-tor will offer a vague assessment such as "good" or "poor" and also recommend a walking plan that will lead to better health. According to these methods, I am a "good" walker and can run a mile in 6 minutes and a handful of seconds, so I should be kicking around for a good long time yet.

But another measure of fitness we should be paying more attention to is muscle strength, according to Steven Blair, a profes-sor of exercise science at the University of South Carolina. "We have accumulated good evidence that muscle strength is strongly associated with functional performance and mortality." He sends me numerous studies that show that in middle-aged adults, muscle strength, independent of cardiorespiratory fitness, has a beneficial effect on all-cause and cancer-related mortality. But the two don't work so independently: We require muscle strength to perform the activities that maintain our cardiorespiratory fitness. Put another way, if I don't fix the muscle imbalances in my legs and get stronger, I'm not going to be able to run longer, in distance or in years.

And Blair points out yet more aspects of fitness that I should work on to retain my youthful vigor, such as flexibility, balance, and adherence behavior. "Self-monitoring is important. You need to know where you are [fitness-wise] and where you want to go," he tells me. "So it involves goal setting. If you achieve that goal, then celebrate it, which is another strategy to develop good adherence [to your training regimen]. Problem solving is also part of that. If you don't reach a goal, look at why and solve that. The core to getting fitter is developing good adherence behavior. And the fitness industry and personal trainers don't work enough on that."

I start keeping a list of Smart Things I Need to Work On when I happen across the catchy acronym and slogan "FACE Your Future," coined by Vonda Wright, the fitness expert for the over-40 crowd whom I mentioned in Chapter 2. Many of the things she urges older folks to work on will help everyone run stronger.

The F stands for "flexibility." The lack of it makes older runners' strides so short that it looks like they're running in a puddle of water. As we age, muscles can lose power, strength, and contractile function and tendons can stiffen, reducing joint stability and the range of motion in joints and, hence, stride length. Reduced joint stability and range of motion can result in strains and even nasty falls. Recent research suggests that dynamic stretching—gently moving a joint through its full range rather than using force to stretch a muscle—is the most effective method of increasing flexibility without overstretching and compromising the springiness of tendons that is required for speed and joint stability.

Wright's *A* stands for "aerobics": moderate to intense running, walking, cycling, swimming, or some other active exercise that elevates your heart rate. Doing aerobic exercise for 30 minutes per day, Wright reports, strengthens the heart and lungs, lowers blood pressure, improves insulin control, increases HDL cholesterol (the good cholesterol), lowers LDL cholesterol (bad cholesterol), reduces triglycerides (dangerous blood fats), and offers protection from about 35 chronic diseases. Most of the benefits come within the first 30 minutes of exercise, with declining results after 1 hour. Typically, I run for longer than an hour, and sometimes for up to 4 hours on Sunday long runs. Running longer isn't necessarily a bad thing, according to Tarnopolsky, though he tells me I should understand that logging this kind of mileage is sport-specific training—acquiring endurance for distance running—that goes way beyond what's required for aerobic fitness. That huge workload can also break down my body if I don't first build it up to withstand that hugely repetitive force load.

Which brings me to the *C* in Wright's age-well recommendations, "carrying a load," such as lifting weights, resistance training with my body weight or rubber bands, or doing strength sports such as cycling or paddling. Isometrics, exercises that involve contracting muscles in a static position rather than in motion, can also build muscle mass and strength, and requires no equipment and potentially less time. A study in the *Journal of Applied Research* says that just 6 minutes a day is the equivalent of 30 to 35 minutes of muscle work on commercial weight machines. Yoga is another great option. While running does build and maintain bone density, it doesn't do a lot to build muscle strength in areas beyond the legs. Tarnopolsky told me that runners' upper bodies can become downright frail, and even the muscles in our legs can shrink as they become more efficient at running. Since muscle mass erodes faster than aerobic fitness as we age, he recommended that I do strength training in order to recapture the functional strength I had my 20s. The payoff now: I will be able to perform everyday feats of strength, such as hoisting Mom's wheelchair into the backseat of my Mini when my Ironman sister isn't around to help me. Wright reports that just 12 weeks of strength training can increase strength two- or threefold. In one study Tarnopolsky conducted, older adults were able to turn back the physiological condition of their muscles 15 to 20 years with just 6 months of strength training.

Finally, the *E* in a fitter future stands for "equilibrium." Working on it is critical as our ability to balance goes out of whack, starting at as young as 25. This is a huge blind spot for many runners, and we often blame our increasing tendency to fall on rough trails, uneven pavement, slippery surfaces, or, in my club, on *me* (I am either some kind of bad-luck charm or I just happen to run along-side a number of aging runners). Luckily, shoring up my balance can be as easy as standing on one leg while I'm brushing my teeth or, even better, while I'm lifting weights. Consider this payoff: After 3 months of working on my balance with weight training and yoga, I slip dramatically on a sheer patch of ice outside the library while I'm carrying an armload of books, yet I am able to right myself without hitting the pavement, wrenching my back, or even dropping a single book. Thank you, Dr. Wright.

○　　●　　○　　●　　○　　●　　○

AFTER GETTING TO WORK slimming down pudgy me, the next obvious thing to tackle on my list of Smart Things I Need to Work

On is my running injury. On the recommendation of a running pal, I take my tortured hams and glutes to a sports physiotherapist at the University of Toronto, my alma mater. I don't know why I didn't seek help sooner. Like many runners, I tried to heal myself while continuing to train, which is laudable on the one hand, as too many aging athletes pull back from sports at the first twinge of pain and, before they know it, find themselves planted on a couch watching sports rather than playing them and suffering even more pain as they overload their joints with the weight they gain. On the other hand, trying to just blast through the pain is not so smart.

I tried the latter approach because I feared that there might not be a fix for my injury or that the fix would be taking time off from running or, worse, that I might have to stop running completely. Given that so much of my social life and fitness are bound up in just one sport, the thought of not running was crushing—perhaps another good argument for diversifying my fitness through cross-training.

As it turns out, there is a fix to my injury, as there is with most of them. But the recommendation for healing strikes me as downright laughable: Essentially, a strain caused by too much repetitive exercise is to be fixed by—wait for it—*yet more exercise*. The prescribed medicine is a daily 20-minute routine of split squats, ham curls, bridges, and clams to strengthen my hamstrings, glutes, and hips. I loathe every single exercise until I tell myself that this rehab work *is training*, and every bit as important as running. Plus, now I can see that there is a way back to running healthy, and it's called cross-training.

Like too many runners starting out, I didn't bother with cross-training because I didn't think of it as injury prevention. Many injuries can be avoided entirely with a little strength training to develop a strong core and balanced muscles. Good running form also helps, and that can be improved with speed training, working with a coach, and studying the form of good runners and trying to mimic them. And definitely get fitted with proper running shoes by a professional at the best running-shoe store you can find, not by a 16-year-old at a discount store.

Until I got injured, I thought cross-training was about giving myself a break from running, like a diversion, and I didn't want one. But my muscles certainly did, the prime one being my butt, which is now missing in action. Literally, I have run it off. This is not a good thing. Being quad-dominant, as many runners are, I use the fronts of my legs, my quads, to drag my legs through my stride, leaving my unengaged glutes and hams to lounge about as if at a picnic. The result? My hindquarters have atrophied pathetically. My bone-flat bum and hamstrings are so laughably weak that when I am lying on my back with my knees bent and my heels planted on the floor, I can barely thrust my hips up *one time,* and not without pain.

Such repetitive-strain injuries are the bane of runners, but they also afflict older athletes doing other sports. A big reason for that is that we become increasingly single directional as we age, doing mostly activities that move us forward (walking, swimming, cycling) while shirking on sports that force us—and our muscles—to move in multiple directions. (Combining several sports helps you avoid this.) And runners who wear high heels are practically begging for an injury. Why, my cranky flat feet ask, would anyone *choose* to be hobbled, foot bound, *disabled* by a shoe? Avoiding them would liberate many runners from associated injuries. A study found that women who regularly don high heels have calf muscles that are 12 percent shorter and Achilles tendons that are 10 percent more rigid than women who wear flat, sensible shoes.

When injuries do happen, what's most frustrating is that the pain and the source of that pain are often not in the same place, making it difficult to understand what our bodies are telling us, even if we have the wisdom of our advanced age to listen to them. Case in point: A University of Minnesota study of shin splints in female runners found that the problem was a lack of muscle strength in their calves. In one study done by the Running Injury Clinic at the University of Calgary, 92 percent of runners with injuries had significant weakness in their hip-stabilizing muscles, even though the pain and injury might be elsewhere. Because power in running is generated by the hips, if those muscles are weak, the hamstrings, groin muscles, and even calves will try to compensate, straining them. Knee pain, or runner's knee, which women may be more prone to developing, given our greater so-called Q angle (caused by our wider hips narrowing to our knees), is often the result of stronger outer quads and weak inner quads, which torques the knee. The good news is that, contrary to popular belief, runners actually suffer fewer knee problems than non-runners, because running strengthens tendons, muscles, and bones. In addition, runners tend to haul around a whole lot less weight, which lightens the load on our joints. Stanford University followed age-matched runners and nonrunner controls for 18 years and found that only 20 percent of runners versus 32 percent of nonrunners developed knee osteoarthritis. Another study showed no evidence that running increases the risk of degenerative arthritis in the hip.

Also contrary to popular belief, women seem to be no more prone to injuries than men: A study published in the *International Journal of Sports Medicine* looked at 3,767 young men and women participating in seven team sports, including cross-country running and several running sports, and found little difference in the patterns or rates of injuries in men and women competing in comparable sports. A study of 629 runners participating in a race in the Netherlands actually found that men were slightly more at risk for sustaining a running-related injury. But little research has been done on gender-related injuries, according to Michael Ryan, PhD, who's working on just such a study with the University of British Columbia, with funding from Nike. He says preliminary research suggests different injury patterns rather than risk levels; for instance, men are more prone to ankle, calf, and Achilles tendon injuries, while women are at greater risk in the knees and hips. Because so many shoes are designed based on men's biomechanics, he told me he hopes more research into women's injuries—and their prevention—might prompt better footwear design for women, and also better injury prevention training.

So far, the best predictors of running injuries for both sexes are bumping up mileage too quickly (more than 10 percent a week), running more than 40 miles (65 kilometers) a week, having a high body mass index (I'm working on reducing that), aggravating a previous injury, and having a low activity level within the past 8 years. But there are a myriad of things that can result in injury: improper footwear, uneven running surfaces, poor cross-training, and the list goes on. Building good overall strength and range of motion, as I am about to find out, offers the best protection.

My effort to recover from my running injury and also prevent further injuries leads me to yet another teacher, Christine Felstead, 61, a marathon runner who turned to yoga in her 40s to heal her own running injuries. She fell for yoga so hard she left her corporate career to develop her own unique practice, which borrows poses from a variety of yoga styles that are particularly beneficial to runners. She teaches in clinics in Toronto, trains instructors at clinics internationally, and is the author of *Yoga for Runners*. I discovered the healing powers of Felstead's brand of yoga through a series of DVDs that she produced for home practice.

When I finally meet up with Felstead in person, she tells me that one of her yoga heroes is none other than Ida Herbert, which made me want to meet the exercise pioneer even more. "I invited Ida to give a workshop," Felstead tells me, "and I asked her if she had any pain anywhere in her body and she said no. That's incredible at 97. But that's what yoga does. Runners think pain and soreness is part of running, and you should just push through it. But aches and pains are not normal, and they don't have to be part of running."

According to Felstead, yoga can serve as both injury prevention and rehabilitation for runners, helping us become more flexible as well as developing our overall muscle strength "in a balanced way," which helps ease inflammation, pains, and strains.

Some running coaches are critical of yoga, claiming it can overstretch muscles and lead to its own set of injuries, often far worse than those caused by running. Felstead agrees. But it's usually not yoga that's the problem, she says, but an ill-trained instructor or an overzealous student who pushes her body beyond what it's ready for. "Yoga is not a competitive sport," she stresses, but rather an individual practice of getting to know your body and tuning in to what it needs.

For me, yoga proves a revelation. From Felstead's DVDs, I develop my own home mini practice of 5 to 10 moves that I try to do daily, and especially after a run, as it's most effective when you do a little yoga each day. Within weeks, my postrun stiffness, which had me walking like a *sedentary* 80-year-old, begins to dissipate. My body grows to crave these moves, with soreness creeping back in if I go 2 or 3 days without them. My daily mini practice, which I can pull off in about 10 minutes, also improves my balance, breathing, and flexibility. I have never been very disciplined about performing a cooldown routine or known how to do one well, but doing a few yoga moves after a run helps ease muscle soreness and restore flexibility.

Once a week, I try to get to a studio for an entire class, both for a more intense workout and to strengthen muscles that can become weak and imbalanced from running—the hamstrings, glutes, back, arms, and shoulders, and also the core, which provides the steady platform for running.

Initially, I find yoga to be slow and all the emphasis on breathing and being new-age-y present in the moment irritating, until I discover that mindful presence is kind of the point. As I once learned to let a run come to me by not starting out too fast, I learn to be content in a pose and open myself to what yoga might teach me, which turns out to be quite a lot.

Yoga is the yin to running's yang. Running exhausts while yoga recharges energy. Running tightens. Yoga loosens. Running exhilarates and pounds. Yoga soothes aching muscles. Running works a few muscles hard. Yoga works all muscles softly. Running drives forward in a headlong rush, providing an amazing cardio workout. Yoga glides in multiple directions, building muscle strength, flexibility, functional strength. Running breathes in a huffing rush. Yoga breathes with control.

What I am learning from yoga is not only helping me heal my body, but also helping me become a mentally stronger runner. When I'm nervous before the start of a race or breathing wildly after that quick acceleration, I can regain control of my breath and calm down by consciously breathing slower and deeper. If I feel a muscle tighten or cramp during a race or hard training run, I don't panic now, but rather simply breathe into it, which, according to yoga gurus, directs energy to the muscle to relax it. However it works, breathing as I have learned to do in yoga can calm me through challenges—physical and mental—and keep me focused on maintaining a fast, even pace from start to finish, which will be critical to whacking off all those minutes in my target marathon in the spring and the half-marathon at the World Masters.

○   ●   ○   ●   ○   ●   ○

IN ADDITION TO doing yoga, I also head to the gym twice a week for an hour-long strength-training session at the insistence of my nutritionist–personal trainer Kirsten Bedard. This accelerates my weight loss, and no wonder—it also ups my overall training load to 15 to 16 hours a week. As Kirsten reminds me, the body has only two storage vessels for food energy—fat cells and muscle cells—but muscle cells burn far more calories a day than fat cells (a pound of muscle may burn up to 15 calories per day com pared to just 2 for fat). So it's clearly better to store energy in muscle. But first, I have to build some.

I can't say I love strength training, but it rapidly and dramatically sculpts my body, giving me incentive to keep at it. I used to practically slather my body in running lubricant to prevent chafing. After a couple of months of lifting weights, nothing chafes. Strength training whacks fat off places I had only thought possible with drastic plastic surgery, i.e., my thighs, cheeks, and neck! Unlike with plastic surgery, however, what emerges in the place of fat is a toned, hard, thin sheath of muscle—and naturally taut skin.

As far as cross-training goes, cycling and swimming might be more fun, but Kirsten says resistance training (using the weight of my body) and eventually training with free weights (once my hams and glutes are strong enough) delivers the most time-efficient, performance-enhancing bang for my effort. It is also teaching me to identify and work specific muscles, lessons I can take into more-fun cross-training activities after this year.

The exercises gradually replace my rehab routine (or rather supercharge it) as I add weights to my split squats, lunges, and deadlifts to strengthen my hams, quads, and glutes. Pressing deep into each squat also increases my range of motion, or flexibility.

Core exercises also do triple duty. Kirsten forbids any core work with forward bending (such as crunches) because running works and therefore shortens more muscles in the front of the body, which is compounded by my sitting hunched at my desk. Instead, she has me do core work that strengthens muscles in both the front and the back, like back-arching supermans (lying on my belly and lifting my arms and legs) and swimmers (lying on my belly and flutter kicking my legs and arms), as well as planks and side planks. Pushups and pullups work my core and back as well as my shoulders and arms.

What all this gym work does not do, however, is indulge my one big vanity. Being gay perhaps liberates me from some of the body image issues many straight women struggle with, but I do have my issues. This one scene sticks in my mind from running the Boston Marathon: In the holding area before the race started, a camera zooming over the crowd focused in on a group of young women, long hair knotted in ponytails or tucked up under caps, dancing to the booming rock music, clearly delighting in their beautiful, strong bodies. When they noticed their images being projected 20 feet high on a screen, they began showing off, flexing biceps and back muscles and what really caught my attention—rippling, sculpted abs. I admit to Kirsten that I want to see if it's possible, after 50, to build ripped abs like those gals had—all in the name of research for this book, of course.

Kirsten's pragmatic response? Those exterior stomach muscles may look good, but they're not particularly useful. Rather, I should focus on turning the interior layer of fat that has been accumulating under my skin and around my belly into a layer of muscle. That thin sheath of muscle, the transversus abdominis, like an interior corset of steel, will keep my posture arrow straight and provide me with core stability for running and daily movement. A recent Pennsylvania State University study said as much, declaring that while crunches build six-packs, planks strengthen more muscle groups in the abdomen as well as the hips, back, and shoulders, and side planks build the glutes and internal and external obliques as well as the leg muscles.

Kirsten wants me to get obsessed with building core strength. She constantly suggests ways to tighten my stomach muscles, as if I'm resisting a punch to the gut, that I can do while I'm walking, running, or making Cavemam feasts. Initially I have so little to flex, I doubt I could resist a poke to the belly. Then, after just a few weeks, there is suddenly a lot to flex. I can actually feel that thin sheath of muscle under my skin—muscle that is teeming with fat-eating, power-generating mitochondria. Pockets of fat clumping at my waist melt away by the day.

And while I don't get my six-pack, I get reasonably defined abs and also manage to pump up two almost entirely brand-new muscles: Within weeks, two fine rump steaks appear on my once bone-flat bum. I have never been prouder of muscles in my life, because I have built them from nothing. Suddenly, I am resistance training everywhere, sucking in that muscular second skin of my core as if I'm giving myself an internal hug and flexing my fetching new glutes while I'm sitting at my desk.

In just a couple of months, I can see the results on the scale, in the mirror, and especially in my performance: My body is transforming into a lean, muscled, fat-burning machine. And yet I still feel guilty that I'm not working out enough! My super-fit-me schedule amounts to 1 hour of strength training on Mondays and Wednesdays (combined with a 45-minute run on Wednesdays), 1½ hours of running on Tuesdays and Thursdays, 1 hour of running on Saturdays followed by a yoga class if I can, and 2 to 3 hours of running on Sunday's long run. I do 10 minutes of yoga after every workout to work on my flexibility and balance and as a cooldown. I take Fridays off, making it a rest/recovery day that gives my muscles time to adapt to the training and grow stronger. However, I try to do some active recovery—stretching lightly, getting a massage, using a roller to massage my muscles, taking a brisk walk—but often it amounts to stretching in our hot tub on Friday evenings, supplemented with a glass of wine, which has to sound wildly indulgent for someone who's striving for super fitness.

Exercise physiologists say it's possible to get super fit on even less time: 5 to 6 hours, including at least two strength-training sessions and five 30-minute aerobic sessions.

Maybe it's my runner's mind-set—always wanting to improve, get stronger, run faster—but I never feel like I'm working out hard enough or long enough. Still, too much training will simply aggravate my injury or cause new stresses from overtraining. Paradoxically, training smarter to stall aging may require *thinking older,* meaning giving my body that rest and recovery time (and yes, massages) to renew itself, which is clearly what's happening. Maybe I am feeling guilty because I am actually feeling so fantastic, even with a far heavier training load. Unlike before, I'm not fatigued, sore, achy, or worn out. Instead, eating smarter and training smarter are rejuvenating me as I suppose they should. I mean, getting super fit should feel good, right?

The pain in my glutes and hams dissipates, and I am able to do hill and speedwork again. Initially, I'm god-awful slow going uphill; my muscled-up hams and glutes seem as lazy as ever, contributing nothing to the climb. Try as I might, I can't think my butt into action.

Then suddenly, with my fall half-marathon just weeks away, as I'm doing a speed workout with my club one evening, my glutes engage. The moment is dramatic. I feel like I have two turbochargers on my butt powering me forward. The new rear-end drive actually changes my gait, pushing me from a heel strike almost up onto my toes. The resulting speed shocks me, as well as my coach and several pals I pass. "You're flying!" they call out.

Trust me, no one has ever said that about my running before.

Looking back over this first segment of my training, I have to admit I've accomplished a lot—more than I ever expected in just 3 months. I've gained muscle while losing nearly 10 pounds of fat and supercharging my nutrition. According to Jack Daniels's training tables (available online at electricblues.com/html/runpro.html), lopping off 10 pounds of lard should slash some 5 minutes off my half-marathon time—and it does.

At my target half-marathon in November, I run a 1:42. I start out at what I think is a blistering pace, 10 seconds per kilometer under the race pace predicted by my VO2 and lactate threshold on my fitness test (see Chapter 2). But less than 2 months after that test, my fitness has improved so much, I blow those predictions out of the water. I feel so great at the end of the race—going faster in the last 5 kilometers than the first 5—that I know I could have started faster and hit maybe a 1:41 or even 1:40.

Getting down to 116 pounds for that race also tips my relative max VO2 from 39 into the low end of the 40-to-45 range of trained college-age women, giving me some claim to having achieved the fitness of a woman in her 20s. Truthfully? I already feel way better than I did in my 20s. I've gone back to *running* errands, because walking now feels too slow. I have healed my sore hams and glutes, gained flexibility, improved my balance, and developed a butt of steel. Most brilliantly (in my mind at least), I acquired teachers and learned to train smarter so I can continue to drive my fitness forward on my own, as well as know when to ask for help when I can't.

Looking back, there's really just one thing I would have done differently, but it's a biggie moving forward.

I sense that my mom, my Ironman sister, and the world's oldest yoga instructor will all have something to teach me about that topic—hence our road trip on the backcountry roads of Simcoe County to seek out Ida.

When I picked up Mom at her retirement home for that excursion, I used my new super-fit muscles to hoist her wheelchair over the side of my convertible Mini and into the backseat. That chair is heavy and awkward, yet I can now lift it with enough ease that Mom doesn't say, "Oh, that's too hard on you. I'm too much trouble." And that is really too much coming from Mom, because she has never shirked on working hard. After contracting polio at age 25, she spent 9 months in a rehabilitation hospital rebuilding her muscles so she could walk again. She had plenty of inspiration: getting better so she could care for her daughter, my Ironman sister, who was just 6 months old when Mom got sick.

When we arrive at Ida's—her house sits on an idyllic knoll overlooking a river and a large pond—we discover she is also recovering, from breaking an ankle 2 months earlier. The ankle is still puffy, though she's back to teaching yoga once a week to seniors at her community center. "Of course, I'm the oldest one there," she laughs.

At age 97, she walks with the vigor of a woman decades younger, even with that still-puffy ankle. She lives alone (her husband passed away and she never had children), and she still keeps house, cooks, and gardens. She has gorgeous snow-white hair and a vibrant face that looks closer to 75. Without knowing that she's nearly 100, many 60-year-olds looking to the future might well choose a body like Ida's to carry them into old age.

"You'll want to see some moves," Ida says, plunking herself down on her back deck without a mat. Even after breaking her ankle, she professes not to feel pain. "I don't know what pain feels like," she says, perplexed by my question. She supposes yoga has helped in that regard.

She has an energetic downward dog, and from a sitting position, she can lift her ankle to her forehead, flop her chest to her thighs, and easily wrap her hands around the foot of an outstretched leg. Of these poses, the only one I can do is a downward dog, and it's not nearly as effortless as hers.

Still, what's most impressive about Ida is her attitude. She has a positive, get-on-with-it outlook, laughs readily, and has eyes that radiate light when she talks about yoga. "Oh, I love it," she says. "Yoga is good for three things: strength, stretching, and your spirit. It's not like running. You're not trying to get anywhere. When you're in a pose, you're still. You're enjoying your body and reaching inside for peace and tranquility."

To stay fit, to age well, her advice is simple: "Keep moving. Even if it's difficult. It shouldn't hurt, but you should just try to do a little bit more each time."

I warn her that I want to ask a difficult question. She warns me that she might not answer. I stumble a bit, ask if she thinks fitness can stall aging indefinitely. Then I finally just blurt it out. "How long do you think you'll live, Ida?"

She responds promptly: "I think about 4 more years."

Age has not left her untouched. She has macular degeneration of the eyes, her hearing is failing, and she jokes that she can never remember where she left her garden shears or knitting. But it would seem that her approach to staying fit—trying to do just a little more each day, even in her 90s—will allow her to live vigorously right up to the cliff's edge and make one final sun salutation before bidding this world good-bye.

"Oh, let's not talk about dying," she says, and leaps up to get her knitting needles. It's clear she would rather be *doing* than talking. "Finding something you love helps you keep moving. But I find pleasure in everything I do. I may not like washing the floor, but I find happiness in doing it. There's a difference between being happy *doing* something [and] finding happiness *in* doing something."

Later, on the drive home, my Ironman sister tells me she tries to teach that attitude in the fitness classes she leads—running, spinning, Pilates, yoga (her activities multiply by the year). "The hump of learning to run is getting through the first 5 minutes. Someone gets to 6, and they feel good. You have to give yourself kudos and allow yourself to accept praise for doing it. If people feel positive, think happy thoughts, they have more energy to do things. Every day, I write down what I've done. I need that proof."

Mom, after my considerable prompting, admits that the exercises she did in the rehab hospital were hard. And her attitude? She focused not so much on her goal—could she even dream of walking again?—but also on *the doing*. She did as much as the drill-sergeant rehab specialist would throw at her. That hospital was filled to the brim with patients after the polio epidemic swept through North America in the early 1950s, and there was little time for soft-pedaling treatment. "Well, we had a phys ed teacher who trained soldiers in the war," Mom laughs, recalling his barked orders. She also remembers the young woman in the bed next to hers who refused to exercise, refused even to get out of bed. "The doctor told her, 'Look, if you're not going to help yourself, you have to leave. You're a waste of this bed.'" To be called a waste of a bed! Yet the woman gave up that bed and her chance to walk again, dooming herself to live inside a dying body. Meanwhile, Mom participated in everything she could. "I was the only woman who played wheelchair volleyball." Then she roars with laughter as she recalls toppling out of her chair while reaching for the ball. "Well," she shrugs, "you just do it. And you always feel better after. That's what I kept in mind."

Mom's still doing it, still going to exercise classes at 88, taking on the challenge of staying fit while confined to a wheelchair. Just like Ida embraces the challenge of living her last years well. And my Ironman sister positively thrives on setting new challenges to keep herself moving like a 20-year-old as she glides through her 60s.

All of them finding happiness in the doing.

Looking back over my first training segment, I now know two things. They may not be deep fitness-guru revelations, but they are profound to me nonetheless. Had I known how well and how fast my 50-year-old body would respond to all my training-smarter improvements, I would have lost the anxiety and guilt that came with always feeling like I should be doing more. Because after my first 3-month training segment, I estimate that I am already halfway to my performance goals for the year, with months and months of training still to go before the World Masters in Italy.

Moving forward, I will try to focus on finding joy in what I am doing so that, like my mom, my Ironman sister, and Ida, I will keep on doing it.

CHAPTER 5

MOTIVATE ME,
PLEASE

THE THING THAT scares me most about my quest isn't failing. It's not the hundreds of miles I will log or the intense hours of strength training. Bizarrely, what really terrifies me is what should be the most fun: the end goal, the actual competition, the start line at the World Masters Games in Italy. How to explain the bizarre fear of racing that I have developed after completing three marathons?

This is not good.

This could make my goal of challenging the front-runners in Italy pretty challenging.

One sports psychologist I speak to about my racing phobia—which seems to me a bizarre condition—doesn't think it so weird at all. Peter Jensen, the sports psychologist introduced in Chapter 3 who has coached Olympians as well as corporate executives on high-performance thinking, suggests that my fear comes from experience: After racing three marathons, I know how painful the last few miles can be. Recreational runners, he says, focus all their

95

attention on training their bodies to handle the distance, yet often neglect training their minds to be strong.

But it's not only physical pain that I fear.

    ○   ●   ○   ●   ○   ●   ○

GIVEN MY FRAGILE MENTAL STATE, I am more than a little surprised to discover that sports psychologists actually study people like me—that is, masters marathoners—believing us to be extreme examples of the extremely motivated. They hope that our determination to log gobs of miles a week might somehow be captured and replicated in a model that can be used to prod couch potatoes into movement and thus stem the tsunami of obesity and chronic disease that's cutting lives short and crashing health care budgets.

In fact, all manner of experts—sports psychologists, exercise physiologists, gerontologists, and sociologists—fan out at the World Masters Games to conduct extensive interviews with participants, keen to learn from older athletes what Olympians can't teach us about elite performance: how to muster the will to compete hard *and* long, as in the long haul, into our 60s, 70s, 80s, and 90s and beyond, perhaps right up to that ultimate finish line.

As a marathoner and masters-age athlete with every intention of running into my advanced years, I am, apparently, a stellar member of both of these camps, a bright, shimmering example of the supremely motivated. On the Motivations of Marathoners Scales—MOMS, for short—I fit the profile of "Running Enthusiast," someone who loves the sport and equally credits four broad categories with veritably drenching me in the sticky elixir of motivation: Yes, I run for health and fitness; yes, I love the psychological well-being I derive from running; yes, I adore the social connections and good friends I have made in my running life; and, yes, I am even motivated by the challenge of competition, as much as it has come to unnerve me.

Interestingly, a greater proportion of women as well as older runners fall into the classification of Running Enthusiasts—or should we be called "superMOMS"?—according to MOMS researcher Benjamin Ogles, PhD, of Brigham Young University. His studies show that younger runners and male runners tend to be more narrowly motivated, running primarily for, say, weight management ("Lifestyle Managers"), to tick one off the bucket list ("Personal Goal Achievers" and the very similar "Personal Accomplishers"), or for the thrill of racing ("Competitive Achievers"). Of course, someone might start running for one reason, say, to control weight, but stick with the sport as she comes to enjoy many more benefits and eventually becomes one of us superMOMS, runners who see advantages in all areas. That, according to Ogles, gives us "a richer set of reasons" to keep at it.

Yet, how to explain me at the beginning of my super-fit-me year, a so-called possessor of the holy grail of the get-up-and-go not getting up to go anywhere, at least not on those first uninspired Wednesday mornings when I was trying to haul my butt out of bed to tackle just one more workout a week? One of the slackerMOMS?

○   •   ○   •   ○   •   ○

DURING THE FIRST WEEKS of trying to launch my super-fit year (albeit before I had developed an actual plan—big problem), I could see little difference between me and millions of couch potatoes when it came to mustering up motivation. Sure, I may have developed a habit of running 4 days a week, yet I struggled

pathetically to add *just 1 more* workout day to my training schedule. For weeks I set the alarm to get up early on Wednesday
morning, only to slam it off and drift back into a weasely sleep, my
thoughts flitting from cursing my lazy-ass, pathetic excuse for a
self to marveling at the strength and gumption of fitness newbies
the world over who were leaping out of bed not just to add 1 more
workout day a week, but 2, 3, 4, and maybe even 5 as they started
an entirely new fitness routine. Statistics suggest only half of the
newbies will stick to it, but that means *the other half will.* How do
they do that?

Marathoner though I may be, grappling with my own motivational shortcomings places me squarely in solidarity with just
about everyone who is trying to start some kind of fitness program, battling to lose weight or stop smoking or quit some other
habit, struggling with a sore knee or any other strain of aging or
even disease, wrestling against inertia to break out of old routines
and take that first gutsy step on the path to wellness. And oh, how
we haul out every excuse to put off starting.

Because in front of every first step to wellness is a psychological pile of steaming self-doubt. Can I do this? Can I stick with
the plan? What is the plan? Can I change the habits that got me
into this unhealthy mess in the first place? Am I worth the effort?
Why does it seem so hard? There's always something threatening
to derail us before we even start, and for me, it explodes into a
confrontation with the very self I am trying to recapture: my
younger self. While physically strong in her 20s, she matured into
a mental tyrant, self-critical to the extreme.

But what woman doesn't wage near-daily battles with a fierce
internal critic? Generally, I feel pretty darn good about myself,
even confident, an impression I manage to convey to many
around me. But when I'm nearing the finish line of a project, a
race, or anything really important to me, who emerges as my

cheerleader? I call her the she-bitch. Stealthily she creeps into my brain when I'm at my most vulnerable and then, once firmly lodged there, she starts sucking at my energy and confidence, which is not at all helpful to the task of finishing.

One of the things I have loved most about running is that it has always been my pure place, full of positive joy and free of stress, anxieties, and judgment; in other words, free of the she-bitch. Then when I began to take running seriously, she started showing up at races, jumping out of nowhere to "cheer" me through the last miles when I was exhausted and in need of a pick-me-up, not a brutal takedown. During a particularly tough half-marathon that was consequential only in that I wanted to do well, the she-bitch exploded with 5 kilometers left to go, savagely ripping into me, ridiculing me for everything from my pathetic effort in that race to my love for the sport—*Nothing but child's play!* she said—and telling me in more censor-worthy language that it was sucking away energy and focus that surely could be directed toward more useful, grown-up endeavors. Her fury zapped nearly all my will to continue running—or ever race again.

The she-bitch had managed to infect my one pure place, my refuge—my running.

And now in this super-fit year, as I am trying to take myself seriously as a runner, she's back, not only spoiling the joy of racing, but also sapping my will to add another training session or two to my week, picking at any loose threads in my superMOMS motivations, and questioning the very worthiness of my goals. Oh, how skilled the she-bitch is. Take this line of reasoning: If there's anything I know after experiencing 50 years of life, it's that a race is just a race. Seriously, the World Masters is not the Olympics. It's not the Nobel Prize. It's definitely not the cure for cancer (though running may be one of the best preventers of the disease). It's not even the most important thing in my life. Even in the year in which

I'm striving to achieve super fitness and personal bests and to compete with the front-runners, I know the journey and meeting a plethora of super-achieving women athletes along the way will be far more meaningful than the actual race. So why work so hard to prepare? Why take the race so seriously? *Why take myself so seriously?*

In all of the training runs and races that the she-bitch has undermined, I know I could have pushed harder, found more speed, finished stronger. And so I am left wondering this: What do I need to do in order to compete hard right to the end, past the pain of charred muscles and ripping-tight hamstrings, through the self-doubt and negative talk that chirps in my head when the lactic acid and fatigue build up, to keep driving hard through those last torturous miles to the finish line? Is finding that mental strength to compete, that grit, for myself and especially at 50, important? Will finding a "finishing drive" spill over into my career? What might it mean for the rest of my life, maybe even for the example I set for others who, as I get older, might—yikes!—look up to me for inspiration?

This is what fascinates me about competition: Racing has ripped open my personal psychology more than therapy ever has. And learning mental strategies to run stronger, and hey, maybe even to win, might prove to be the more effective treatment.

○   ●   ○   ●   ○   ●   ○

LUCKILY, THE BOOM in women's running means that even older runners like I now have mentors who have sweated through the very questions that plague me, and they have come to understand something about this motivation thing, so ephemeral yet so essential to success.

At age 50, Leith Drury, PhD, set a goal even more ambitious than mine—to become a professional athlete and a world-champion triathlete. She walked away from a successful career as a business executive to dedicate herself fully to achieving her dream. She traded consulting for coaching, scraped together her savings, cut her living expenses, and marshaled sponsors, all to hire a support team and train full-time to achieve her dream of winning the world championships in her age group at the Olympic-distance event, a 0.93-mile (1.5-kilometer) swim followed by a 25-mile (40-kilometer) bike ride and then a 10-K run.

Her motivation, she tells me, was ego—and unfinished business. As a teenager growing up in the 1950s, she had been a gifted athlete and talented downhill skier, but her well-to-do family sent her off to boarding school, making it clear that education came first and that young women should not waste time on sports. She always wondered what she might have achieved. So at age 50, in full control of her own life with her children grown up, and confident that she could be successful if she put in the training, she set out to make herself a world champion.

At that point, she had already run some 20 marathons, yet with additional training, her finish times and fitness improved well into her mid-50s, until she finally achieved her goal at age 55, in 1994. She still gets emotional talking about that win, even though she quickly realized that winning the International Triathlon Union World Championship "wasn't the most important thing." Learning to compete with everything she had in her was.

During her pursuit, Leith became fascinated by how people develop into high performers. After her triumph, at an age when most people drift toward retirement, she returned to university to pursue a doctoral degree in sports psychology. Now in her 70s, she's well into an entirely new career, coaching Olympic, university, and masters athletes in high-performance thinking. Her story, while exceptional, is not unusual. She says that excelling at athletics gives women incredible confidence, empowering them to take control of their lives, whether it's ending a bad relationship, switching careers, or pursuing big dreams and making them happen. "That same kind of ethic and passion required to compete in sport is necessary to achieve goals in all areas," she tells me.

Leith is a sports psychologist at the university where I teach, which is how I came to know her. In her work with athletes there, Leith noticed that women often underestimate their abilities and need to be convinced that they're ready to compete, that they have trained hard enough. She says the opposite is more often the case with men, and her challenge is to convince them that they have to work harder during training to be better prepared for competition. She believes the same is true of runners. "Women runners are easier to get hooked on the journey as opposed to the destination [i.e., the race]," says Leith. "Men are more outcome oriented, but they can get injured and burn out more quickly than women." But motivations evolve. Women, she says, may take up running for one reason—to become fit, to manage weight, to relieve stress, or because friends drag them into it—but as they become stronger, fitter, and faster, they soon discover that they, like men, have that "competitive gene." For women, competitiveness flows from competence.

A big challenge for women, Leith says, is to own our competence, to put ourselves in a position to compete and win. The good news is that she believes older women have psychological advantages in this regard. We're great multitaskers, persistent, and mentally strong, and we tend to know our bodies better and "run within ourselves," making us great pacers.

When I tell Leith about my goals to supercharge my fitness and compete with the front-runners at the World Masters, she agrees to help me with the mental side of my training. We meet for our sessions in the café of a beautiful concert hall and teaching facility, so appropriate to Leith's approach to coaching as she seeks to engage the whole athlete in her performance—brain, body, imagination, heart, spirit, even sense of humor. And clearly, she throws her entire self into coaching. From under a sheath of white hair, her face lights up at every motivation issue I raise. She ruminates over each one, spins it through several solution models, then lobs the problem back to me so I must solve it with my own particular strengths, making the solution uniquely, potently mine.

Working with Leith, I begin to acknowledge and own the successes I have had on the road to becoming a SuperMOMS marathoner. I also learn how to supercharge that motivation, to become a stronger, even a fearless, competitor.

○　●　○　●　○　●　○

IN TRAINING TO BECOME mentally stronger, I tap into the vast experience at my running club and talk with other runners about strategies they use.

Apparently, my admission of fear and weakness makes me, along with many women, an "ideal candidate" to train for marathons, according to one of my running friends, Jean Marmoreo, MD, an author, a doctor specializing in women's health, and a five-time age-group winner of the Boston Marathon (posting ever-faster times in her three wins between ages 65 and 69). She didn't take up running until age 50. At age 60, after completing several marathons and regaining the fitness and strength she enjoyed as a teen, she and her husband and running partner, Bob Ramsay, cofounded Jean's Marines, a clinic that trained hundreds of women to run marathons over its 5-year existence. Jean, now 71, still works full-time, still enjoys hiking and cross-country skiing adventures in remote mountain ranges, and still wins at Boston (setting a new Boston women's 70-plus age-group record of 3:48:57 in 2013). She says women showed up at those first clinics of Jean's Marines terrified and full of doubt, but after miles of training they became supremely confident in their physical abilities, which flowed over into other areas of their lives. Overweight and sports-phobic women suddenly became triathletes, cross-country skiers, and trekking adventurers. "There was no longer a question of 'Can I do this?' but 'What are we going to do next?'" says Jean. "Women own their imperfections and fears or whatever their start places are. What makes women good [at marathoning] is that they have patience, self-discipline, endurance, and also the capacity to build social connections. The thing that gets women out running and keeps them going is the connections they make with each other. Put women together and they start talking, sharing, empathizing, and supporting each other, and they can run for hours."

Researchers refer to this phenomenon as "social contagion," and what women runners catch from each other is mostly good. Catherine Sabiston, PhD, an exercise psychologist and professor at the University of Toronto who studies women's cancer charity running groups and dragon boat racing teams, says women are more influenced by the moods of those around them than men are. "If you're running with others [who are] in a good mood, you're in a good mood. You may push yourself harder, go longer, and do more." Thankfully, running tends to tip women into a positive mind space; if we happen to be running with someone who's had a crappy day and she spews it out all over us, our effort may feel harder.

Of course, I didn't know any of this when I joined a running club, which I did out of panic. I had no idea how to train or even any confidence that I could keep up with other runners. The coach of my club, Elaine McCrea, has developed an incredibly inclusive and positive group to share the running contagion, welcoming men and women, gays and straights, old and young, running novices and age-group winners, and folks from the diverse corners of Toronto, one of the most multicultural cities in the world. The inclusiveness enables a variety of personalities—chatty, shy, serious, out for fun—to make what they want of the club, whether it's forming a subgroup, developing one or two close training pals, or remaining solitary while enjoying the structure and pace of group runs. For me, an extrovert who spends most of my day in solitary confinement (i.e., in my office writing), the club is like a United Nations watercooler, offering a world of personalities to meet, each with unique stories and miles and miles to tell them in. When I joined, I loved meeting whomever my pace introduced me to, and catching up with new pals was a huge incentive to hit the trails. Now my running pals are among my very closest friends, and I look forward to our training runs as much as I would to meeting up for martinis—or even more, since I know I'll also get a good hit of exercise.

○   ●   ○   ●   ○   ●   ○

I DON'T KNOW WHAT MOMS category sheer panic falls into, but it's a powerful motivator. When I set the big, scary goal of doing my first marathon, I reconnected with my running club with gusto. I was so terrified of that monster distance that I never missed a Sunday long run. And I was so afraid of those long runs that I never missed a mile of training during the week.

Then, somewhere along the way, I began to confront even deeper fears.

Running the so-called trophy race was never on my bucket

list—that is, until I turned 48, stared down the barrel at 50, and saw dark bullets scudding toward me.

This age range is a particularly tough time for women. We're already two times as likely to suffer from anxiety and depression as men. Toss wildly fluctuating hormones into the big bag of midlife stressors (kids leaving home, kids still at home, retirement on the horizon, retirement savings flat as the horizon, and on and on) and, according to the Harvard Study of Moods and Cycles, which followed 460 midlife women for 6 years, even women without a history of depression double their risk of developing it during perimenopause.

And what can I say? I have a history.

Scratching in the back of my mind was my father, who had died 12 years earlier after suffering for years with Parkinson's dementia, which had crept up on him—oh, yes—during his 50th year. I was just 15 then, a helpless witness to his short-term memory dissolving, his mood darkening. He begged doctors to fix him—or free him from the torment of losing his mind. Of course, they could do neither. He used to beg my mother to take him to the cemetery, as if he could just lie down and be done with things. She hid the bullets for his shotgun. I idolized my father so much that while he thrashed about for ways to off himself, I made it my mission to figure out what might make life worth living, for both Dad and myself. Not surprisingly, a heaviness descended on my teenage years that infected my thinking in odd ways. I did well at school, but how could I celebrate achievement, especially intellectual achievement, when Dad was losing his mind? How could I be happy when Dad was not? How could I admit to any sort of deep unhappiness and inflict yet more stress on my family, especially on Mom, who was dealing with so much already?

My story has its individual quirks, but I'm certainly not the only woman to have suffered trauma during those tumultuous teen years. Is it even possible to get through them without experiencing some mental anguish or abuse or flood of cultural messages that makes us doubt ourselves, measure all the ways we don't measure up, even believe we're number two to the happiness or suffering of a supposedly more important father, brother, husband, or other male figure? Through therapy, analysis, or endless discussion with friends, we can come to understand the pain of our teenage years and even put it behind us *rationally,* but dealing with how that stress has rewired our brains can remain a lasting challenge.

For me, nothing particularly bad needs to happen to unleash a flood of stress chemicals in my brain. Weirdly, good things can, too. Luckily, I have been somewhat physically active throughout most of my life, which has helped me flush out the toxic stew on a regular basis and keep depression at bay. Until, that is, 50 loomed. Having worked hard to achieve a life that I really enjoy living, time suddenly seemed to be running out. There was so much I wanted to write, and it seemed like I was just getting around to the projects I really wanted to do. The stress chemicals started whirring in my brain until the she bitch was nearly screaming: *Dad lost his mind at 50 and now you will too!*

Okay, all this turmoil wasn't just about staring down 50. It was also about tipping into menopause. Nouns started dropping out of my sentences as fast as estrogen was leaking from my brain, which scared the hell out of me. Maybe it makes sense that the Teen Trauma that took root in my brain when estrogen was flooding into it would return with a vengeance as estrogen was being sucked out? As I struggled to ask someone to pass the thing that holds the wine, I found myself again floundering in that stew of teenage angst, missing Dad, and chewing on that old search for what gives life meaning. I picked up my old social smoking habit—Dad smoked, of course!—with such dedication that I didn't need anyone to smoke with.

And then, out of nowhere, the crazy idea to run a marathon rushed into my head. Perhaps it dropped into the empty space that had held the word for the thing that holds the wine. Or maybe it popped into a cartoon cloud of smoke swirling over my head, making me believe that running a marathon was the only way to definitively drop that habit. However it came into my mind, once the idea was there, I could not get it out. It teased and taunted me: Did I really think I could outrun a midlife crisis, stay ahead of the dark waves lapping at my heels? Irrational as it may be, I decided I could—or at least that I would try. I had some hunch that the marathon had something to teach me about coping with my anxieties, and maybe even something about writing, my career, and that old search for what makes life worth living.

Who knows why middle-aged people suddenly decide to climb mountains or run crazy-long distances? But feeling the angst of my teenage years in middle age is not exactly rational, so why seek a so-called rational solution, like counseling or medication? Instead, I turned to running as my therapy, as so many have in this women's running boom.

Pamela Paul went through something of the same experience at age 49—a sneaker awakening? While running a half-marathon in St. Petersburg, Florida, "likely in a state of clinical depression . . . from a shattered-dream experience," she decided that she would not be in this space at age 50, feeling alone and hopeless. A certified coach and psychotherapist, she too reached for running as the lifeline that might keep her from having a "total meltdown." In the midst of that race, this idea came to her: As a 50th birthday present to herself, she would offer a gift to other women, writing training plans for any who would run a half-marathon with her on her 50th birthday. The response to her Fab 50 Women on the Run group was overwhelming in the numbers who flocked to it, their age ranges (11 to 70), and the psychological and physical transformations they went through. "There is something magical that takes place when you train and achieve a milestone in life," Pamela tells me. "Ninety percent is getting your head on straight [understanding that you can go from couch potato to running a half-marathon in a few months], and my training programs help them do that. They do the physical training, then they see their lives change. They get fit. They feel good about themselves. They get their confidence back. They're more on top of their game, more focused on careers, families, relationships. They care about their lives again. They have hope. Some husbands come to me and say, 'Thank you for my Fab 50 wife.' And, I say, 'What do you mean?' And they say, 'She's happier. She's just happier.'"

Pamela was so astounded by the changes she saw in her group that she started recommending running to her therapy patients. "I have clients in my private practice with weight-management issues. They're trying to diet, and it's not working, and they're depressed. They come to me for therapy, but I started thinking, *Let's not waste time here.* I tell them to join the running group. They do, and they don't need therapy anymore. The way you eat and treat your body has a huge impact. These women come to realize, *If I don't exercise or eat healthy, I will start to spiral into that gray cloud.*"

But the therapy is not simply in the running, Pamela believes. "Running is the door to community. It is about women making relationships with other women from all walks of life, from all socioeconomic backgrounds, across all ages. You're running and sweating together. No one's wearing makeup. No one cares. No one's comparing. You're not competitive with each other. There's not that cattiness or jealousy that women can have. The women are positive, encouraging, and supportive of each other. It's a very safe dynamic for women.

"So many women say they couldn't do this on their own. Most women don't have that intrinsic motivation to drive themselves. But when they have support and community, they can do it. This is electric. It's real. It's powerful. It's why they come [to the running group] and why they stay. "

Pamela sees such a powerful model for physical and mental wellness in the group that she is making it, rather than individual counseling, the core of her work. "Physical conditioning is the foundation. [If] you get fit, then you can fight depression and drive for a higher level, reach for spiritual engagement. . . . So many people tell me, 'This group saved my life.' It helps manage the stress of life. It gives women a sense of empowerment to take control of their lives and go after their dreams."

Countless studies back up Pamela's observations. We live in a society that loves to medicate behavior and mood issues—especially in children and women—yet James Blumenthal, PhD, a psychologist at Duke University, has done several studies with patients who volunteered for aerobic exercise that show that it can be as effective as antidepressants at treating major depression, with longer-lasting results and none of the nasty side effects. And you don't have to be clinically depressed to enjoy the benefits. In a study comparing healthy middle-aged people who started exercising and a sedentary group of people, Blumenthal found that those who started exercising exhibited less anxiety, tension, depression, and fatigue, and also reported more vigor.

However, for exercise to continue to be effective, as recent research breakthroughs in neuroscience suggest, we need to approach that exercise like athletes—that is, continually intensifying the dose as we reach higher levels of fitness.

And that takes considerable motivation.

○   ●   ○   ●   ○   ●   ○

WHILE TRAINING FOR my first marathon, as I stepped up both my mileage and the intensity of my training, I realized that I really could outrun my midlife crisis. I found myself gaining energy, optimism, and a calm sense of control. But the magic is not just in the marathon. Those just starting to run or do some other aerobic activity—as long as it brings on a hard sweat a few times a week—will get similar benefits.

Exercising hard enough to stress the body triggers the pituitary gland to release human growth hormone. According to the authors of *Spark: The Revolutionary New Science of Exercise and the Brain,* your production of growth hormone decreases over your lifetime until it's but a trickle at middle age—unless you're shocked into stepping up your production by either starting to exercise or stepping up its intensity. One session of sprinting, as our ancestors might have done fleeing from a predator or chasing prey, can elevate production for up to 4 hours after. And that growth hormone not only burns fat and builds and repairs muscles, but also performs the same rejuvenation work in our brains. According to a study conducted at the Montreal Heart Institute, adults (of an average age of 49) who began twice-a-week exercise-bike and circuit training significantly lowered their weight and percentage of body fat and also significantly improved their cognitive function.

Pushing my distance from 18 miles (30 kilometers) a week divided over 3 days up to 55 miles (90 kilometers) over 5 days and adding hill work and speed intervals turned my pituitary into a veritable geyser of human growth hormone. While stress and depression erode neural connections and shrink parts of the brain, exercise literally rewires the brain by elevating and balancing levels of feel-good neurotransmitters such as serotonin, norepinephrine, and dopamine, the same neurotransmitters that antidepressants target. Exercise also stimulates production of brain-derived neurotrophic factor (BDNF), which the authors of *Spark* call "Miracle-Gro for the brain." A sprinkling of BDNF on neurons, like fertilizer on plants, causes them to grow more and stronger connections between them, which is critical for learning and preserving memory.

And wouldn't you know it, that superheroine hormone estrogen also plays a role in the production of BDNF, making it even more critical for menopausal women to exercise. In fact, exercise can pull off the same benefits as hormone replacement therapy, with none of the side effects: While our bodies stop producing estrogen, we continue to produce DHEA (dehydroepiandrosterone), which helps the body make estrogen. Produced in the adrenal glands, ovaries, and brain, DHEA is the most abundant circulating steroid made by your body *and is boosted by exercise.* Increasing the amount of DHEA can protect women from the serious consequences of estrogen loss—increased risks of heart attack and stroke, muscle loss, dangerous fat accumulation in the belly, as well as an increased risk of dementia. In tests of brain function in more than 100 menopausal women at the University of North Carolina, those who were physically active scored higher. An Australian survey of more than 800 menopausal women found a strong correlation between exercise and less intense physical symptoms of menopause as well as reduced rates of depression, stress, fatigue, and tension. The maximum benefit seems to come from hour-long bouts of exercise on 4 days a week at 60 to 65 percent of the maximum heart rate—the pace of an easy to moderate jog—plus 2 more days of more intense activity, like sprinting, intervals, hill work, or long runs. That's very close to the dose that my running coach prescribed for me for my marathon training.

Did I develop new superpowers of concentration? That might be a stretch. But I cowrote a screenplay for a feature film that would be produced, and I started on a dream project I had been putting off for years, writing a novel. And 3 weeks after running my second marathon and shortly after my 49th birthday, I joined an all-women climb of Mount Kilimanjaro. The physical and mental challenges didn't faze me. I had begun to feel that I could accomplish anything I set my mind to.

○　●　○　●　○　●　○

THREE MONTHS BEFORE that first marathon, my partner and I took a mini sabbatical, 4 weeks holidaying on the east coast of Canada, a beach holiday with few commitments and gobs of free time, which enabled me to structure my days around running. The first thing I did once I was away from my regular routine was give up my secret smoking habit—it fell away with ease—which gave an extra jump to my step that seemed to accelerate all the adaptations my brain and body were going through. Nearly every morning, I set out on a different route, along hilly country roads that hugged the coastline or meandered along tidal rivers. I ran through mind states that veered from whoa-this-is-tough to a dreamy calm to raging euphoric happiness—all within a single run. I was running farther than I had ever run before, and I was on my own, and my body thrived on the work. That's another reason I came to love long-distance running: I like the adventure, the sense of freedom, the sheer physical work, the feeling of achy muscles and being plain spent after several hours of going hard at it. How else can we get that in our modern, deskbound lives? The sensation takes me back to summers growing up on the farm, when I was in perpetual motion from morning to night, riding my horse, swimming in the pond, helping Dad and my brothers with the farmwork, serving as my mother's legs by running errands for her, and playing sports. With each stride I took that summer, I felt younger, stronger, freer.

Before that mini sabbatical, I had never experienced such a fierce runner's high, and I suspect that's because we have to run long—and hard—to unleash it. After returning from morning runs, my brain seemed to be feeding on happy pills, and the joy extended through long afternoons at the beach, allowing my anxious self to relax in a way that had been nearly unbearable before.

Researchers still don't understand what chemicals produce the so-called runner's high, but it's very likely a cocktail of neurotransmitters, endorphins, BDNF, and endocannabinoids (which sound like "cannabis" for good reason, as they share similar chemical makeups). Researchers also don't know why running, more than other forms of exercise, produces this rarefied state of transcendent clarity and calm and extreme well-being. One theory posed: Our hunter–gatherer ancestors needed to stay serene and positive to persist in running down animals on the hunt. Another theory: The constant pounding breaks blood vessels on the bottoms of the feet and triggers the release of the heady chemical cocktail to both fix the damage and numb the pain, perhaps another evolutionary adaptation to allow success on the hunt. If so, my flat feet may well explain why I get such a rush after a long run: My soles take added punishment from slapping against my stiff orthotics.

When I returned home in September, my running pals marveled at my sudden improvement in pace and threw out outrageous theories, as if I had returned from some Kenyan training camp. I was too embarrassed to explain about the smoking habit I had just shed.

Perhaps as penance, I badly flubbed my first marathon, the Washington, DC, Marine Corps Marathon. I made every rookie mistake possible. Spent too much time on my feet sightseeing the day before. Didn't eat properly. Arrived at the race late and panicked over getting to the start. Went out too fast. Burned out my quads charging downhill. Had no mental strategy to deal with the she-bitch when she exploded as I passed the Pentagon, with miles yet to go.

And yet, the dramatic improvements I had made in training made me believe that, with a little more training, I had a shot at qualifying for the Boston Marathon.

○　　●　　○　　●　　○　　●　　○

I ALSO BLAME MARY SPECK for making me believe I could do it. When she joined our running club, I immediately sized her up: She was my age, had a similar running history, was my height (though quite a few pounds lighter), and had achieved what I wanted—she had qualified for Boston on her first attempt!

Call it the Oprah effect in action: I reasoned that if Mary could do it, then I could too. My new training strategy for the upcoming Boston-qualifying marathon became this: Stick to Mary like glue.

Often my new pace had me running alongside another couple of runners more experienced than I: Danielle Beausoleil, 4 years older and Boston runner once before, and Phyllis Berck, a decade older and a talented athlete with plenty of speed from running track in her youth. Given my background in team sports, I gradually turned us into a team as I raced to keep up with Mary. The strategy, such as it was, paid off. Danielle and I ran our next marathon side by side, pacing each other to qualify for Boston by a whopping 16 minutes under our age-group time. Phyllis had already qualified on her first attempt, by running New York in 4:11:57 at age 59. And Mary requalified for Boston at Boston, something that fewer than 40 percent manage on the tough, hilly course.

Over the next year, our connection deepened into a full-blown, codependent running sisterhood as we planned, plotted, and plodded toward our new big goal: running Boston together. Every workout, I swear, we fell deeper in love with the strengths that running brought out in us.

Danielle, a French professor, astonishes us with her determination to execute each workout to the demanding specifications of our coach, all the while looking fantastic with a perfect Parisian flip of bang extending from her running cap—even as she torpedoes a runner's wad of spit onto the road.

Phyllis, fearlessly feminist, still getting faster, and brimming with fun and fight into her 60s, constantly inspires us. And with a vast trove of contacts from working as an activist with a national association that promotes women in sport, she can rip through her vast cranial Rolodex to come up with experts to help us in our quest.

As well as being the rabbit we chase, Mary emerges as the Dorothy Parker at our running roundtable, cracking us up with self-deprecating accounts of juggling her roles as a "suburban housewife," manager of a research lab, and mom to a precocious preteen daughter.

As for me, I suppose I'm like the little sister making us a family, eager for everyone to get along and be happy, because what we have going I'd like to keep going for a very long time. As our coach likes to say, "If you could bottle what you guys have going, it would be powerful."

According to evolutionary psychologists who study such matters, we are a prime example of how women connect: We compete as a community rather than individually. We form closer relationships involving greater emotional intimacy and sharing for mutual benefit, which is also the reason why competition can be so fraught for women and, apparently, why we may be less willing to compete against each other than men. Rivalry could well disrupt the social bond we value so much.

In other words, during the 4 months and nearly 1,200 miles (2,000 kilometers) we put into training for Boston, we were work-

ing stuff out, as many women do in running groups, trying to figure out this competition stuff—specifically, how to become
stronger competitors without corroding our connection.

The four of us are all pretty driven personalities, yet the beauty
of training with a club is that we can leave alpha duties to our
coach. She sets out the workouts at race clinics, leaving us to join
ranks to bolster and support each other as well as pull other runners into our fold, such as Katherine Landell, more than 2 decades
our junior, whom we're training up to become fast and feisty.

Running together through a stormy winter morning, snow
swirling around us, wind biting cold, our connection can feel ele-
mental. Like a pack of she-wolves chasing after the same dream,
we compete hard, though not against each other so much as with
each other. We push each other to go faster on hill and speed
workouts, heap loads of positive feedback on each other, yet also
use each other to measure our own progress. If someone else is
doing well and I'm snapping at her heels, then I have to admit that
I'm doing okay too, and my confidence builds.

Between twice-weekly club runs, we maintain our tight connection by exchanging a laughably huge slew of cc'd e-mails,
teasing each other about overly active bladders, sharing training
tips, reporting on the miseries and highs of our individual runs,
and consoling each other during times when life gets in the way
of training, though always with a wry, slap-upside-the-head
comment—usually from Mary—to stop whining and get back on
the road. Through our connection, we amplify the importance of
our goal and our commitment to it and, hence, our effort. We even
nicknamed ourselves after our goal—the Boston Beaners—as in
Boston baked beans, which was how we felt when we finally
arrived in Boston to face the sweltering heat wave of 2012. Running together as a group and marshaling every bit of group

wisdom, we slowly but sanely paced each other through that 90°F scorcher, working our way from the third wave to pass faster runners who had started earlier, in the second and even the first wave, but had staggered to a walk by the end.

Women in running groups like ours tend to think we are creating a new model of running, although we are actually rejuvenating a very old one, running as our ancestors did and as the world's best distance runners still do—the Ethiopians and Kenyans, who train together, drawing on the pack for motivation and energy. In 2 years of running together, we have made extraordinary progress. We set personal bests nearly every time we race. Phyllis has become one of the top masters distance runners in the country, regularly winning her age group. Mary often places in the top three of our 50-to-54 age group. I'm starting to flirt with podium finishes, as is Danielle as she moves up into the 55-plus category. As our running improves, our ambitions rise—to go even faster, perhaps even win. We are certainly on the "compete" end of any motivation scale—logging, year-round, close to the 31 to 50 miles (50 to 80 kilometers) a week required to race to our top potential, far more than the 23 miles (37 kilometers) that women typically run in a week, according to a 2010 Running USA survey.

○   ●   ○   ●   ○   ●   ○

THAT I HAVE BECOME so competitive catches me by surprise, and I attribute it to the social contagion of my running pals. Perhaps that's another benefit of the women's running group—it's a safe place for women to own their competitiveness and learn to compete harder, lessons boys grow up learning while playing sports with friends.

Not learning how to compete may hold us back in significant ways. Statistics suggest that men are more motivated to train and compete hard for good results in road races. Evolutionary psychologist Robert O. Deaner, PhD, argues that those stats show that men have an "evolved male predisposition for enduring competitiveness," which explains why men are "overrepresented in the arts, sciences, and sports." In other words, boys, by their very nature, compete hard in sports and grow up to be men who compete hard to win in life.

Distance running, Deaner suggests, is the ideal domain for showing this sex difference in competitiveness. Perhaps more than in any other sport, men and women can pursue running with relative equality, because they have roughly equivalent intrinsic talents that span settings, cultures, and time periods. In addition, distance running allows objective comparison of men and women by their race finish times. Deaner calls running a "true meritocracy" because doing well requires talent as well as "motivation to engage in dedicated training for an extended period." According to a 2010 Running USA survey, men typically spend 15 percent more time training than women do. The result? In a study of 343 road races in the United States between 1981 and 2006, three to four times more men than women ran fast relative to their sex's world-class performance records. That performance discrepancy occurs consistently in recreational, high school, collegiate, and professional populations, with three times as many males running within 10 to 25 percent of male world records for every female running within the corresponding female world records. This, Deaner argues, is why men often do better than women off the road, in their careers: They work harder and compete harder.

Deaner's hypothesis is tough to stomach. Certainly, it's no surprise that women are still underrepresented in power positions, a fact that persists despite women now typically outnumbering men at universities and many professional schools. But his conclusions seem to suggest that we deserve our lowly place due to our lower competitive drive, and that there is little we can do to boost it since it's shaped by years of evolution.

I could contest his arguments on a number of levels: Opportunities for men and women runners may be roughly equal, at least in North America, but there's still great disparity in incentives, predominately that of social recognition, which is what Deaner says drives male status seekers. Sports media coverage remains almost entirely dedicated to the glorification of male athletes, and their opportunities in pro sports abound, whereas women don't usually grow up thinking we can make careers in sports. As a result, women may dedicate our competitive efforts to acquiring an education, establishing a career, and investing time in family, friends, and community.

But in matriarchal societies where women enjoy more advantages and higher social status than men, a study of competitive drive suggests that women may be every bit as competitive as men, and maybe even more so. One study that Deaner kindly sent me, led by the University of California–San Diego's Uri Gneezy, PhD, and published in *Econometrica,* found that Khasi women, dominant in that matrilineal tribe in India, were twice as competitive as the men, and even slightly more competitive than Maasai men, who are dominant in their patriarchal society in Tanzania. Interestingly, the wealthier the women and men were in their respective societies, the more eager they were to compete in a game that involved tossing a ball into a bin, suggesting that confidence and social status also influence competitive drive.

Research on masters athletes shows that men and women may be equally competitive—at least as older athletes. According to a study by Diane Gill and colleagues published in the *Journal of Sport Behavior,* among adult sport and exercise participants, young men tend to prize competition and winning more highly than do young women, who hold such things as fitness and social affiliation in higher esteem. However, in terms of what motivates them, the gender gap in competitiveness tends to disappear with age, with masters athletes of both sexes scoring high on competitiveness: They set personal performance goals and work hard to achieve them.

That's certainly my experience with my running pals. When I mentioned my goal to become super fit and travel to Italy to test myself at the World Masters, they immediately rebranded themselves the Fagioli and signed on for the journey.

Given that distance running is one of the few sports that women and men can compete in on the same course and at the same time, it offers an incredible opportunity for both sexes to learn competitive strategies from each other, and to create the winning conditions for all to reach their full potential. Men certainly benefit from the sociability and fun women are bringing to the sport, and may well learn from us how to be longer-living competitors—healthier, happier, and more well rounded. And women might learn strategies for competing harder that would be helpful in both racing and career.

○　　●　　○　　●　　○　　●　　○

AS I STOOD on the precipice of my new goal to compete with the front-runners in Italy, much like a newbie starting a fitness program, I found myself struggling to find the motivation to step up my training and putting it off for another week as I questioned my goals, my will, myself. Do I really have what it takes to drive hard? Can I develop that competitive drive, and how? And is pushing harder, especially at 50, even wise? Could it lead to burnout or injury? Could it derail my larger goal of running happy and healthy for the rest of my life? How much is too much, and how will I know? And what's the point of taking it so seriously when, after all, it is just a sport?

Caring so much about a sport and driving so hard at it, especially at this stage of life, with my athletic prime supposedly behind me, may seem silly. Yet the competitive zeal that keeps us pressing hard in training bolsters our fitness, which triggers the release of feel-good chemicals, which contributes to greater psychological well-being as well as supercharging us with the heady cocktail of chemicals and hormones that stalls aging and keeps us young. My running pals, in setting similar goals and striving with me to achieve them, have become even closer friends, and our camaraderie inspires others to join our pack, which fosters even more social connections.

Upping our competitive drive is like spreading a thick layer of icing over every MOMS motivating factor that keeps us running.

But as our competitiveness increases, so do our performance anxieties. We face our fears head-on as many women do—by getting together for dinner and discussing them over wine. Turns out that my half-marathon from hell, when I ripped myself mercilessly for not performing better even as I staggered to a personal best, is not so unique. Others admit to similar woes of slowing down when the going gets tough, experiencing negativity when exhaustion hits, which makes pushing through the pain and fatigue even harder. They also admit to feeling let down after some races.

Phyllis cracks a joke that we might need therapy, which in fact turns out to be precisely what we need: a good dose of sports psychology, what the pros call "cognitive coping strategies." And so started our serious pursuit of effective mental training strategies in books, picking the brains of other runners at our club, and consulting with sports psychologist Leith Drury.

In my first session with Leith, I tell her about my goals and admit that I am struggling with both the motivation to increase my training and my anxieties about racing. For many years, I trained for half-marathons but never entered races. I just didn't "get" racing. Growing up, I was plenty competitive, but I played team sports. I can compete hard for a team, but I find it difficult to compete hard for myself. When I admit that, it sounds pathetic, yet Leith is quick to point out that this is how many women compete— more for the community and family than for themselves. When it comes to running, women may feel guilty taking time away from their families, friends, or careers to train. They may need justification for it beyond their own fitness or enjoyment, such as racing to raise money for charity or setting an example of active living for their kids.

The first task Leith assigns me is to find a purpose in my running goals—as in the Big-Picture Purpose. She urges me to work with my team-oriented personality and suggests several strategies. I could enlist my friends in my mission to do well at the World Masters, for example, perhaps by establishing a team time target that requires a personal-best contribution from each of us. Or my purpose could be to train and compete hard to help my country's standings at the Games.

Quickly, I realize that my motivational issues in running are not so different from the ones that dog me in my career. One of my first bylines—in the university student newspaper—was cut from several copies and plastered over my residence door, courtesy of my friends. Rather than being proud, I felt embarrassed for standing out. If truth telling is in order here, I had a feeling back in my 20s that it would take me until my 50s to finally have the time and focus to get to the writing that I really wanted to do. And that's been true: I have let too many other things take priority over my goals. I have mired myself in constant training as well as constant questioning of the worthiness of my goals and, yes, of my abilities, too.

With this book, my challenges in writing and running have come to a head: Running is no longer an escape from the pressures of my career. Running and my writing career have become one. Yet I am reluctant to even write this sentence, to admit that I want to learn how to compete harder and "win" not just in running, but also in my career. But why not win? Why do women have such difficulty putting ourselves in the mind-set, let alone the position, to win?

I started training for my first marathon because I had a sense that it might teach me something about my career and writing, and here I am, stumped by Leith's question: What is my purpose?

It took me awhile to come up with this.

Truly, I run because I love life. I love throwing myself headlong into experience and adventure, as you do in running. I also want to stall aging and stay young in body and spirit, primarily because I want a shot at an entire second act to my writing career and life. I am just hitting my stride. I want this to keep going.

I also write because I love life. Being limited to living just one life has never seemed fair to me. Through writing, like a cat living nine lives, I can explore and inhabit many lives as well as reliving my own.

My challenge for this year of writing about my running journey lies in turning the seemingly solo sport of writing into a team game. I need to sweat through the challenges of supercharging my fitness and learning how to win so I can share that to help women around the world run into stronger, happier lives.

I could well take the purpose for this book, for this year, from a short story I wrote when I was 16 and my father was first hospitalized with a so-called nervous breakdown: "Writing should have some saving quality about it."

Finding my purpose for running and this book and wrestling it into words feels like pulling on a suit of armor. The she-bitch may well rear her ugly head again, but it's hard to imagine her winning against my Big-Picture Purpose.

○ • ○ • ○ • ○

THE NEXT STEP, Leith tells me, is to develop a plan to achieve my Big-Picture Purpose, with clear, achievable, measurable short-term goals along the way. Up until now, I've relied on my running coach to make my training program. But I need to take charge of my overall fitness, and develop a yearlong plan as well as a daily schedule with running, cross-training, and recovery sessions all plotted out. (I will focus on the running journey here, but of course all of this can be applied to a career as well.)

Leith also counsels me to develop a goal for each training session—not just a training goal, but a learning one. "Treat each workout and race as if you're running a science experiment. You're testing yourself, to learn something about technique, nutrition, ability to hold a pace, your mental imagery, or whatever. You want to know what worked, what didn't, what can you take away from this, what can you change to improve? Every time you train or race and don't learn something is a missed opportunity."

That exercise also endlessly complicates running, making it not only a physical and emotional challenge, but also an intellectual one, which makes it more engaging for older athletes.

As for my concern about training too hard—which seems rather laughable at the start of the year, when I am doing more thinking about training than actual sweating—Leith gives me an active-recovery strategy that involves checking in with myself on four levels of energy. After each training session, I am to rate how the exercise left me feeling in terms of my physical energy (with a 1 for exhausted to a 10 for super energetic), emotional energy (a 1 for "oh my god, I'm down" to a 10 for really enthusiastic), mental energy (a 1 if I'm negative and distracted to a 10 if I'm focused and positive), and spiritual energy (a 1 if I'm questioning why I'm doing this to a 10 if I feel closely connected to the Big-Picture Purpose).

Then, to help me recharge my energy on all levels and get into positive recovery mode, she instructs me to identify something positive about my performance or the training session, something I can feel grateful for, maybe something I've learned about training or about myself or simply enjoyed, like the weather or the scenery. Finding the positive will help put training in proper perspective and reconnect me with my Big-Picture Purpose. "To train strong, you need high energy, and that's connected to a strong sense of purpose," says Leith. "If you're in negative recovery mode, the psychological—the self-doubt, the negativity—will reveal itself before physical tiredness."

Of course, I can substitute "writing" for "training" and apply the same active-recovery strategies to keep me performing positively on the page. Leith concurs. "You need to be emotionally powerful and inspired to perform well at whatever you do."

But she warns that older athletes (and no doubt older writers too) have a special challenge: a lower boredom threshold. Boredom can mask itself as fatigue. So, before letting myself off a training session, Leith recommends committing to just starting. If after 10 minutes of a session I can't shake off the fatigue or shift into a positive space, that's an indication I may need to scale back or schedule in more recovery time.

When Leith says this, I immediately realize that boredom is a major issue, though not with running, with cross-training. Doing that core work and resistance training solo isn't exactly appealing, given that I already spend vast numbers of hours alone writing, and that may well lie behind my resistance to adding extra workouts. So I book times to work out at the gym when I'll have company. Plus, I prioritize those strength-training sessions in my schedule and start setting and tracking performance goals as I do in my running to keep me emotionally and intellectually engaged and make these workouts a key part of the Big-Picture Purpose. Truthfully, dear reader, you have helped me get through more than a few weight-lifting sessions, as I submit to being your guinea pig on the road to wellness—incentive for those days when my own motivation flags. In time, the extra workouts become a habit and I no longer question whether I'll go or not. I just go.

○　●　○　●　○　●　○

BEFORE MY FIRST BIG RACE since starting to work on the mental side of my running, I bring my running pal Mary along for a joint sports therapy session with Leith to discuss race plans. With all the progress I am making in my first training segment, a rate of improvement that continues through marathon training in the second, I have finally caught up to Mary in pace. Since we do virtually all our club training runs together, we decide to run our next two races together—a tune-up 30-K and then our target spring marathon. This is the first time anything I say actually throws Leith. She's not a fan of this strategy. She's concerned that we will distract each other or compromise our pace by expending energy talking or looking after each other. We assure her that this will be no trip to the nail salon. Our plan is to work together like

Kenyan or Ethiopian front-runners, using each other to set a strong, steady pace and then, in the last quarter, to drive each other into the ground trying to beat each other.

"Ah," Leith lights up. "You are worthy opponents, then."

She instructs us to develop extensive race plans, committing every detail to paper—time goals, performance measures, what we want to learn from the race, as well as logistical details such as what time we'll get up, what we'll eat, what we'll pack for the race, and when we'll arrive—to alleviate anxiety and ensure that everything goes as smoothly as possible.

As part of that plan, and to help us deal with the enormous distance of a race, she recommends breaking the course down into sections (perhaps by distance or geographic features) and developing a plan for each section, including pace, split times, strategies for navigating course challenges, when we'll drink and fuel. That plan should include how we'll be racing, meaning what we expect our bodies to be feeling as well as what we should be thinking during each section. For instance, we should develop imagery for each part of the race. It could be an animal, a favorite color, a mentor, a mantra, a hero, a memory of a past triumph. The purpose is to come up with powerful imagery that will key us in to how we should be racing in each section (for example, saving energy at the beginning or pushing hard at the end) as well as what we should be feeling and thinking. Leith tells us she's a fan of animal imagery, and this speaks to us. Mary and I regularly steal each other's imagery: Her eagle hauls us up hills, my childhood horse helps us run fast on the flats.

Finally, Leith teaches us a fatigue-management plan, a strategy used extensively by Canadian speed skaters, who typically dominate the winners' podium at the Olympics. It helps them push through exhaustion and the pain of lactic acid buildup, so they can maintain their top speeds for longer. At the first sign of fatigue or discomfort or negative self-talk, we must cycle through three problems.

First is a technical problem, requiring me to check how I'm running, my posture, my stride, my arm swing. Maybe I need to relax my shoulders, loosen my grip, breathe into a muscle that's tight or cramping. Adding imagery—say, of a deer running effortlessly—can create a visual for how I should be running.

Second is a tactical problem, such as how I should run this section, if I can pass someone, or whether I need to take in fuel or water.

Third is a mental or emotional problem involving, for example, determining what imagery or positive self-talk I need at that moment. Like the imagery I will use, I have to prepare that positive mantra before the race, committing it to my race plan so it will be there to draw upon should the she-bitch suddenly spring out from behind a bush to trip me up.

Working through these three problems will usually divert the mind from focusing on the fatigue or discomfort, Leith tells us. If not, she says, we should cycle through the three problems again. And in our training sessions long before the race, we should practice using our fatigue-management strategy.

The technique helps create a state of focused awareness, concentrating the mind on what the body needs to run strong in the moment, making it what sports psychologists call an "association strategy." Research shows that competitive runners tend to utilize association, and that it enables them to run at higher intensities for longer. They anticipate that the end of a race or certain sections will be tough and develop strategies for dealing with those challenges rather than, say, turning pain or fatigue into a catastrophe. Recreational runners more often dissociate, meaning that they distract themselves from the work of running by daydreaming or thinking about something else, but shifting their focus away from running usually causes them to fall off pace and slow down.

For women, positive association strategies seem most effective. In one study led by Benjamin Ogles, marathoners were given two association strategies. One group listened to a positive-imagery tape twice a week for 6 weeks before a race, hearing a voice talking them through every aspect of the race and telling them they were doing great and feeling great in each section. Another group listened to a tape offering coping imagery, with a voice warning them about challenges they might encounter (such as hills, crowding on the course, fatigue, cramping) while also giving them coping methods to get through each challenge. The study showed little impact on the men's finish times, with both groups actually running slightly slower than usual, though the group using coping imagery did slightly better. Women, however, ran faster with positive imagery, a whopping 9 minutes faster than the coping group. As Ogles explains, "The women told us that the coping tapes brought up negative things they hadn't thought of before, so it made the race more of a challenge. For them, thinking positive is a more effective way of imagining themselves running the race." This, he says, is in keeping with meta-analyses exploring sex differences in coping in situations other than running. "Men are more likely to see problems as controllable and use problem-focused strategies. Women are more likely to see problems as less controllable, and they tend to ruminate over a problem, seek emotional support, and use positive self-talk and emotion-focused strategies."

Interestingly, while association strategies may help a runner go faster, dissociating may be more beneficial if the goal is to run healthy. That seems contrary to common sense, which says that a runner with greater focus would be more likely to avoid injury. But studies show that runners who associate actually have more injuries. Ogles says it's possible that those runners are more com-petitive, so they train more intensively and log more miles, which can lead to more injuries. "If you want to be healthy into your 80s, is running a faster marathon better?" Ogles wonders. "Other strat-egies may be more helpful. We just don't have good data."

As I start to work with imagery, fatigue-management strate-gies, and game plans for training and racing, I realize it's possible to use association strategies to go easy on certain runs. If the goal is to recover—mentally and physically—from hard training the day before, then I can queue up easy running imagery as well as positive self-talk to remind myself to tone down the intensity and enjoy the outing. I can also give myself permission to daydream on those runs.

The beauty of the fatigue strategy that Leith teaches us is that, unlike the association tapes with canned generic talk, I have to draw on my intellect, experience, and creativity to develop my imagery, self-talk, and game plan, which makes it all the more potent.

Mary and I realize that we are extraordinarily fortunate: How many great friends also share a similar pace, race goals, com-petitiveness level, and wacky sense of humor? She jokes that during her first year with our club, when my strategy was to stick to her like glue, she told her husband that she spent all her time trying to run away from a lesbian. Now that I'm getting faster, she finds herself chasing after one. That's our connection: We shower each other with encouragement as much as we tease each other.

One of my greatest fears in learning to compete stronger is actually getting faster than Mary and losing my training buddy. Luckily, she's just as determined to get stronger and faster, so we can continue to push each other.

Through the fall and early winter, my racing improves dramat-ically thanks to all my training-smarter improvements and the motivational techniques Leith teaches us. I have never been fast enough to finish on the podium, but suddenly, I win my age group in two small races and finish third in another, and then place fifth in that fall target half-marathon while knocking 5 minutes off my previous personal best. And even better, the she-bitch didn't put in an appearance, not even once. Using sports psychology techniques, I am training my mind to recognize negative thoughts when they come up and shift to positive imagery, and even cheer myself on.

As for Mary, who regularly finishes among the top three in her age group, she starts to race even stronger, scooping up a couple of first-place finishes as well as a third in that fall half-marathon, 2 minutes ahead of me.

For all the so-called drama women have about competition, perhaps the best antidote is simply winning. After a few brushes with the podium, my confidence builds, and I start looking forward to racing. In fact, I begin to think about not just competing to achieve a personal best, but also placing in my age group, and even winning.

At Leith's prompting, Mary and I write extensive race plans for our upcoming race, the historic 30-K Around the Bay Road Race in Hamilton, Ontario, an 18.6-miler that claims fame as the oldest road race in North America, even "older than Boston," as the race shirts boast. Many use it as a tune-up for Boston or another spring marathon, as we are. So we're not feeling much pressure. But Leith encourages us to be rigorous with our race plans for this 30-K so we can test them, see what works, and revise them if need be before our target marathon 6 weeks later, when we will attempt to reach the toughest Boston qualifying standard for women, the 18-to-34 age group.

Our goal is to start out together, running the first 5 kilometers 10 seconds slower than our marathon race pace, then kick up to marathon race pace through the next 20 kilometers. That pace still feels intimidating—just 2 years ago, it was my 5-K race pace—so we're eager to see how our bodies will feel after 20 kilometers of it. Heading into the last 5 kilometers, we will release each other and become free agents, allowing ourselves to hang on at marathon pace or slow down if it's too tough. But if we're still together at the end, we will race each other to the finish. Other than checking in with each other to check our pace, we will not talk, in order to conserve our energy and focus for racing.

Almost immediately after the start line, I use my fatigue-management plan, though not because I'm tired; rather, it helps me stay on target pace. The imagery I conjure doesn't just cycle through my mind, it comes alive. A fox trots alongside me during the first 5 kilometers, reminding me to run relaxed, to be calm, to conserve energy. My mantra for this section is to stick to the target pace—and wildly, I imagine Joan Benoit Samuelson appearing beside me, reminding me to run easy, to rein in the pace as she did in her 1984 gold medal run in the Olympics before breaking away from the pack. I need the imagery and the mantra because it's a struggle to control my speed, and we run faster than we intended to through this section. Training has gone well. Mary and I both feel stronger than we ever expected.

During the second section, we pick up to marathon pace as we run through a series of low, rolling hills. My childhood horse appears now, offering rides uphill, making the physical work easier. On the downhills, a hawk swoops in and carries me in her talons, reminding me to glide down rather than pound on my quads. And another running hero appears, Kathrine Switzer, the first woman to officially run Boston, telling me to be fearless, just as she was in her historic run, and that I have the strength and guts to hold this marathon pace.

Then, ahead of us, at about the 23-kilometer (14.3-mile) mark, another running hero appears, this one in the flesh in the form of my coach, who is being paced by another runner in our club, Bruce, who's also a close friend of Mary's. The coach is struggling with a blister. We don't know this. What I do know is that I never, not even in my wildest dreams, imagined being able to catch her. Now I make it my goal to reel her in and pass. When we do, on a downslope, I get a crazy surge of adrenaline and whip past the coach and Bruce, which also leaves Mary in my dust. This isn't in our race plan—going faster than our marathon pace or starting a surge so early.

Suddenly I am alone heading into the final difficult section, which starts with a wicked hill, then a 4-kilometer stretch into a headwind. This is when the she-bitch usually bares her fangs and starts sapping my will. Instead, thanks to my fatigue-management plan, a dolphin appears beside me, lunging through the waters of Hamilton Bay, sucking in air and smiling and laughing, which keeps me focused on breathing, moving fast, and connecting with the joy that running gives me.

My marathon pace feels easy so I press a little faster, focus on people ahead of me, on catching and passing them. The men are the easiest to pick off, likely because they went out too hard and are now flagging at the finish. Passing them feels awesome, floods me with yet more energy.

And suddenly, completely off my race plan, a bleacher pops up at the side of the road, and it's jam-packed with all my running heroes: Joan Benoit Samuelson is there. So is the indestructible marathoner Linda Somers Smith. And ultramarathoner Pam Reed, who outright won a 135-miler, nearly 5 hours ahead of her nearest male competitor. There's also Sister Madonna Buder, the Iron Nun, who, at 82, became the oldest person, man or woman, to complete an Ironman. Canadian marathon record holder Silvia Ruegger is also screaming encouragement. Leith is there too, reminding me to focus on what I'm learning from this race. What I'm learning is that this imagery stuff is powerful, hallucinogenic even, because now my heroes are all on their feet, cheering wildly for me, like it's the goddamn Olympic marathon I'm about to win.

I get another surge of crazy energy and step up the pace again, though I can't help but think of my race buddy, Mary, and wonder how she's coping with me pulling so far ahead, how she could possibly conjure up anything to compete with my bleacher full of heroes. But, it turns out, she has her own secret weapon. Bruce broke away from our struggling coach to pace Mary, and doggedly, determinedly, they have worked their way up to catch me until, suddenly, Mary is beside me. The first greeting out of her mouth? "Bitch." I congratulate her for catching me. We bump fists. Then, as we promised Leith, we start plotting to race each other through the last 3 kilometers to the finish.

Bruce is now ahead of us, trying to pace us both in, but he's comically out of the loop on our plan to race each other into the ground. This is an entirely new experience for us. In the past, we have focused on trying to hold a pace and finish in a certain time. Though we've been in many races, we haven't actually *raced*. We have never gone head-to-head against someone and tried to win.

Though Mary has always been faster, I feel stronger than I have ever felt at the end of a race, and I am certain I can beat her today.

I throw in a surge, pull past Bruce to get ahead of Mary. Mary responds, reappears at my left shoulder. A shocked Bruce struggles to get ahead of us again. I throw in another surge. Again Mary responds. When Bruce gets back out in front this time, he murmurs something about killing each other if we keep this up, though it may really be self-preservation he's worried about.

With 200 meters left, I break into a hard sprint, more than I can usually muster at the end of a race. I see Mary respond and Bruce give up trying to stay with us. But I have opened a few paces between Mary and me, and then gain the inside corner on the ramp into the stadium finish, a tactical move that forces Mary wide. I'm certain it will get me across the finish line first. But Mary, far from giving up, somehow finds an extra spurt of speed to cross the line right beside me. It is, for all we can tell, a photo finish.

After we receive our finishing medals, Mary throws up in the nearest trash can (it's a routine; I hold her hair), and then we grab each other in a huge hug, laughing that this is, by far, the most fun we have ever had in a race. With the extra adrenaline that comes from racing against a person rather than time, we threw everything we had at the road and ran faster, harder, than we thought possible.

Later, as my running club celebrates over beers at a pub, someone checks the online results and there's a wild roar—not because the clock gave me the win over Mary, but because I was ahead by just 2/100ths of a second. They can hardly believe we raced each other so aggressively and wonder, no doubt, what this might do to our close friendship.

But we are both ecstatic. We hardly care who came out ahead (well, maybe just a little), only that we both did so well. Training partners, now fierce rivals, still best friends, we know that we have developed the mental strength to compete hard right to the end and win—with everything we have in us. And that feeling is sublime.

Still, once my runner's high wears off (it seems like days later), I have questions. Will we be able to compete as hard in our spring marathon, especially if we're not together at the end to race each other in? Can I muster up that intensity on my own? Will my bleacher full of running heroes appear again, or will that powerful imagery wear out, as Leith says it can? How can I come up with anything more powerful? But I will have to, not only to cheer myself on through the last difficult months of training for the World Masters, but also to help myself train even harder and to summon within myself the belief that I might actually be able to challenge the front-runners. For as well as I ran that 30-K, I only finished 11th, a far distance from the podium. One thing is certain: This business of learning to compete hard and win will require ongoing work.

CHAPTER 6

STRONGER

THE HAPPIEST MAN at the 48-mile aid station of the Bighorn Mountain 100-mile ultramarathon is out of the race, a knee heavily bandaged. He wears a cockeyed smile of relief as he gazes at a fellow runner laid out on a stretcher, shaking uncontrollably and retching up the warm soup that a medic is trying to spoon into him. A few hours ago, just before nightfall, the two male front-runners checked through, both looking strong. Since then, guys have been staggering into the massive tent after 9 or more hours of running, many looking miserable and bone-cold from the plunge in temperature from 70°F at the start line to near freezing at night. A few are nauseous from scrambling up to 8,800 feet of altitude, and perhaps also at the thought of running another 52 miles through the cold night and most of the next day to reach the finish line. One 50-something guy, unable to warm up despite the blanket and warm drinks I've been fetching him, knows his race is over. He wears a thousand-yard death stare that could drop a moose. As a volunteer nurse so aptly put it later, the aid and food station was beginning to look more like a MASH tent for the hypothermic.

And then the women start trickling in. To my shock, they are smiling, exuberant even, gushing about the beauty of this wild mountain range they have just run through and how much fun they're having. Faces glowing, they could have walked right out of the *New England Journal of Medicine* study that reported the endorphin levels of ultrarunners are among the highest ever measured. Among the first 10 women is Meaghen Brown, just 24 years old and a former ballet dancer. She will go on to finish third woman overall (in any age group)—in a time of just over 28 hours—and will tell me later, "Some of the happiest running I've done in my life happened out there on the course."

This is why I have flown to this race in the heart of America's Old West, Wyoming, USA, to see firsthand how strong women runners can be. The so-called weaker sex may not be as fast, but we are more likely than men to complete these grueling ultradistances and will often be in better condition at the end. More than a few researchers studying their extraordinary ultra performances believe that when it comes to endurance, women are the stronger athletes. Through the winter and the second training segment of my super-fit year, as I pumped weights to prepare myself for an attempt to run the fastest marathon of my life, I became obsessed with the unique qualities of our strength. How and why are women so strong? How is it possible for older women to maintain that strength and endurance? And how can we get even stronger?

I called up Pam Reed, one of the top ultrarunners in the world, and she shared training advice, much of it motivational, then invited me to shadow her in this 100-miler, crewing for her at aid stations and pacing her through the final 20 miles or so. Pam has the distinction of being the only woman to win what's been called the world's toughest footrace, the Badwater Ultramarathon, a 135-mile (217-kilometer) grunt through hell on earth, California's Death Valley, where temperatures have spiked to 134°F, giving it the distinction of being the hottest place on the planet. That race ends with a brutal 4,760-foot climb to the trailhead of Mount Whitney. The first time Pam attempted Badwater, in 2002 at age 41, the tiny runner—just 5 foot 3 and 100 pounds—won the thing outright, trouncing her nearest male competitor by nearly 5 hours. Many called it a fluke. So she returned the next year and won it outright again. A month after this 100-miler in Bighorn, at age 52, Pam will complete her ninth Badwater (she attempted but dropped out of two others). She will finish second woman (13th overall)—but nearly 2 hours faster than ultrarunning legend Dean Karnazes, 50 at the time of the race and also hailed as one of the fittest men on the planet. She will also beat 38-year-old Navy SEAL David Goggins. "It feels good to be able to do that," admits Pam.

At Bighorn, she arrives at the 48-mile aid station at 11:45 p.m., a little behind schedule, and plunks herself down on a folding chair, right between Happy Man and Retching Man, and is oblivious to both. "The trick to running 100 miles is to reach 50 feeling great," Pam had told me earlier. I couldn't fathom that, yet here she is with the same live-wire energy she had when she started running more than 12 hours ago. Retching Man and Happy Man are both a good 15 years younger than Pam, yet she's the one still in the race. And she is focused on one thing now: getting back on the trail as fast as possible.

I go into crew mode, fetching her warm clothing, food, drinks, extra batteries for her headlamp and iPod. She eats a couple of cheese quesadillas, sips from all four drink options I hand her (who knows what will sit well after 12 hours of running?) and, 14 minutes later, she heads out into the night doing her "funny little jog," as she calls it, a gait she can keep up for days, as she once did in setting a world record for running 301 miles without sleep. That feat took her just under 80 hours—3 full days and nights, plus nearly 8 hours more of continuous running without stopping for more than a few minutes in every 25-mile loop. A precautionary hospital checkup an hour after she finished revealed that she suffered no more than a small blister and sore hamstrings. Pam herself could not believe how good she felt.

○   ●   ○   ●   ○   ●   ○

JUST AFTER MIDNIGHT, I drive back down the mountain to get a few hours of sleep before returning in the morning to pace Pam through the final stretch of the race. While she's out there running through the night, I can barely keep my eyes open—until a moose staggers into my headlights, forcing me to veer sharply to avoid smashing into it. Awake and with my adrenaline pumping now, I try to imagine being out there with Pam, running through the darkness in a mountain range populated with moose, black bears, snakes.

When I spoke to Pam before the race, she made running 100 miles seem *almost* normal. "You can't think about the distance," she advised. (And perhaps not the wildlife either.) "If I thought about what I was doing, I wouldn't do half of it. It's big. But if you go out and do it and experience it and let it happen, it happens. A 50-K ultra is a glorified marathon. A 50-miler will teach you to run slower. Running a 50-miler is so enjoyable because you're not pushing yourself. You're jogging and having a good old time. See how you feel after that 50. How did you recover? You'll find out what your body is capable of. If you're brave, you'll do a 100. Go into it with zero expectations, maybe just to finish. You can do a lot of walking and it's totally doable. With experience, you get better. It doesn't have to be such a big deal."

But at the awards ceremony after the Bighorn race, when I ask the woman who finished second overall, Gwen Scott, if most women could run a 100-miler—not saying me or anything, but *most* women—she answered with a definitive *no*. "You have to *want* to run 100 miles. And most women don't want to."

○　●　○　●　○　●　○

ULTRAS—DEFINED AS anything longer than a marathon and with no upper limit—have been hyped up as extreme, brutally tough, male-dominated events. Yet, in competing head-to-head with men, women are proving they can hold their own. It's not unusual for women to finish in the top 10 and occasionally even win the race outright. While the differential between world-record times for men and women is about 10 percent across most race distances, that shrinks to about 5.3 percent at 100 kilometers (62 miles), and it seems that the longer and tougher the race, the better women can do. When women started running the Leadville 100-miler, which winds through the Rocky Mountains of Colorado and boasts extremes in weather, they were more likely than men to complete the race. Some 90 percent of them brought home a prestigious finisher's buckle, compared to only 50 percent of men. The race director from 1984 to 2010, Merilee Maupin, says the women who attempted the 100-miler in the 1980s were more often experienced ultrarunners—one reason for their high finish rate. But she also believes women are stronger pacers and "just tougher." Evidence of that: In 2012, a 53-year-old woman—Liz Bauer—broke the world record for completing the most 100-milers in 1 year (36), a record that was previously held by another woman, Monica Scholz, at 25 races.

Remarkably, these exceptional results are being produced within a much smaller talent field. Women still comprise only about 20 percent of ultrarunners, which shrinks to maybe 10 percent in the most difficult races. And yet major stars have emerged, one of the trailblazers being Ann Trason, a high-school science teacher from California who won several ultras outright and finished as the top woman 14 times at the Western States Endurance Run, the world's oldest and most prestigious 100-miler. Scotland-born Ellie Greenwood, among a new generation of greats, broke Trason's Western States women's course record in 2012, covering the 100-mile trail in an incredible 16:47:19. American Krissy Moehl has amassed 46 wins—2 outright—in 96 races and held the women's record on the Ultra-Trail du Mont-Blanc until fellow American Rory Bosio eclipsed it by nearly 3 hours in 2013, when she became the first woman to crack the top 10 in what is considered the world's toughest trail ultra, a 104-mile romp that spans three countries (France, Italy, Switzerland), crosses some 400 summits in the Alps, and dishes up 31,000 feet of vertical punishment, higher than Mount Everest. And how's this for astonishing: In one 4-week blitz, Brit Lizzy Hawker won the 2012 women's Ultra-Trail du Mont-Blanc and the women's 100-mile Run Rabbit Run in Colorado and set a course record for women in Greece's 155-mile Spartathlon Ultra Race.

Studies suggest that women ultrarunners are getting even better while men may be plateauing. One study out of the University of Zurich found that in each year between 1998 and 2011, the 10 fastest women increased their running speed by 3.2 percent while running speed stayed the same for the top 10 men. It also revealed that masters runners—both men and women over 30—produced the fastest times, predominantly due to steadier pacing. Some research suggests that after the age of 50, women may slow down more than men, but that may well change as the massive numbers of talented women who took up the sport in this running boom continue into their 50s. Indications are that women are continuing to get faster and are still conquering these unfathomable distances well into their 60s, 70s, and even 80s. At age 60, American Gunhild Swanson set a new women's 60-to-69 age-group record at the Western States 100-miler, completing it in 25:40:28, and is still running ultras at age 69. And American Helen Klein, who only started running at 55, ran eight ultras at age 80 and set age-group world records in two of them.

Then there are the self-described "ordinary" women who attempt 100-milers, such as a fellow Canadian I met at the sign-in for Bighorn, Lori Herron, a strikingly attractive woman with supremely toned muscles and long blond hair. Spotting her across the room, I guessed her to be in her late 20s. Knowing the competing demands of family for younger women, I asked her how she found the time to devote so many hours to training. She blushed and quickly fessed up that she's 53, with two daughters in their 20s. Her work, she told me, is perfect training for the ultra. As a letter carrier, she lugs 40 to 50 pounds of mail while walking 6 to 9 miles (10 to 15 kilometers) a day. On top of that, she puts in a couple of shorter runs during the week, 4 hours on Saturdays, and up to 7 hours on Sundays. This was her seventh 100-miler. She says she does them because she loves running, loves the outdoors, loves being strong. And she loves challenging herself.

Too few women runners possess that "physical curiosity" to see just how strong and fast they can be, thinks Kathrine Switzer, the first woman to officially complete the Boston Marathon. She is also the author of several running books, a TV commentator, and a deep thinker on the sport. As we discussed the potential of women runners, she told me she considered herself good but not particularly fast, yet trained like a fiend to see just how fast she could be, hoping to break 3 hours in the marathon. She got down to 2:51. But too few women push themselves to explore their potential, she says. Though Switzer doesn't believe the best women will ever run faster than the best men in the marathon, that speed advantage does not make men better runners, she contends. "Women are not better or worse runners," she says. "We are *different* athletes. But races are all designed to showcase men's unique strengths—for speed and explosive power. Races have yet to be invented that test women's unique strengths." She then ripped off a list of our feminine superpowers: the ability to endure heat and cold, sleep deprivation, intense pain, stress, and extreme-distance running.

I dread what such a race might look like: perhaps a 1,000-mile migration across the African savanna (about the distance we can walk on our greater fat stores) through sizzling hot days and frigid nights while breastfeeding a baby, herding a passel of children, and—drawing on our great powers for empathy and self-denial—forgoing our own needs to give whatever paltry food is available to the youngsters. And to think that the fastest man in the world—showered with riches and fame—gets to go home to a hot meal and warm bed after sprinting a mere 100 meters.

○   ●   ○   ●   ○   ●   ○

SINCE WOMEN HAVE blasted onto the ultra scene, researchers have been trying to understand why women are proving to be such exceptional endurance athletes. After analyzing performances in the 56-kilometer Two Oceans Ultra in South Africa, sports physiologist Tim Noakes, author of *Lore of Running,* once predicted that women who could run as fast as men at marathon distances would actually *outpace* those men beyond 41 miles. He has since reneged on that prediction. A catch in the study: It was based on recreational runners. Elite male and female marathoners have more similar body weights, while male recreational runners are often 22 pounds heavier than their female counterparts, which means they have more mass to move, and that becomes increasingly difficult over longer distances. Current ultra research shows that the men's field runs faster than the women's field, sometimes by as much as 20 percent, but there could be a catch to that data as well. The superior speed of men could be attributed to training, as men generally put in more mileage while women are often more reluctant to take time away from family and friends. One study showed that female ultrarunners trained, on average, just 12½ hours a week, less time than I spend preparing for marathons.

And perhaps that makes the considerable success of women in the sport all the more intriguing. Handicapped by slower speed, less training, and a smaller talent pool, women still turn in exceptional performances. How? Why?

Physiologically, women bring amazing endurance traits to ultrarunning. We generally have a higher percentage of slow-twitch muscles, which, though less powerful, are far slower to fatigue. Women's muscle tissue may also have greater fatigue resistance. One study of isometric contraction showed that while young men (ages 18 to 35) were stronger, women of the same age took longer to reach task failure in low-force fatiguing contractions of the sort we use to hold a baby or ourselves upright. In older adults (ages 65 to 80), the fatigue resistance was similar between the sexes. Certainly, our higher percentage of fat, while a drag on speed, provides superior insulation when racing in cold weather, handy in high-altitude and overnight ultras. Fat is also the major fuel used on long slow runs, and countless studies show that the female body is particularly adept at burning that fat and sparing glycogen in muscles—perhaps the reason why women often look "fresher" at the end of endurance events compared to the drained, haggard look of men who have burned through their stores of glycogen. A Turkish study showed that in response to exercise, women produce more glutathione, an antioxidant that makes us more resistant to oxidative stress, which can damage muscle. We can also shed heat more readily without copious sweating, which also staves off dehydration. Certainly, men have numerous and obvious advantages—bigger lungs and hearts, greater oxygen-carrying capacity, bigger muscles—but women's smaller bodies can be advantageous on hillier courses, as they're lighter to haul up steep slopes. One of the best male ultra competitors in the world is Spaniard Kilian Jornet Burgada, who is just 5 foot 5 and 125 pounds but a brilliant mountain runner. Pam, who is even tinier, says her favorite section of Badwater is a wicked 20-mile uphill where she methodically picks off competitors to pass.

Pam's mental grit testifies to the psychological strengths women bring to ultrarunning. Olympic historian Karl Lennartz, PhD, argues that women are more patient, steadier pacers, often finishing an ultra moving at the same speed or slightly faster than they were at the start. Men, hyped on adrenaline, often go out too fast and flame out. A study in the *Journal of Strength and Conditioning Research* showed that "even pacing" is the most effective strategy in both marathon and ultra events, and that women are "optimal pacers." In a variation on that theme, sports psychologist Bruce Gottlieb has said that men think "harder, faster, stronger"— great for shorter races—while women "think with more determination and tenacity," which are handy traits for handling soul-sucking, never-ending miles. Running journalist Andy Milroy goes so far as to suggest that women bring an evolutionary psychological advantage to the sport, possessing the capacity to endure greater pain and stress that is helpful during childbirth as well as ultras, where athletes can hit the so-called wall not once but multiple times.

When I spoke with Pam before she started the Bighorn Ultra, she attributed her massive first win at Badwater to her ability to run in extreme heat, steady pacing, and a strong race crew who came up with a litany of tricks to cool her down and keep her properly fueled. But she also believes women, especially older women, can be stronger mentally. "Women who sign up for Badwater tend to complete it. A lot of men might not show or drop out. When women say they are going to do something, they do it. And with age, you get stronger in your mind and you know your body better." She agrees with Kathrine Switzer that a good male runner will usually beat a good female, but she believes women too often sell themselves short. "All we want to do is beat other women or win our age group. Why don't we try to win? I want to pass everyone, man or woman. When I pass someone, I get their energy and I can use that to pass someone else." As for how women can get stronger, she says this: "Get to the finish line. It gives you that much more confidence and strength for the next time."

○　●　○　●　○　●　○

BUT GETTING TO THE FINISH LINE is not a given for Pam, not today. Some 40 of 166 runners will drop out of this tough 100-miler, including, surprisingly, the two front-running women. The leader was forced out during the night when a medical check at an aid station revealed she had lost too much weight to continue safely—she blamed faulty scales and a change to lighter clothing, but also admitted later that she felt pretty shaky. This was her first 100-miler.

The new leader reached the Dry Fork Ridge aid station—at mile 82½—early in the morning and plunked down on the grass, her knees trashed. Someone carried two children to her open arms and, to the awe of runners and volunteers, she breastfed the baby while her older child danced around her. Perhaps contemplating the needs of her young family and the toll another 18 miles of largely downhill slogging would take on her knees, she too dropped out.

Meanwhile, as I wait at Dry Fork Ridge, Pam is nowhere on the horizon. After an hour, I calculate the cost of adding a few more miles to my pacing duties and decide to run back along the course to meet her and hopefully bring her some energy. It shocks me that I have the confidence to pace in an ultrarunning legend without having done an ultra myself, let alone any mountain running. I attribute it to the weight lifting I did over the winter, mostly targeting my legs but also my overall strength and, apparently, supersizing my ego.

During this "stronger" segment of my super-fit year leading up to a spring marathon, in addition to running 5 days a week (building to 59 miles, or 95 kilometers), I hit the gym twice a week to lift free weights, the most efficient and targeted way of building strength, though, for me, not nearly as exciting as running. But I dug deep into my motivational bag of tricks and persevered, and I'm thrilled I did. One study suggests masters runners can increase their running economy—the ability to run faster with less oxygen— by about 6 percent by doing strength training for their legs.

My personal trainer, Kirsten, came along on my first day since I knew virtually nothing about pumping iron and found the lingo of "sets" and "repetitions" mystifying. She showed me four different lifts as well as the proper form for each lift (critical to avoid injury as well as work the right muscles) and started me on weights heavy enough to exhaust my muscles after 8 to 10 lifts, apparently called "repetitions," or "reps," that together constitute a "set." She prescribed 3 sets of each lifting exercise and, between those, exercises to work my core while I gave my lifting muscles a rest. The constant movement kept my heart rate up, giving me a hit of cardio as well. Even better, constantly working rather than standing around resting got me out of the gym in under an hour.

My goal was to pump up my speed and endurance for the marathon, but I also wanted to build overall strength to avoid developing that frail upper body that runners can have. According to a study at McMaster University, lifting heavier weights targets fast-twitch muscle fibers (great for speed), while lifting lighter weights targets the slow-twitch fibers (great for endurance, though running gives us that). Benefits will come whether lifting a lighter weight for more repetitions or piling on the weight and doing fewer reps. What's most critical to building muscle is volume—3 sets rather than 1 or 2—and also working the muscles to exhaustion. That stress is what provokes the chemical reaction that repairs, builds, and strengthens muscles.

For older women, muscle researcher Mark Miller believes there's benefit in working the muscle to exhaustion by doing more reps with lighter weights. His research shows that our muscle tissue may age differently from men's, maintaining similar strength but losing more power. That means that with age, our muscles may not contract as fast. He thinks endurance-style weight training—lifting less weight for more reps—may help preserve power, but has yet to prove that theory with a full-fledged study. One 80-year-old sprinter I spoke to has been covering both bases: In one session she lifts heavy for strength, and in another session she goes light for power.

From my limited time at the gym, I see women's greatest challenge in building strength to be *owning* our strength. A number of women at the start of the Bighorn ultra had no trouble flaunting that attitude, wearing running shirts with slogans like "Strong Is the New Beautiful" and "Strong Is the New Skinny." These runners, along with so many in the sporting sisterhood around the world, may well be ushering in a new wave of feminism, laying claim to an equal right to be physically strong by throwing off the shackles that have been placed on women's strength, from foot binding to constricting bodies in black robes in desert heat to, in North America, touting impossible thinness as a sign of sexiness, which is really just another way of tarting up feminine weakness to make men seem even stronger by comparison.

My gym is located in the most multicultural neighborhood in Canada, and I work out during women-only hours, when women from diverse cultures take over the exercise room and claim the right to be healthy and strong. Aerobic strength is clearly in: Many plug away on treadmills and exercise bikes while wearing headscarves and hijabs. But no matter what culture, only a few women do strength training, and even then most crank away on puny weights as if lifting a yo-yo, as if they believe they are inherently frail or are afraid of building Mr. Universe–sized muscles. That's just not going to happen for women, unless they're juicing on steroids.

Pound for pound, our muscle can be every bit as strong as men's, but men have larger muscles (that's the reason they can run faster and carry more weight) and more testosterone, which enables them to build those bigger, bulkier muscles. For women, it's a challenge to build muscle at all, let alone bulky ones. Lifting weights creates lean, strong muscle and improves the quality, tone, and power of the more than 650 (counts vary) we have in our bodies. Ignore those muscles and it's like ignoring a major part of your body mass. Ignore them, and those muscles actually fill up with fat, like the thick white gelatinous wedge surrounding a steak. And while both men and women may lose up to 40 percent of their muscle mass between the ages of 30 and 80, women are more prone to frailty because we start out with less muscle mass in the first place.

But here's the thing: *We don't have to lose that muscle.* Sedentary living contributes more to the loss of muscle mass than aging, according to a study that compared the muscle masses of

65-year-old-plus masters athletes with those of sedentary controls and younger athletes. Masters athletes—both men and women—who exercised over a lifetime retained both muscle mass and strength that were comparable to those of *athletes* decades younger. In fact, the muscles of a 70-year-old triathlete looked pretty much the same as they did in a 40-year-old triathlete. The study found that for both men and women athletes, strength did not start declining until 60 and then not significantly, even into their 80s.

Recent studies are now also showing a relationship between muscle fitness and mortality. One, published in the *European Journal of Preventive Cardiology,* looked at the ability of adults ages 51 to 80 to sit down on and rise from the floor, an exercise that tests the muscle strength and flexibility of the entire body. Researchers broke down the participants' scores on the test into four units; each unit of improved ability to haul oneself up off the floor conferred a 21 percent improvement in survival rates.

The great news for those who haven't been doing strength sports or lifting weights is that we can build muscle strength at any age—and fast. Numerous studies show that both men and women can quickly rebuild lean muscle mass without making an outrageous amount of effort. A Boston University study put older athletes on a 12-week strength-training program, and they improved their muscle strength by 40 percent. A Marquette University study of 217 adult women across a range of ages compared their responsiveness to a 12-week strength-training program. The researcher on that study, Sandra Hunter, PhD, says older women—from ages 70 to as old as 90—were able to increase their maximum strength by 41 percent. "Some older women gained 6 years in strength. After training, their muscle became younger. The contractile machinery acted more like a young person's." In yet another study, frail elderly people who did weight training three times a week were able to increase their strength by 5 percent *per training day.* They followed a protocol similar to mine, doing 8 repetitions with 80 percent of the maximum weight they could lift once.

So how much stronger did I get? I already felt pretty robust from running and the sports I played into my 40s, but in the 3 months before my 51st birthday, I improved from lifting 65 pounds on the squat and deadlift to lifting 95 pounds; from holding 10 pounds in each hand on the split squat to holding 20. At first, I struggled to do 10 pushups, but was soon ripping off 25 in each of 3 sets. Holding a plank for 30 seconds had me shaking like a wet dog initially, but soon I was doing one-arm-and-one-leg planks to make a 90-second plank feel hard, and I repeated that 3 times. While I remained pathetic at the most wondrous exercise of all—the chinup, which works just about every muscle in the body—I kept at it, working my way up from nothing to a shaky 3.

Besides vastly increased strength, I enjoyed another unexpected benefit. That Boston University study of older athletes showed that building muscles also builds stronger minds: Participants reported having less anxiety, improved mood, and more confidence. I felt the same wonderful boost in overall well-being—especially right after weight training—and that makes sense. Exercise-science professor Sandra Hunter told me to think of our muscles as a single endocrine organ that "pumps out a lot of hormones." All the good stuff that floods through our bodies after a weight-training session to repair, rejuvenate, and grow muscles also benefits other cells, for instance by spurring on the growth of new neurons in the brain, which can lead to improved cognitive function.

Yet building strength remains a mental challenge because there is no end point. *We must keep doing it.* Like running, as soon as we stop, we start losing benefits. For runners, it's particularly critical to strength train. In addition to our oft-neglected skinny upper bodies, the repetitive act of running develops some muscles and undertrains others, throwing the musculoskeletal structure out of balance, which can strain and injure muscles that are overused. As well, one study showed that the muscle fibers in the legs of highly trained distance athletes who have continued training for more than 20 years were actually smaller and weaker than those of sedentary controls. The smaller fibers are an adaptation to distance running, which requires fast contraction and sustained submaximal power over a long period, but not necessarily a lot of strength or power. The trick to strength training over the long haul may well be finding something we will enjoy doing over the long haul. Alternatives to lifting weights include isometrics and strength sports such as yoga, paddling, rowing, cycling, kettlebell, and swimming.

For me, feeling and looking strong is powerful motivation to keep at the weights. After a mere 3 months, the layer of fat under my skin that I could not shed while just running seemed to turn into a thin sheath of muscle. Little wonder. As my personal trainer and nutritionist Kirsten is always reminding me, the body has two storage containers for the energy we eat: fat and muscle. It's better to have muscle to pack excess energy into, since fat is deadweight while muscle is a metabolic workhorse. Per pound, muscle burns between 6 and 15 calories a day compared to the measly 2 calories that a pound of fat operates on. Adding muscle mass cranked up my sluggish metabolism and my weight dropped down to 113 just before my target marathon. My abs, shoulders, and arms took on enough definition to elicit "wows" from friends taking winter dips in our hot tub. And I have to fess up: I passed way too much time standing naked in front of the mirror admiring my new buff self. That's something I just never expected to happen at age 50, especially given that I'd spent the previous 3 decades avoiding the mirror.

As my marathon approached, I worried that lifting weights during the ramp-up in mileage would exhaust my legs. The opposite proved true. Though I was working far harder, the training felt far easier. My body wasn't nearly as sore and cranky after tough runs. I recovered much faster. Day to day, I had more energy. I had way more enthusiasm for the longest runs and toughest speed and hill workouts. And building strength delivered the jackpot I was hoping for: improved speed. Three months before my target marathon in January, I hit a marathon race pace that would bring me in at my sub-3:35 goal. But my heart rate was banging away at 166 beats, barely under my lactate threshold, and I felt like I was sprinting. After a month of lifting, when I repeated that 2-kilometer race pace trial, my heart rate hummed along at 160, well under my lactate threshold, and the pace felt far easier.

What role did strength training play in that improvement? I put that question to Jason Vescovi, who tested my VO2 at the beginning of my super-fit year. He said strength training alone won't increase VO2, but being stronger would enable me to run harder and longer, which could boost that ultimate measure of cardiorespiratory fitness. He also sent me a study that showed that although triathletes who supplemented endurance training with heavy weight training for 14 weeks did not improve their VO2s, they did increase their overall strength and running economy compared to triathletes who did only endurance training. Running economy, apparently, refers not to the amount of money I spend on sneakers each year, but rather to the efficiency of my stride: Being stronger enables me to use less oxygen per stride.

At the start of my super-fit year (see Chapter 2), Vescovi had measured my relative max VO2 at 39, which was well above the 29 that sedentary women my age typically score. He had warned me that with aging, VO2 can decline by 2.5 percent a year in trained endurance athletes such as myself, but if I could forestall that decline and maintain my VO2 of 39 through the year, I could consider it a training win. Instead, training scored a *decisive* win. My relative max VO2, which I had tested again, this time a month after my spring marathon, had gone up to 43.2. My absolute max VO2—which does not take into account the pounds I had shed and is a better measure of true cardiorespiratory fitness gains—increased from 2.05 liters per minute to 2.33, a significant increase of 13.7 percent.

That kind of increase is not unusual for sedentary folks who embark on training programs. Studies show they can boost their VO2 by as much as 11 to 15 percent in just 4 months. But it's tougher for older endurance-trained athletes like myself to boost VO2 because we have already trained ourselves to a degree closer to our maximum potential. Yet I managed a pretty big increase, suggesting that so-called age-related decline in VO2, like a decline in muscle mass, may also be due more to a decline in physical activity.

So let me pause here to pull out the scorecard on my super-fit year so far. The bump in my relative max VO2 to 43.2, measured a month after my 51st birthday, now gives me the cardiorespiratory fitness of trained, athletic college-age women, who typically have VO2s in the 40 to 46 range. On paper, at least, and with just more than 2 months left to train until the World Masters in Italy, I achieved my goal to recover the fitness I had as a 20-something university athlete. On the scales, I can lay claim to being in even better shape— I now weigh 25 pounds less and am significantly more toned. Perhaps more fabulous is what all this strength and aerobic training has done to my head because, honestly, I *feel* like a 20-something kid bursting with energy and confidence as I scamper back along the trail at Bighorn in search of ultramarathoner Pam Reed.

○   ●   ○   ●   ○   ●   ○

WHEN I FINALLY MEET UP with Pam on the trail, nearly 24 hours after she started running, she's struggling at the bottom of a long, steep slope, her funny little jog barely faster than a walk. The heat on this mid-June day is starting to build. She's 2 hours off her time goal, and her mood shows it. She's angry—at the course, at herself, maybe even at me. "Ugh," she responds to my greeting. "I would have dropped out by now if you weren't waiting for me."

I don't know how to respond to that, if her staying in the race is a good thing or not. To build her strength, Pam does hot yoga, cycles, and swims—she hates lifting weights—but she remains rail thin at the best of times and looks skeletal now.

"I'll carry your pack," I say.

She readily rips off her hydration pack that holds her water and, with a burst of energy that seems to come from a grunt of frustration, starts running up the hill.

For the next hour, I trot alongside Pam, blathering about whatever comes to mind—the happy guy, the retching guy, the moose that almost destroyed my rental car—anything to try to lift Pam's spirits and distract her from the pain of braking with nearly every step as the trail now plunges down some 4,000 feet into Tongue River Canyon. I can sympathize. My legs may not be trained for this steep descent, but there are still 80 fewer miles on them and the agony explodes in my quads with every footfall. Perhaps even tougher for Pam, streams of runners are passing us now, a few from the 100-miler, though most from the 50-mile and 50-K races that started on the same course earlier that morning.

"I need to listen to music," Pam says, finally releasing me from my hapless attempts at cheering her. She puts in her earbuds and retreats to whatever place it is that runners go to during the darkest moments of a race.

For Pam, that's doing battle with her "anorexic brain," as she calls it. She has struggled with the condition since the age of 14 and writes candidly about it in her book, *The Extra Mile*. She has been hospitalized on several occasions, but considers running her best treatment. Her love for the sport keeps her fighting to stay alive. To run, she must fuel her body. And yet, while I gobble down sandwiches and pizza slices at aid stations and urge her to take at least a gel, she will eat nothing over the nearly 6 hours and 20 miles I pace her. She will barely drink any water. She will not glance at the plunging canyon walls, the river gushing below us, the high alpine meadows painted with spring flowers, a sky so blue it yanks my heart into my throat. For her, the race has narrowed to the few feet of trail in front of her. And to me, her race now seems more about punishment than joy, a theory I will float out to her later, long after it's over.

"Our subconscious is wild," Pam will say. "I still struggle with anorexia. But I don't starve myself. I eat what I want. But still these times come up when I'm unable to eat at times I need to eat. It's like I'm sabotaging myself." As for brutally long races being another way of being hard on herself, Pam says her goal in life has always been this: "I do not want to be average. I want to be different. If it's not hard, it's not worth doing. What you saw, I'm like that in 98 percent of things. It's really hard. That's why I do it. Bighorn is one of the toughest. People drop out. Finishing it gives me power and pride."

At Bighorn, I never doubt that Pam will finish. I just dread how much longer it might take her. Two younger women pass us, almost apologetically. They shout out to Pam how much they like her book. It brings a small smile to her face.

Then another runner passes us, Pam's husband, Jim, who is racing the 50-K. He mumbles a "How's it going," barely slowing to hear her answer, which is a frustrated shudder. "We'll catch up to him on the road," she vows.

I dread that thought too.

In her book, Pam writes that in a marriage of two competitive athletes, "there's going to be drama." On the drive to the start of the 100-miler yesterday, Pam and Jim, parents of five boys, got into a spat that was bigger than their usual bickering. Pam and I were struggling to locate the start line on the map and Jim, who was driving, lost it: "Pam," he shouted, "you don't know what the fuck you're doing." She hardly seemed to hear the outburst and directed him to do a U-turn.

I thought, *What a way to send your wife off on a 100-miler.* Now I wonder if it was his fear shouting, his frustration with her driving need to compete.

"If I listened to Jim, I wouldn't do half of what I do," admits Pam.

This is what Pam did in her 2013 racing year: a 15-mile snow bike race in January; a 30-K skate ski race and a 55-K run in February; a 50-mile run in March; the Zion 100-miler in April; a Half Ironman triathlon in May; the Bighorn 100-miler in June followed by a full Ironman the very next weekend; the Badwater 135-miler in July; the Leadville 100-miler in August and an Ironman a week later; in September, another Ironman, in which she would finish first in her age group to qualify for the world Ironman in Hawaii; in October, the Yellowstone 100-miler, her fourth 100-miles-or-more race of the year; in November, a Half Ironman; and in December she pulled on her race director's hat and "rested" by putting on the Tucson Marathon. Often, she'll throw in "little halves and marathons in between" ultras and triathlons, which she does "for speedwork," as she hates going to the track. She also hates doing long runs—bizarre coming from an ultrarunner. Instead, she trains by doing hour-long runs up to three times a day. "I think breaking it up helps keep me from being injured. And you can also go a little faster on each run." Her cross-training, she believes, also keeps her strong and injury free.

"This is my lifestyle," she will tell me after the race. "Men don't get a hard time for training hard, but women do, and women give each other a hard time. This is what I love doing. I will do this until I die. That's my plan. I don't think I'll live to 80 and I don't care. I want to be able to run until I die."

○　　●　　○　　●　　○　　●　　○

PAM IS NOT THE ONLY ultra athlete—or marathoncr, for that matter—to use running as a place to pour restless, obsessional energy, yet excessive training and racing can take a toll on health. One world-record distance runner I called for advice gave me plenty, along with a cautionary tale. Diane Palmason ran track as a teen in the 1950s, when women weren't allowed to compete in anything longer than 200 meters. She was good enough to race on Canada's national team at age 17, but knew her real talent lay in longer distances, so she grew disheartened and quit. At age 37, after hearing that women were now running marathons, she blasted back onto the scene, throwing off years of thwarted ambition as well as the stress of a bad marriage. That year, she ran her first marathon, a 3:54, on just 6 weeks of training (her best marathon time is 2:46). She went on to break nine world masters records and so many Canadian records in distances from 100 meters to 80 kilometers that she has lost count. Then at age 72, she began feeling off, having to slow down in races, even fainting at the end of one. Her doctor had little more to say than "Well, you are 72 and still running." But it turns out she had developed what's being called a "runner's heart," not an especially endearing term in the medical sense as it refers to a myocardial injury that is linked with excessive training.

A 2012 study for the Mayo Clinic found that "chronic training for and competing in extreme endurance events such as marathons, ultramarathons, Ironman-distance triathlons, and very long-distance bicycle races can cause transient acute volume overload of the atria and right ventricle" and "elevations of cardiac biomarkers." All of these changes return to normal within a week but, in some individuals, months or years of repetitive injury may lead to damaging structural changes such as stiffening of arteries, scarring of the heart muscle, a dangerously low resting heart rate, and arrhythmia (an irregular heartbeat). While the authors of the study concede that "lifelong vigorous exercisers generally have low mortality rates and excellent functional capacity" and that more research needs to be done, they wrote that "a safe upper-dose limit [of exercise] potentially exists, beyond which the adverse effects of physical exercise, such as musculoskeletal trauma and cardiovascular stress, may outweigh its benefits." The lead author, cardiologist James H. O'Keefe, MD, has since become an outspoken critic of extreme endurance training: "You reach a point of diminishing returns," he maintains, if you push beyond 30 to 60 minutes of cardio activity a day.

I first heard about this "dark side of running" from Mark Tarnopolsky, who gave me so much advice on "training smarter." When we set out for an early-morning run, the longtime endurance runner, also 50 at the time, told me he had developed atrial fibrillation, which he calls more of a nuisance than a concern. He's had two ablations, a procedure to destroy the area of heart muscle causing the abnormal rhythm. He takes medication that prevents his heart rate from going above 120 beats a minute, which makes it difficult to "keep up to the young bucks" in a race, though he still tries. A few kilometers into our run, we met up with a running buddy Tarnopolsky has trained with since university, who had also developed runner's heart. He had a pacemaker installed to keep his resting heart rate above 30 beats per minute. He still races as well. "The normal adaptation to marathon training is the heart rate goes down and the stroke volume—the ability to pump blood—goes up," Tarnopolsky told me. "But some will get into pathology. The heartbeat slows so much and the heart fills up with so much blood, when it beats, it's like a tiny explosion. You need to do 12 to 14 hours of training a week with high-intensity intervals to do the sport. Either you don't do the sport or you expose yourself to those risks." His advice? "If you feel trashed, if you're tired, your legs are heavy, take a day off. Mix up your activities to give your heart time to recover."

Diane Palmason was also diagnosed with atrial fibrillation and had a pacemaker installed. Now 75, she decided to stop competing. She attributes her heart problems to "distance, intensity, duration of running, and maybe some genetic predisposition"—her father died of a heart attack at 81, and her mother suffered a stroke, albeit at 91. But Diane admits to doing some pretty crazy things in her running career. She once ran a 2:55 marathon and, trying to break 2:50, ran another 2:55 marathon the next weekend. At age 49, she competed in a 1-day event that included five races: a 10-K, a 100-meter, a 400-meter, and a mile and concluded with a marathon. "It was exciting, but maybe not too smart," she admits now. "From 40 to 50, I wouldn't put any restrictions on my running. I was really pushing hard and not giving time for my heart muscle and leg muscles to recover and heal. If I were paying attention, I would have allowed more time for recovery after a hard effort."

Still, she doesn't regret her running career. It helped her leave her first marriage, introduced her to her second husband and countless friends, and also gave her a career as a running coach. Though she no longer races, she still runs four or five times a week near her home on Vancouver Island, poking along at a comfortable

pace and stopping when her standard poodle catches an interesting scent. "It's all very pleasant. And I have no chronic injuries, so
I did a few things right in my career."

Though excessive and intense distance running may have an
impact on the heart, it still seems to be far healthier than not running at all. In the United States, 600,000 people die of heart disease every year, making it the leading cause of death for both
men and women. According to one study of marathons and mortality, between 2000 and 2009, 28 people died while running
marathons or during the critical 24 hours after finishing; of those,
6 were women. All 28 had preexisting heart conditions. While the
number of participants in marathons vastly increased during those
10 years, the rate of mortality did not. And given that there were
more than 3.7 million marathon participants, such cases of sudden death are exceedingly rare—less than 1 percent—and only
about 0.5 percent for the half-marathon. Compared to the 1 in 7 in
the United States who die of heart disease, the 1 in 7 who die of
cancer, and the 1 in 28 who succumb to respiratory disease, I
vastly prefer my chances of survival as a marathoner.

○   ●   ○   ●   ○   ●   ○

AS FOR PAM'S STRUGGLE with obsessional tendencies, when
she talks about anorexia, it's almost as if she's talking about an old
friend who's annoying as hell, but has also given her a kind of
strength that's useful for running ultras. Pam has an amazing ability
to withstand deprivation and pain. She once ran 4 days after having a Caesarean, and is now driving herself forward, seemingly, on
sheer grit and willpower.

At about mile 95, the Bighorn trail connects to a wide, flat gravel road for the final 5 miles. That shift to flat terrain is a huge challenge to the ultrarunners who prefer trail running. But when Pam's feet hit the flat, she rockets out of her funny little jog and launches into a determined run. She is clearly more at home on the road, as I am. Of some use as a pacer now, I run alongside her, raving over her pace, calling out encouragement, and Pam responds, gaining even more speed.

It feels great to stretch out our legs, and we start picking off runners who passed us earlier, 100-milers who have staggered to a walk on the road. We even pass 50-milers and 50-K racers, who are also struggling to hold any kind of pace.

And finally we catch Jim.

"Where's the speed coming from?" he hollers as Pam passes him. With barely a shrug, she presses on, reeling in more runners.

I can hardly believe Pam's speed and wonder how long she can keep up this pace, after 96, 97 miles of running. As we pass water stations, I try to whip up excitement, get them cheering and clapping, to keep Pam's energy surging. "Hundred-miler coming through," I shout out. "Pam Reed, ultramarathon legend, coming through."

The two women runners who passed us earlier scream out as Pam passes them now: "You go, Pam!"

Pam mutters some encouragement back and, astonishingly, picks up even more speed. She is finding the stride she used during a "Boston double" one year, getting up early to run from the finish line to the start, which she did in 3:36, then turning around to race back, completing the official marathon in 3:30. At Bighorn, no one can answer Pam's speed. I have lost count of how many runners we have picked off, how many places we have moved up. What I do know is the finish line, so agonizingly far away all day long that I could not let myself think about it, is now less than 2 miles off.

And then, against all odds, Jim catches up to Pam. "Wouldn't it be nice if we finished together?" he suggests.

No, no, no, I think, my mind flashing back 28 hours to the start line, to their squabble over directions, spiked by mere frustration and nerves. In this last push, Pam is struggling with sleep deprivation, fried muscles, mental exhaustion, disappointment over her performance, and now she must deal with the rivalry between two athletes who happen to be wife and husband, one of whom devotes her life to her sport and one of whom puts his training second to pay the bills of raising five kids and the thousands of dollars Pam incurs racing every year.

And Jim is battling through his own dark space, I'm sure, provoked by resentment in moments like this and the fact that he's struggling to keep up with someone who has nearly 99 miles in her legs compared to the mere 30 in his.

About half a mile from the finish line, Jim wants to walk. And he wants Pam to walk with him. "What difference does a minute make!" he shouts as he slows, falls behind again.

There are so many strengths that racing demands: the ability to endure pain over an improbable distance; the heart to believe in the worthiness of the challenge and in the self to meet it; the confidence or self-love to put yourself first when the moment demands it, which can be so difficult for women.

I see Pam faltering, slowing, her energy being pulled into a spat about the meaning of a minute that's pregnant with decades of life.

I don't know where Pam is in the standings or who might catch her or what difference a minute might really make in this race, but I do know this: With her muscles seared from nearly 29 hours of running and this last scintillating hour of speed, changing gaits now will undo her, and we're oh so close to the finish.

I take a deep breath and marshal up a few strengths of my

own, thinking fast and taking charge. "Look," I say, running between them and slightly ahead as we veer off the road and into a park for that last push to the finish. "We are going to run to the finish line. And we are going to finish looking strong!"

Then I shout out to the fans gathered in the park to cheer in runners: "Husband-and-wife team coming through," I scream, raising my arms to get them going. "Let's hear it for the husband-and-wife team!"

The fans erupt, clapping and cheering them on. Caught in that spotlight, Pam and Jim do their best to look the happy couple and direct their energy into running strong to the finish.

My pacing duties done, I step aside and watch them cross the finish line together.

A few minutes later, Marta Ostler, 45, runs past me with her five children trotting alongside, cheering her through the last steps of her first 100-miler. She wears a massive smile as she crosses the finish line, yet bursts into tears when I ask her why she wanted to run 100 miles. "I just wanted to show my kids that they can do anything they set their minds to," she says.

○   ●   ○   ●   ○   ●   ○

A COUPLE OF HOURS LATER, back in my hotel room, I crack open the biggest, coldest bottle of beer I could find in the town of Sheridan, Wyoming, then sink into a tub full of hot water. My feet, knees, and quads—untrained for the unrelenting descent—are now repaying me for the punishment I gave them over the last 5 hours.

As I sip on my beer, begging my muscles to unknot, I decide that my pitifully flat feet will never allow me to train for a 100-miler, though that's what I said of the half-marathon, and then the marathon. Still, after this weekend, I am intrigued by the idea of trying a 50-K, maybe even a 50-mile trail ultra. The challenge isn't what entices me. With proper training, I'm sure I could do it. It's the adventure that calls, the opportunity to run in wild landscapes like I did today and share that exhilaration with other runners. As Pam suggests, I could do it as a slow jog or fast hike, only with aid stations along the way to provide the lunch. But given the hours of training required, I would not get hooked, *I could not get hooked,* though I said that about the marathon too, and I just completed my fourth 3 weeks ago, a month after turning 51.

That was the target race I had been training so hard for during this second training segment of my super-fit year: my attempt to prove I could attain the fitness of a 20-something athlete by running under 3:35 and achieving the toughest Boston qualifying standard for women.

The morning of the Toronto Marathon, a heat wave blew into the city, spiking the temperature well above the winter temperatures we had been training in and well above the perfect marathon temperature of 51°F—the point at which the exercising body doesn't have to work to warm up or shed heat. Midrace, the temperature reached 70°F, and felt like 80.

My running buddy, Mary, started out with me. Our plan was to work together to hold our pace of 7:38 a mile (5:03 per kilometer) until friends met us at the 20-mile (32-kilometer) mark to pace us in the last 6 miles (10 kilometers). We had written out extensive race plans, and everything about our training indicated we could nail a sub-3:35. But nothing felt quite right on race day. Maybe it was nerves. It was definitely the heat. I couldn't get my hamstrings to loosen up. Mary struggled with nausea. I neglected to drink enough at water stations and stopped sweating early on.

Just more than halfway through, heading from the east side of Toronto through downtown to the west side of the city, my heart pounding in my chest, I could not believe how fast we were running, and for such a very long time. It's good to get the heart rate up. The world's oldest Ironman, Lew Hollander, recommends going anaerobic every day, *every day,* and he still races in his 80s. And it's good to run long distances. Researchers identified a "blue zone" on the island of Sardinia in Italy, home to the world's longest-lived people, shepherds who travel countless miles a day herding livestock through this mountainous terrain; a centenarian woman living there claimed she walked 19 miles (30 kilometers) to her work on a farm and the same distance back, a veritable ultra every day over that hilly terrain, for much of her working life. But what's the magic combination of intensity and distance for good health, and how much is too much? While many marathoners can't imagine running 100-mile ultras no matter how slow the pace, many ultrarunners can't believe the intensity some marathoners race at.

When we picked up our pacers, Mary started to fall back. There's a history of heart trouble in her family, and she has a pre-teen daughter. Mary pushes herself hard in training and races, but she also has a strong instinct for self-preservation that seems more common in older runners, especially women. We call it knowing when to push it and knowing when to back off. Pam puts it this way: "I run to protect my running."

At 20 miles, I was still on pace and feeling pretty good. I was running hard, pushing right up against my lactate threshold and close to 90 percent of my max heart rate. My legs and heart take a pounding during a marathon, so I strike a deal with them: No running for a week after a race; no fast or long runs for a month after a marathon. I also try to limit myself to one marathon a year, though in some years I've done two. Current sports psychology seems to be all about overcoming the mind to push the body beyond what we think we can do, but I consider my brain a valuable companion on any run. My goal is to get brain and body on the same side, to perform to my fitness potential on race day, but without crashing the system.

At 22 miles (35 kilometers), as we ran alongside Toronto's waterfront, my left leg started cramping. Then my right leg started cramping. My pacer, Jennie, who runs marathons and ultras, told me she knew how much pain I was in. I begged her not to say the word "pain." I did not know it then, but I was badly dehydrated. My brain, my body–mind signaling mechanism, my central governor, or whatever dressed-up term I call common sense, was telling me this: If I pushed the pace, I would cramp up totally and end up at the side of the road, out of the race. But I wasn't about to give up, either. I kept pressing, albeit slower, but as hard as I could. I still had a pretty good time going, and as I had learned from my talks with Pam leading up to this race (and as she had demonstrated so superbly in the Bighorn ultra): Stay strong; do not give up on yourself; do not give up on the race; *anything can happen.*

Our coach calculated that the sudden spike in heat would add as much as 5 minutes to our finish times, and it did just about that. I finished in 3:38, 3 minutes over that elusive 3:35 and 5 minutes slower than the 3:33 target pace would have brought me in at. Mary finished just a minute behind me. Yet, during those last couple of miles of running through that brutal heat, as I badly fell off my pace, I still passed 41 people while only 1, a woman, passed me.

When I crossed the line, I accomplished something I could not have imagined when I started marathoning. Me, the short, stocky, still-smoking, flat-footed wonder who was too slow as a kid to make the elementary school track team: I had placed third in my age group, just 4 seconds behind the second-place woman and 6 minutes out of first place in my age group. And though I just missed that toughest Boston qualifying standard for women I was chasing, five age groups down from my own, here's some solace that a 51-year-old can take away: Of the 1,653 finishers, I was the

55th woman, faster than 582 other women and 678 men. Put another way, if the dinner bell rang out during the great migration across the African savanna, I would not be the frail one straggling behind, providing the feast. In fact, though I may be of postmenopausal, grandmotherly age, I could clearly still do my bit for the survival of the species by helping run down dinner.

Admittedly, I pushed myself hard in the race. Running pals who greeted me at the finish line insisted I go to the medical tent. They had a point. When I sat down, I couldn't get up on my own, my stomach and legs were cramping so badly.

In the tent, the only medical attention I received was a sports drink to help me rehydrate. I sat beside a younger woman who was in greater pain, albeit psychological. Sobbing, she told me she had missed that sub-3:35 Boston qualifying time, only she was under 34, which meant she would not be going to Boston. I didn't tell her that I ran an 11-minute personal best and had easily qualified for Boston in my age group, with 21 minutes to spare. Instead, I commiserated with her, as women do. I told her that I missed my time goal too, and it sucked but, hey, we ran a damn fine marathon in brutal heat, and, there's a silver lining here: We still have a goal to shoot for. Boston is a powerful motivator, and we still have that to keep us training hard over the next year. And if we were strong enough to run this time in this heat, we know we can nail our goal in the next marathon.

She perked up and smiled at me. I felt like I had paced in another sister, helping her find her strong. And that felt awesome.

BACK IN WYOMING, when I finally haul my aching body out of that hot tub, my legs are even stiffer, if that is possible. This is not good. I am heading into my next and shortest training segment—working on increasing my speed to compete with the front-runners at the World Masters—and this exercise in punishment will knock off nearly a week of precious training time. My aching quads will not let me run for 5 days.

Pam, however, seems no worse for the 100 miles of wear and tear on her body. She has left a text on my cell phone. She sent it an hour ago from a downtown restaurant, inviting me to have dinner with her and Jim. The next morning she will run the 3 miles from the hotel to the awards breakfast to accept a Bighorn award—an engraved rock—for finishing first among women in her age group and fourth among all women, just 17 minutes behind the third-place winner, the former ballerina who is just more than half Pam's age. I tap out "Thanks, but I am dead" in reply to Pam's text, then hobble across my hotel room to collapse in my bed, where I will sleep for 10 hours.

CHAPTER 7

FASTER

OF COURSE, THE DAY AFTER my marathon, my mind fixated on how to get 3 minutes faster, to finish sub-3:35. But getting faster is not easy. Trying to get faster can be hugely humbling.

Take this practice sprint at a high-school track on Canada's west coast. Beside me on the start line is a 76-year-old great-grandmother, Christa Bortignon. Let that sink in for a moment: *76 years old*. More than a quarter-century older than I am. Just 4 years shy of 80, If I need to point that out. Yet I already know this race won't be much of a contest, given that she is the fastest 75-plus woman in the world.

I manage to stay even with Christa for, oh, maybe three strides. Then she powers forward, bounding as if on springs, surging like white froth on rapids. When she flies across the 60-meter finish mark, I am a good 25 meters behind.

In my defense, I am trained for endurance rather than speed, and Christa regularly outruns trained sprinters two and three age groups younger. Since the semiretired accountant took up running 4 years ago—yes, at age 72!—she has won some 80 medals at various masters games. In the past 2 years, the 5-foot-1

102-pounder has broken 14 age-group world records and now holds world records in virtually everything she competes in, which is a lot: sprints, hurdles, triple jump, long jump, and the heptathlon and pentathlon, which are multievent competitions involving sprints, jumps, and weight throws. In 2013, she won gold in every event she entered in world competitions and bested her own world record in the 200 meters eight times. Little wonder that World Masters Athletics, the international masters-competition governing body, hailed her as the best masters woman competitor in the world for that year.

When I first saw Christa compete at a national indoor event, her start in a 400-meter sprint brought a group of university students to their feet. "Look at her run!" they screamed, all but forgetting their task of timing the athletes. "She runs like a teenager!" Indeed, at a provincial track meet where Christa was seeded by time rather than age, she held her own against 14-year-old junior-high students. After the race, her ponytailed competitors swarmed around, asking for her autograph. Christa looks closer to 60, and physically, she's so toned and spry she easily blended in with the teen sprinters. "They told me they wished their grandmothers were more like me," Christa says proudly.

Perhaps they could be, *if they tried*. Though few will have Christa's exceptional talent, training for speed will keep us younger. And latecomers to masters track-and-field sports are not unusual. Take Christa's mentor, Olga Kotelko, 94. She started training at age 77, after deciding it was time to give her place on her coed softball team to a younger person. She fell in love with her new sport and soon discovered she had considerable talent. She has since won more than 700 gold medals and set 26 age-group world records in sprinting, weight throwing, and jumping events. Reading a local newspaper article about "Olga the Great" inspired Christa to check out masters track after her doctor ordered her to stop playing tennis due to arthritis in her wrists. Christa thought, *If Olga can run at her age, surely I can at 72.* So she looked up Olga in the phone book and gave her a call. "Olga can be a bit pushy," Christa laughs. "She told me to meet her at the track in 10 minutes and she would teach me some stuff."

Olga proves just as willing to "show me some stuff" when I drop by after my training session with Christa. Less than 5 minutes after knocking on Olga's door, we are in her car, and she is driving us to the local high-school track where she practices her events two or three times a week, on top of doing aquafit three times a week and bowling once a week, all while following a daily exercise routine at home and puttering nonstop in her garden and around her house.

At the track, the bespectacled grandmother pops open her trunk and hauls out a discus, a shot, and a hammer, which is a 4½-pound weight attached to a 3-foot-9-inch length of cable and a handle. Throwing the hammer is the retired schoolteacher's favorite event. I must admit it is humbling to watch a 94-year-old swing the thing in a whirring circle above her head several times, winding her body around as she does, before hurling the weight some 49 feet through the air—especially when I am too nervous to try throwing it lest I wrench my marathon-tight muscles or misdirect the hammer into the camera guy I brought along to record my day with the super seniors.

At least on the track, I can hold my own with Olga. She also looks a good 20 years younger than her age and moves like . . . well, what is a super-fit 94-year-old supposed to move like? Or behave like, for that matter? Few that old would jump on a plane and travel to another continent, let alone compete in the long jump and high jump, as Olga will do later in the fall at the World Masters track-and-field games in Brazil, and again the next year, when she will turn 95 and surely set a slew of new records in that age group. Tired of explaining her exceptional youthfulness, she has shared her secrets in a book about her fitness journey, *What Makes Olga Run.* "I always wanted to feel young and capable and vibrant and, yes, sexy," Olga tells me. Her mantras are "Love your aging body" and "It's never too late to achieve optimal health." She's quick with a joke, her eyes sparkle with laughter, and she teasingly flirts with my camera guy, who's less than half her age and charmed by her sense of fun. But on the track, Olga's a determined competitor. Though just 5 feet tall, she is sturdy and muscular, a strength athlete built for throwing events, but she competes in sprints of up to 800 meters (as well as the long jump and high jump) and often beats women a decade or more younger.

From a standing start, Olga quickly powers up to top speed. I run beside her and figure we're moving slightly faster than my 5-K race pace. Later, doing a few calculations based on her 100-meter time of about 25 seconds, I estimate we hit a top speed of close to 9 miles (14 kilometers) per hour, a pace swift enough for a 3-hour marathon. But no way she's running that distance. She closes down the sprint after 50 yards. "Hey, don't forget I'm 94!" she laughs, slapping my arm as she sucks in air, catching her breath. Then she walks back to the start to do another heat.

○　●　○　●　○　●　○

DURING THIS FINAL SEGMENT of my super-fit year—building speed to prepare for the half-marathon at the World Masters Games—I set out to run with world-class sprinters and middle-distance runners ranging in age from 50 to Olga's 94, obviously hoping to pick up a tip or three. A few things stand out about these runners. They love racing. They love competing. And while they challenge themselves by chasing after new world records, this ultimate goal stands out: Christa wants to be like Olga, and 50- and 60-something runners want to be like Christa. In other words, their primary goal is to live young and run strong, for as long as they can. And they figure speed is their golden ticket.

Like many in the women's running boom, I got a late start, coming to regular training at age 42 and serious training at 48. Now 51, I am dramatically fitter and faster—and still getting faster. It's heady and more than a little empowering, getting better at something after 50. Unlike other sports, in which we so often experience a discouraging erosion of skills, runners, no matter what age they start at, usually have a 10-year window to improve, believes Joan Ullyot, MD, a doctor turned runner, author, and early champion of the women's running boom.

My running pals would seem to be proof of this. Phyllis Berck, a track runner in her youth and athletic all her life, took up distance running in her mid-50s. At age 61, she set personal bests in distances ranging from the 5-K to the marathon. We have brilliant pictures of Phyllis waving at the camera as she races to the finish line while men 10 and 20 years younger are flailing after trying to keep up. Another member of my running club, Jean Marmoreo, a family doctor specializing in women's health, started running at age 50, determined to get back some of the fitness she enjoyed as a teen. Between ages 65 and 69, she won her age group at the Boston Marathon three times—and she got faster each time. After setting a new Canadian women's 70-plus marathon record she told me this: "If I can run that fast, then I can run faster."

A top 10 finisher in the first-ever women's Olympic marathon, Sylvia Ruegger, now 52, believes it's possible for a woman to take up running in her late 20s or 30s, put in the decade of endurance training required to develop her cardiovascular potential, and compete with the world's best into her 40s and maybe even 50s. She would know. In that first women's Olympic marathon, Joyce Smith, then 46, finished 11th, less than 3 minutes behind Sylvia, who was 23 at the time. Smith, a middle-distance specialist, had actually retired and then made a comeback when women were allowed to run the marathon. She won the women's division of the London Marathon 2 years running, at ages 43 and 44.

I have the cool opportunity of running regularly with Sylvia, as I volunteer with a national children's running and reading organization that she directs. Though she only runs for fun and fitness now, keeping up with her is a faint hope of mine. She strides like a deer while I bob along like a waterlogged cork in a stream. When I ask Sylvia if she thinks I can get faster, she bursts out laughing, apparently meaning to be encouraging. "Of course you can," she says. Then again, she thinks pretty much everyone can. "For women who didn't get a chance to compete in their teens and 20s, whether for lack of opportunity or they were sidetracked by family, they might discover later on that they have a real talent. And that older runner comes to the sport with fresher legs. An older runner might not challenge for a world record or win, but a marathon is about more than speed. On any given day, it's weather and course conditions and racing strategy, and an older runner can be competitive."

Several studies support Sylvia's assertions. After a rapid improvement in women's running times in the 40 years since our official inclusion in the New York City Marathon in 1971 (the world record improved by 46 minutes and 17 seconds, a 25.5 percent improvement, compared to the 16.9 percent one that men managed between 1908 and 1948), the fastest women marathoners have now plateaued, but not the older women. A 2012 French study concluded that we are indeed getting faster. That study analyzed finishing times of the top 10 male and female runners between 20 and 79 years of age in the New York City Marathon from 1980 to 2009 and showed that running times for women older than 44 improved, as did those of men older than 64, while all other age categories had plateaued. Over the past 2 decades, women in the 60-to-64 age group had the greatest improvement—7 percent. A similar study, an analysis of running times of nearly 195,000 participants in a Dutch 15-K road race between 1995 and 2007, showed that, with age, the erosion in men's performance was greater than women's, by 5.9 percent.

Exercise physiologist Sandra Hunter, who studies sex differences in performance, says improved running times stirred up speculation that older women might possess some advantage— whether physiological or psychological—when it comes to speed and endurance. Unfortunately for me and my older running sisters, that's not the case. Hunter's research shows that faster running times result when the number of participants increases. More participants, she explains, increases the genetic potential in any field—the more well-trained women there are in a race, the greater the probability there will be more *fast* well-trained women. Between 1980 and 2009, the NYC Marathon has seen an explosion in masters' participation, far more so for women than men. Many of those pioneers of the women's running boom have now put in the 10 or so years of training required to reach their potential. And when they stick with the sport into older age categories, these well-trained women make their age groups more competitive. Take my 50-to-54 cohort. As chuffed as I may be at qualifying for Boston 21 minutes under the standard required for my age, my time of 3:38 wouldn't even crack the top 100 among finishers in my age group at the 2013 running of Boston, or even the top 5 of 60-year-olds. The top 50-plus finisher—at 3:06—could be back at her hotel enjoying a beer by the time I huffed across the line. And the 2:36 marathon that Linda Somers Smith ran at age 50 would have won Boston with a half hour to spare.

Rather than discourage me, these far superior finish times absolutely thrill me. In the ultimate race of our lives, I don't want to be some genetic outlier. Rather, these incredible finish times show our collective potential to maintain speed, strength, and fitness into very advanced ages. Our steadily improving speed also begs the question, How much faster can we get? And given that women are such complex thinkers, I'll throw out this question: Why is it important—beyond ego, beyond the narrow measure of time—to strive to get even better?

○   ●   ○   ●   ○   ●   ○

PHYSIOLOGICALLY, IT WOULD SEEM that women are built more for endurance and men more for speed. Typically, men have larger hearts, less body fat, greater hemoglobin concentration (and hence oxygen-carrying capacity), more muscle mass per unit of body weight, higher max VO2 (making more oxygen available to feed working muscles), and, on average, more fast-twitch muscles, all giving them considerable advantages for running fast. Yet, the performance difference between men's and women's world records in the 100 meters is just 7.3 percent, versus the 10 percent across most other distances, from 1,500 meters to the marathon.

Performance-wise, women sprinters appear to be slower to fatigue and have faster recovery, according to a study done at St. Ambrose University in Iowa. It looked at the responses of men and women to three bouts of eight 30-second sprints. While men ran faster, their speed deteriorated faster over subsequent sprints. Women produced a lower concentration of lactate, which likely enabled them to recover faster and preserve their running speed.

Health-wise, women seem to be particularly responsive to

speed training. Two recent Swedish studies comparing the responses of men and women to three 30-second bouts of sprinting separated by 20 minutes of rest (which to this marathoner sounds like a day at the spa) revealed that women produced more insulin overall, built muscle while men did not, and reached peak levels of human growth hormone secretion faster than men.

This is worth unpacking. First, spiking insulin clears the blood of glucose (sugar), preventing it from being converted into fat, hence checking weight gain. That sprinting can help women build muscle mass is also a very good thing, as it is more difficult for us to do even lifting weights—and where muscle erodes, the double whammy of fat and frailty rushes in. But I immediately wanted to hit the track when I read that sprinting provokes the body to release growth hormone (GH), because if the goal is to stall aging, you want this stuff coursing through your body.

The downside of the Swedish study is that participants were all *young* men and women, but after his review of current research on GH and its potential effects in elderly populations, Richard Godfrey, PhD, a senior lecturer at London's Brunel University, told me that there is significant evidence that GH diminishes much less in people who remain active, particularly in those who continue high-intensity exercise.

Many of us have only heard about GH from sports doping scandals, but this "youth drug," as it's often called, is secreted naturally. Produced in the pituitary gland, the conglomeration of proteins helps children grow into adults. Beginning in our 30s, GH production gradually falls off, by a magnitude of four- to sevenfold over a lifetime, a decline that coincides with the reductions in testosterone in men and estrogen in women—and often with reductions in the volume and intensity of exercise. Sex hormones interact with GH, signaling the body to renew itself. But exercise, as researchers have discovered, can play that role as well. High-intensity training in particular—such as bouts of fast running—is akin to throwing the body into crisis, and robust secretion of life-revitalizing GH is the body's response. GH then signals cells to reproduce and regenerate, renew muscle mass, and rebuild bone and also collagen, which is the connective tissue in tendons and ligaments and also a major component of skin—the reason why exercise literally helps us look younger. In the presence of cortisol—which is also released when we run—GH also increases fat metabolism, helping us check weight gain and keep our youthful figures.

Godfrey, who has worked extensively with Britain's Olympic athletes and now specializes in GH research and aging, argues that exercise for older adults should focus on promoting GH release to reduce "some of the deleterious effects of aging."

And what does that antiaging, GH-promoting exercise look like? A moderate effort will do, but for the most powerful stimulus, think of an all-out mad dash to chase after a child who's about to run in front of a moving car or a sustained effort like those our ancestors made to hunt down dinner (or to run away from an animal intent on making them its dinner). Mustering up the motivation to move that fast without a crisis instigating the effort is not an easy thing.

Scientifically, Godfrey describes the exercise that elicits the greatest sustained rise in GH as repeated efforts "at an intensity above lactate threshold (about 70 percent of maximum heart rate and above) and for a minimum of 10 minutes." That 10 minutes can be alternated with brief rest periods or light exercise, as long as the total period of intense effort adds up to 10 minutes. He says to achieve "an absolute peak in GH, 30-second sprints would provide the greatest concentration of GH, but this level would fall rapidly" after the exercise session, while the slightly slower but more sustained effort can keep GH spiked for up to 90 minutes after exercise. Cycling, Godfrey says, is better for GH secretion, but running is better for fat oxidization. For his own routine, he does a variety of aerobic exercises in a high-intensity interval training (HIIT) session as well as other exercises to build strength and endurance. But if he's pressed for time, he forgoes endurance and focuses on the HIIT to reach that 10-minute threshold of intense effort.

A specialist in HIIT research, Martin Gibala, PhD, chair of McMaster University's Department of Kinesiology, says numerous studies that his lab and others have conducted over the past 10 years suggest we may actually be able to replace the recommended 4 to 5 hours of aerobic training a week with just three 20-minute sessions of high-intensity training per week and get the same health benefits. And those benefits are significant, with a study in the *Journal of Aging Research* showing that endurance training over a lifetime improves life expectancy by anywhere from 2.8 to 8 years. One of the good things that come out of HIIT-style exercise is weight control: A Laval University study showed that intense workouts burn up to nine times more fat than traditional aerobic training; one at Appalachian State University found that the after-exercise calorie burn remained elevated for 14 hours following a vigorous 45-minute cycling workout, but that effect wasn't seen after less vigorous workouts. A University of Bath study revealed that a single spurt of sprinting for 30 seconds generated a sixfold increase in GH. And a study comparing 50 sprinters, 19 middle-distance runners, and 109 long-distance runners competing in the European Masters Games found that the sprinters, whose training basically consists of HIIT-style sessions, had greater bone density and leg muscle size due to the higher-impact nature of fast running. HIIT, like endurance training, also improves cardiovascular health, boosts VO2, and reduces the risks of developing aging-related diseases. If retaining youthful looks is an aim, researchers conducting a study of age 75-plus world-record runners at McGill University noted that older sprinters tended to "look fresher" than their long-distance counterparts. In that very small study, both sprinters and distance runners retained an impressively high max VO2, though the distance runners had an edge there.

Trying to derive all the health benefits of endurance training from high-intensity running alone isn't for the faint of heart. As Gibala warns, "You have to be willing to work hard." He recommends doing intervals at 85 percent or more of your maximum heart rate, but the specific nature of the intervals isn't critical. "There's no magic formula that's most effective," says Gibala. "You can change up the variables and there's lots of variety and that's part of the appeal." HIIT can be cycling, running, swimming, speedwalking, or any other activity that forces the body to really move. Variables could be a 30-second all-out effort repeated four or five times with a minute of recovery in between, or 3 or 4 minutes of intense exercise within a 15-minute window of easy exercise, or 10 repetitions of 1 minute of hard running followed by 1 easy minute.

Any good half- or full marathon training plan will include at least 1 day per week of HIIT-style training—400- or 800-meter repetitions, stretches of fast running within a continuous longer run (a fartlek), and hard uphill running, all of which boost your VO2, your lactate threshold, and, ultimately, your running speed. But distance runners can't simply replace all those training miles with fast running, or our endurance will suffer. Still, Gibala believes distance athletes tend to do too much aerobic training. Classic distance-training plans call for 15 to 20 percent of the mileage to be either above race pace or over that lactate threshold of 70 percent or more of your maximum heart rate. Gibala says it may be more effective for performance to push that to

25 percent, but cautions that we can't simply add more fast running; we must replace some slow runs with fast sessions or risk overtraining and injury. The other caveat is that runners, especially older ones, should be fit enough to run 4 or 5 days a week before attempting all-out sprints—and even then should ease into them to avoid injury.

Given all the health benefits that come with HIIT workouts, reducing both mileage and training time and racing over shorter distances and even sprinting would seem to be a godsend for women runners, who are often pressed for time. Yet masters track competitions that stage sprints and shorter races (1,500 meters, 3,000 meters, 5-Ks, and 10-Ks) have not benefited from the women's running boom. At many meets, fewer than 1 in 10 participants is female. That may change as more discover how welcoming these competitions are and also that track offers something most distance runners usually don't get to experience. While distance runners tend to compete against themselves for personal time goals, on the track, sprinters get the thrill of actually *racing,* competing head-to-head with age-group peers and trying to win.

A third speed-training session at a university track on a soft spring evening will leave me even more in someone's dust when I go up against a sprinter my own age. Karen Gold, 51, is a marathoner recently turned into an 800-meter specialist merely good enough to help set an indoor world record as part of a relay team of 50- to 54-year olds. She was no slouch in the marathon either, qualifying for Boston several times. She tells me distance didn't agree with her: She was constantly suffering injuries. While rehabbing her latest with light running at the track, a coach saw her and encouraged her to try shorter distances. "I was only going to do it until [my injury] got better," says Karen, "but I fell in love with it." The transition to speed training has been life changing, she adds. She credits it with making her stronger physically and also mentally.

I get the physical part during 3 repetitions of 300 meters, then 3 over 600 meters, then 3 more 300-meter efforts, in which Karen cruises far ahead of me. During this workout, we will run a third of the mileage I put in on my lightest training day, but the speed takes its toll: Just halfway through, my hamstrings ping and my abs and my glutes ache (there's a reason sprinters have bigger, firmer butts than distance runners).

During breaks between repetitions, we chat as women do on longer runs, and Karen tells me about the mental toughness she has gained racing on the track. The senior marketing executive admits that at work, she tended to back down when she found herself competing with men for projects, clients, or promotions, to the extent of switching jobs. Not so now. On the track, she races not so much by pace, as distance runners do, but to pass runners and try to win. Given the low number of women at some competitions, Karen is often seeded in a field with men, and that experience, she says, "toughens you up mentally." Men may run faster, but her finish time is what determines her ranking in her own age and sex category. "Guys might be running ahead, but I learned to keep pushing hard right to the end. You learn not to give up." With her newfound strength and determination, she also left a lengthy marriage that hadn't been working for a long time.

○　　●　　○　　●　　○　　●　　○

INSPIRED BY KAREN'S STORY and her excitement about masters track, I confront my own track phobia and enter a small regional event at the university I attended. The popularity of these sporting events has exploded—at least among men—since the masters athletics movement began. The Masters Mile in 1966 and the US Masters Track and Field championships in 1968 steamrolled in popularity, inspiring the first World Masters Games in 1985, which are Olympic-style multievent games held every 4 years, and also World Masters Athletics (WMA) track-and-field championships (indoor and outdoor competitions are held in alternating years). Cities around the world vie to host these events, much like the Olympics, albeit at a fraction of the cost. WMA sanctions masters track-and-field world records at these events and also regional ones.

Perhaps women mistakenly think these competitions are only for elite athletes, but there is usually no qualifying standard. The primary emphasis has always been on participation and love of sport. While about half who compete are lifelong athletes, the other half are either new to a sport or returning after a long layoff. Given the high ratio of men to women at masters events, if I were on the lookout for a fit guy, I'd consider taking up masters track!

The atmosphere is friendly and hugely supportive, especially among the women, who often offer each other informal coaching during events. Still, many masters athletes take competing seriously, often more so than serious collegiate athletes, notes the University of Ottawa's Bradley Young, PhD, a professor and researcher who studies masters athletes. He told me that older athletes compete not to please others, improve their social rank, or score scholarship money, but because it pleases them to train, be fit, and compete. They keep training at an intense level because they love it. "We see exceptionally high performances in running," he said. "People have been training consistently, 48 weeks a year for the past 15 years. It's remarkable. We study loss and dysfunction [relating to physical aspects of aging], but I think it's imperative we try to understand the more adaptive end of the spectrum." He believes governments should do more to support and promote masters events, to increase their visibility and encourage participation, which, in turn, could produce massive health benefits for our aging population. Joseph Baker, PhD, a York University researcher in Toronto who has attended numerous masters games to study the athletes, also believes we should consider advocating high-performance sport as the healthiest way to age. "There's a wide range of performance levels [at masters competitions]," he says, noting in particular the supportive atmosphere. But he believes peppering that participation with competition increases the health benefits. "The competitive aspect provides a challenge to continually push ourselves, which maintains functional capabilities. . . . We've looked at aging as an inevitable cascade of declining function, but masters athletes are busting down those stereotypes."

Those who want to soak up the intense, yet friendly atmosphere of these international competitions—and can afford the costs—can jam-pack their calendars with events at summer and winter World Masters Games, masters regional indoor and outdoor games, the WMA indoor and outdoor track-and-field competitions, as well as individual sporting federation events such as masters cycling and swimming competitions.

At this regional 2-day track-and-field meet, I sign up for the 1,500 meters, which at least demands some endurance rather than all-out speed, and I go into it pretty confident—that I won't do well. For that low expectation, I can blame school physical education classes for their emphasis on sprint competitions and timed lap runs, which left slow kids like me bringing up the back of the pack. For too long, I thought fast was the only way to run, and if I couldn't run fast, I couldn't run at all.

I can also blame my parents for my less-than-blistering speed. World-record sprinters are, in many ways, born, inheriting a genetic mother lode of fast-twitch muscle fibers, which, compared to their slow-twitch counterparts, are bigger, more powerful, and faster to contract, though also quicker to fatigue as those fibers work anaerobically, meaning without oxygen. The rest of us mortals are born with more slow-twitch muscle fibers, which, though smaller and slower, can deliver power for extended periods because they are packed with oxygen-carrying capillaries and energy-producing mitochondria, allowing them to work aerobically, or with oxygen.

But we're not entirely prisoners of genetics, for training can restructure muscles. Long runs will build more slow-twitch muscles in anyone. While speed training may not add fast-twitch muscles, it can wake up what we have inherited and also build two subcategories of them, one that gives sprinters endurance and another that provides distance runners with speed. Speed training (as well as strength and explosive-power training) can also stall the impact aging has on muscle structure, preventing the age-related shift in the ratio of fiber types to favor the slow-twitch as well as preserving the size of the fast-twitch fibers. In one study, elite masters sprinters between 53 and 77 years of age had no age-related differences in fiber distribution compared to elite 18- to 35-year-old sprinters. Muscles, observed Ball University's Scott Trappe, PhD, in a study of masters athletes, have a "high degree of plasticity" and will adapt to the type of exercise being performed.

As I discover personally, speed training is making me faster, even at the advanced age of 51 and even after plodding through years of slow running. Speed training is also showing me that there are a myriad of ways to run and stay fit—and I am just beginning to discover my own particular strengths as a runner.

Even though I don't train specifically for the 1,500 and didn't taper my training to prepare properly for this hard effort, I do not finish last *by that much*. Not that it would matter if I did. At these masters competitions, a great performance by a silver-haired speedster will bring an audience to their feet, but the predominant vibe is a celebration of all athletes, at all levels. Indeed, there's a tradition of cheering in the back-of-the-pack runners, which is how I know my place in this race. Still, I heed Karen's advice: Don't give up; keep pushing right to the end. And every time I pass the stands, people cheer and even scream my name, which is really odd given that I don't know anyone other than a marathon pal, Bruce, who came along. But it seems everyone I crossed paths with at the meet—those who signed me in, gave me a bib, scrawled a big fat 50 on that bib so others in my age group would know who to target and pass—have all rushed to the sidelines to cheer me into the finish. It feels great.

And before I can even catch my breath after the race, a group of women urge me to join their makeshift relay team for the 4x100-meter race, with none other than world-record-holder Karen Gold running the first leg. "You saw how slow I am," I remind them. "I'm a marathoner. I'll look like I'm *jogging* out there." They protest that it doesn't matter. It's just for the experience. *It's just for fun*. Racing 100 meters for fun? Racing on a team, like I didn't get to do in public school because I was too slow? I tell them I'm in. The field is a mixed bag of women's and men's teams across a range of ages. The race is a blast even though our team loses badly, primarily because of my contribution. As my buddy Bruce put it, charitably, I think: "You only looked slow because everyone else was so fast."

○　●　○　●　○　●　○

THOUGH I HAD ALREADY been doing interval-style training with my running club, I add a second speed workout to my week and sneak in "speed tricks." While brushing my teeth, I do butt crunches (squeeze and relax the glutes) to build up those essential muscles for sprinting. Instead of jogging to my gym, I amuse people waiting for the bus by doing plyometrics along the sidewalk—springy leg hops such as high knees, butt kicks, side running, and bounding—all to build leg strength, power, and quick turnover. Waiting for lights to turn at cross streets, I skip or hop on one foot. And I try to do this blazingly simple speed trick once a day: Where younger runners might add on a second run, I go for a walk, which keeps the metabolism revving and stretches out leg muscles. I also cycle around the city as much as I can—some think it helps with speed, others not—but I find it stretches out the legs, and I can throw in spurts of speed to get that growth hormone spiking.

I learn many of these speed tricks from masters women runners who have set world records and also coach. One, Diane Palmason, who holds the women's 65-plus 400- and 800-meter records and still runs for fun at age 75, is a stickler for form. She urges me to get my weight forward and strive for a quiet midfoot-to-forefoot landing—and to practice that soft landing by running barefoot in the grass after a run. She also recommends varying speeds within a run: "Throw in 300-meter and 75-meter repeats of fast, relaxed running. You strengthen different muscle fibers, so when one muscle type gets tired in a race, you've got another type beside it to recruit. It's fun and you can't run sloppily."

Karla Del Grande, who set three world records in 2013 and also coaches at a kids' track club, personifies the importance of setting goals to keep focused and energized. When the retired schoolteacher turned 60, she decided to go after all the indoor and outdoor world sprint records up to 400 meters in her new masters age group. She nailed the 60, 200, and 400 indoor records. At the 2013 WMA outdoor meet, she managed it in the 200 and 400, but a glitch with the timer nullified her 100-meter record. She's hardly upset. She'll chase down that record during the summer season when she's 61. Plus, there's a deeper motivation to her goal setting. "I love showing what women over 60 can do," she says. "I love that the kids I coach say, 'Gee, you're fast,' without adding 'for someone your age.'" Sprint training, she tells me, "gives you a sense that you can do anything. It gives you a sense of being strong." No surprise, she emphasizes strength training, but also giving the aging body more rest. She's getting better results doing less, limiting her track workouts to 3 days a week and lifting weights on the same days. That gives her a recovery day after hard training. On those easier days off, she still *moves*, by doing yoga, cycling, or working out on a mini trampoline at home, which is great for core strength and provides a gentler surface for jogging and bounding. Her training formula is clearly working. As a track athlete in high school, she ran 200 meters in 25.2; 40 years and a 30-year running hiatus later, her world-record time is 28.11.

Helly Visser, who set world records in the indoor 1,500 and 800 at age 80, believes her success and longevity in the sport have come from speed training and developing great running form. She is such a huge proponent of posture that she cowrote a book on it, *The Guide to Natural Posture Running*. She also teaches clinics. "You need good posture to shift weight from one foot so the energy goes through the body to the head, so you're running smoothly, effortlessly, and relaxed," she tells me. "Imagine a straight line running from your ankles to your ears. You have to be aligned, with a slight forward lean, but at the ankles rather than the hips. If you stick your bum out, the energy from your foot strike stays in your bum and creates injury." She urges me to think consciously of my stride, landing on my mid- to forefoot, using that slight forward lean to spring forward. Arms and legs should swing in a light, fast pendulum without overstriding: "It's easier to swing a short pendulum than a long one." To develop that beautiful stride, she suggests running short intervals (200 or 400 meters) at paces slow enough (3-K and 5-K race pace) to practice balance, form, and relaxation, yet fast enough to focus on the spring that comes out of the foot and into the body. The goal is to have a light, elastic running style. "For me, the moment I became a good runner was when I could relax my shoulders and let my arms swing in a motion that my body initiated. That took 4 years for me to discover. But I loved that. I realized how interesting running was mentally and physically. You make discoveries about yourself."

What I discover is perhaps more basic: For me, training for speed is more difficult than training for distance. I can do pretty big distance on my own, and hills too. But fast intervals? It's tough to muster the mental energy to tackle those by myself. They are also physically exhausting.

I should have taken the advice Karla offered me. And Helly, too, who told me a variation of the same: Don't train so hard on tough days that you can't train at all the next day. Perhaps another thing I discover about myself as a runner: I need to hear a lesson three times before it sticks. But coming off marathon training, and facing less distance on my half-marathon schedule, I figure I can just tuck in more speedwork on my regular runs without reducing mileage or dropping 1 of my 5 running days. Not so. The extra speed training leaves me feeling wiped, and on cross-training days, I struggle to get to the gym. As the schedule wears on, those gym days turn into unintended rest days—or guilt days following one too many glasses of wine the night before. But with spring easing into summer, there's life to enjoy too. Maybe it's not the wisest decision, but I opt to keep both speed and distance and back off on strength training. That's not a balanced training plan for the long term, but I'm hoping I can get away with it for the next 2 months heading into the World Masters in Italy. Having just missed my target in the marathon, I'm more determined than ever to perform well in the half-marathon.

As hard as the extra speedwork is, it's also exhilarating, especially when I'm doing intervals with a group of similar-paced runners in my club, and even more so when we're at my favorite track in a park on a high hill that offers an incredible view of downtown Toronto, its thicket of skyscrapers, and Lake Ontario beyond. On those soft summer evenings, with the sun setting over the lake and casting us in a crimson light, we take turns leading the pack, pushing and pulling each other along as Kenyans and Ethiopians do, going faster with that collective energy than we ever could on our own.

One night is particularly thrilling: Men that I once struggled to keep up with are suddenly struggling to keep up with me.

○　●　○　●　○　●　○

IN JUNE, A LITTLE FITTER, a little faster, my running pal Phyllis and I head to the historic women-only New York Mini 10-K to race with one of the greatest-ever masters runners, Kathy Martin, 61. The *New York Times* has called her stride "classic" and "a fluid parting of the empty air, almost balletic." That's a long way from her first attempt at running at age 30, when she collapsed in the middle of the road, almost begging a car to run her over. The former nurse, though skinny, realized how haplessly out of shape she had gotten, and committed to training with her runner husband, Chuck. In time, he became her coach and she a remarkable talent, blasting off 17-minute 5-Ks by her late 30s. Now a real estate agent and mother of two adult children, she has set dozens of American and world records for the age groups spanning 40 to 60 years old at distances from 400 meters to 50 miles.

To understand how performances like Kathy's compare to those of elite runners in their prime, masters associations use a handy age-grading formula (a calculator is online at www.mastersathletics.net) that crunches age, sex, race length, and finish time and then adjusts that performance to compare it to the world records for that race distance. That gives you the time your masters performance may have translated to in your prime and allows fair comparisons of the performances of runners of different ages. For an idea of how I stack up against Kathy, my best marathon time of 3:38:14 age-grades to a 3:02:27 for an age-performance percentage of 74.22 percent; that means that if I had been this fit in my prime, I would have verged on being a regional-class athlete, maybe challenging the top runners in small local races for the win. When Kathy won her age group in the Philadelphia half-marathon at age 60, her blistering 1:28:28 age-graded to a 1:06:20 for an age-performance percentage of 99.25. Scoring close to 100 means that if she were in her running prime, she would be a world-class athlete challenging for Olympic gold and world records. She usually scores percentages in the high 90s, incredibly, over all distances.

Does Kathy ever look back at what might have been had she run track as a teen? Like most masters athletes, she likes that she is running *now*. She also thinks it's important. "Women understand at a deep level that we have to be the role model for generations coming." She points out that this is the first generation of children who will have shorter life spans than their parents because of obesity. "So women are saying, Let's get out there and be the role models."

At the New York Mini 10-K, Kathy turns out to be an amazing role model, not that she will be recognized for it. Our projected finish times place us in the first corral, just behind the elites, who are showered with attention at this race. There's an amazing energy at these all-women events, and the excitement here is particularly buzzy. When it was founded in 1972, fewer than 100 gutsy pioneers took part. Today, some 5,500 from around the world flock to it for the opportunity to race through Central Park with the tribal sisterhood of women runners—and measure themselves against some of the world's best. In this showcase of women's running, international elites will be vying to be the first to break the finish-line tape, not just be first woman across. I see them right ahead of me—the Ethiopians, Kenyans, Brits, Americans—leaning in for the starting horn.

I get caught up in that frenzied excitement, adrenaline shooting through my legs, and I go out way too fast. After the race, Kathy Martin will tell me that she thinks the 10-K is the toughest race to run, demanding speed, endurance, and meticulous pacing. She will finish within 4 seconds of her projected race time. Unfortunately for me, almost all my race experience is over longer distances. At the half, I'm on track for a 5-K personal best; in the second half, I die. Still, I finish in 47:40, good enough to crack the top 20 in my age group, for an age-graded performance of 73 percent. Competing in the same age group as Kathy, Phyllis finishes fourth in 50:46, for an age-graded performance of 78.34. Though a decade older than I, Kathy finishes well ahead, in 40:56, and wins her age group by some 5 minutes. Overall, she is 69th, but according to the age-grade calculator, her 97.16 percent bests the entire field.

But the New York Mini 10-K only recognizes the top elites—quite wrongly, I believe, for at the awards ceremony after the race, one of the best masters runners in the world is just another face in the crowd. Kathy shrugs it off, though she thinks top masters finishers should get acknowledged in some way. Not that she wants the attention. Quietly confident, she races for the fun of the challenge, not the accolades. But it's that example thing again, the opportunity to show what older women are capable of. "It's not about this one race," she smiles. "It's about fitness for life."

We gather up our spouses and friends and head off for brunch, where Kathy talks about her training, which, interestingly, is based more on speedwork than long runs. "I don't go into a marathon with a lot of distance," she says. "My friends do those 20- or 22-mile runs and their body is too beat up. They get to the starting line tired." Kathy seems to have a greater capacity for training than I—or she has built it up. She runs 6 mornings a week: 2 speed workouts (intervals, mile repeats); a hard, hilly run; a long run of between 12 and 16 miles (19 to 25 kilometers), sometimes pushing that to 18 miles (28 kilometers); and two easier recovery runs of 6 to 8 miles (9 to 13 kilometers). She also does resistance training and yoga. Chuck describes her as "ridiculously fit." She shrugs again. "He's the one who obsesses over my training and records. Going after them is a challenge. It keeps me from becoming bored. But the number one thing for me is fun." Using age-graded calculators is another way of keeping the fun in the run, she says, as it levels the playing field, enabling people of different ages and sexes to compete. "The guys I run with sometimes bet me bottles of wine." Rather than the lowest time, the best age-graded performance wins. Kathy admits she wins a lot of wine.

○　●　○　●　○　●　○

IN A SMALLER 10-K on a brutally hot July evening, I accomplish something rare, at least for me: I win my age group. While my time isn't any better than in New York, it's not any worse—an improvement, I think, given the heat. And what is much stronger is my compete level—I battled harder. From the start, I try to keep up to Ed Whitlock, who happens to be merely the fastest marathoner over 80 in the world. When his flowing white hair disappears ahead of me, I settle into a speed that's saner for me in this heat. Then, when my pace starts breaking down in the second half thanks to the stifling humidity, I ignore my time and focus on actually *racing*—trying to pass runners and not letting anyone pass me. That will be handy grit to take to Italy, where we'll also be dealing with heat and competing not so much for a time but against our age-group peers for places on the podium.

Then, finally, in a 5-K race, I get some proof that I have gotten faster as a result of all my speedwork. Seven months earlier, at the end of my first training segment in this super-fit year, I set a personal best in the 5-K. In July, on a tougher 5-K course and in hotter weather, I run a 21.46 to shave more than a minute off that previous best. Over such a short distance that's huge, translating into a nearly 10-second-per-kilometer improvement in pace.

That gives me some pause. That forces me to reevaluate my entire identity as a runner. I would have bet Kathy Martin an entire case of wine that my strength lies in endurance rather than speed, that my best chance of winning a race would be to extend the distance indefinitely, until all my competitors dropped out, whether from exhaustion or boredom. But fed into the age-graded calculator, my 5-K time translates to 78 percent, a good 4 percent better than at any other distance I run, suggesting this short distance is actually my best.

Unfortunately, my target half-marathon at the World Masters Games in Italy is now mere weeks away, and it's too late to enter the 5-K!

It's time to take stock. My super-fit year is drawing to a close. My race performances over the year show that, although I am older, I have become a stronger, faster, and more confident runner. I set personal bests at every race distance I attempted and even made it to the podium in a few. That has sent my compete level skyrocketing, which bodes well for competing with the front-runners in Italy. As I've learned this year, a race isn't just about speed, it's about strategy, weather conditions, who shows up, a competitor's bad luck, hopefully my good luck, the determination to race hard right to the end—never giving up on the race and definitely never on myself.

But the intensity of the year is also taking its toll, not so much physically as mentally. I catch myself fantasizing about *after* the Games, the break in training, what I will do when this super-fit year is over, and this biggie: How much longer can I keep up this intense training?

CHAPTER 8

OLDER

WHAT DOES GETTING OLDER really mean when, biologically at least, time seems to be spinning backward? Let me go back to the few weeks before I ran the fastest marathon of my life in May, and specifically to the day before my 51st birthday, when the answer to that theoretical question appeared before me in flesh and blood, in the form of 85-year-old world-record marathoner Betty Jean McHugh—or BJ, as everyone calls her. In the moments before BJ entered the lobby of my Montreal hotel, I was contemplating the cold rain outside—so typical around my April birthday—and that ominous threshold I was about to cross over, which would put me closer to 100 than the sparkling start of life, and yet my mood was shockingly *jubilant*. Birthdays usually bother me—and mightily—but after months of working to achieve super fitness, I felt that I have made an impossible birthday wish come true: to possess the hard-earned wisdom of my years but the vitality, physique, and fitness of a 20-year-old. Could a birthday present get much better?

Then I spot BJ across the lobby. We had spoken on the phone, but this is the first time I am meeting her in person. My first thought: *Our body types are so similar, she could be my mother.* My second thought: *She could be me!* We are exactly the same height and virtually the same weight. Though we are both shy of 5 foot 1, few would describe us as tiny given the breadth of our shoulders, a certain muscular sturdiness to our frames, even our outsize personalities that have us as ready for a laugh as a challenge—or a glass of wine, as I will soon find out.

Unbeknownst to BJ, she offers me an even more amazing birthday gift: this glimpse into my future, to how I might be at 85, which is mind-blowing because BJ looks decades younger—about 65—and she has managed to retain the physique of a very fit 20-year-old.

The notion that I could slow the speeding train of aging like BJ has is thrilling—and a bit daunting. Even though, by many fitness barometers, I have cranked back the clock on my biological age, I still catch myself thinking like a 51-year-old, wondering what I'll do when this super-fit year is over. How long will I keep running marathons and half-marathons—another 5 years, 10 years? How long will I keep up this business of striving for ever-faster times and better fitness? The answer—if I want to look like BJ at 85—would seem to be this: *Never stop.*

Since taking up running at age 50, BJ has not let up. She ran her first 10-K at age 52 in a time of 43:52 and could lay down 44-minute 10-Ks in her 60s. While some of her world-record times have since been surpassed, she posted 9 of the 11 fastest 10-K finish times in the world for women ages 70 to 74. In the marathon, she posted the second-fastest finish times in the world in the 5-year age categories for women 70 to 74 (4:08:00), 75 to 79 (4:08:54), and 80 to 84 (4:36:52), according to the Association of Road Racing Statisticians. Then in 2012, she became the fastest female marathoner on the planet over the age of 85 when she ran the Honolulu Marathon in 5:14:26, more than 20 minutes faster than Helen Klein's previous world record of 5:36:18 set 4 years earlier. BJ's world record age-grades to 2:14:70—consider that against Paula Radcliffe's 2003 world record of 2:15:25, set when she was 29.

When we spoke on the phone prior to meeting up in Montreal, BJ admitted that it has been tougher to muster up her old enthusiasm after losing her husband of 60 years just 9 months ago. Yet she has signed up for two half-marathons this spring and yearns to do another marathon. She has no plans, no intention, not even an inkling of ever giving up running.

Now BJ has been summoned to Montreal to undergo intensive testing by a team of McGill University researchers looking for clues to how the octogenarian keeps ticking along at her frantic pace, apparently defying any normal aging process. Is it genetics? Have decades of running conferred some antiaging superpower on her? Is it her tremendous appetite for exercise that keeps her training like a 20-year-old? Perhaps some individual quirk of physiology is protecting her from the usual ravages of aging?

Since setting eyes on BJ and realizing how similar our bodies are, I have a self-involved question or two of my own: If I keep up my present level of training, can I retain my 20-something fitness into my late 80s as BJ has done? I also want to know how I can muster the motivation to keep training that hard and even upping my game, for as I am about to find out, BJ is, in many ways, fitter than I am.

○   ●   ○   ●   ○   ●   ○

BJ IS THE MOST RECENT of some 15 world-record holders over the age of 75 who have travelled to the Canadian city to take part in the yet-to-be-published Montreal masters athletes study, a pilot project launched by husband-and-wife research team Russ Hepple and Tanja Taivassalo. The two exercise physiologists, whose research interests focus on aging muscles and mitochondrial dysfunction, respectively, started scheming up a new approach to aging research when they attended the 2009 World Masters Athletics outdoor Track and Field Championships in Finland and this thought dawned on them: While aging research tends to focus on disease and disability, why not focus on how to prevent disease and preserve ability? And where better to search for models of successful aging than among these senior super athletes?

The two were at the track meet to cheer on Taivassalo's then 70-year-old father, who was competing in the marathon, but the athlete who grabbed their attention was a diminutive, then 91-year-old Canadian, Olga Kotelko, who started her track career at age 77. Throughout the meet, the sturdy, sub-5-foot nonagenarian sent crowds into a frenzy as she determinedly banged down world records in the 200-meter sprint, javelin, discus, long jump, and throws pentathlon (javelin, discus, shot, hammer, and weight). Though just showing up could earn her gold medals since she is often the only 90-plus competitor, Olga doesn't just show up to competitions. In Finland, she sprinted 5 seconds faster than her nearest competitor in the 100 meters. At age 91, she raced two age groups down and still helped a women's 80-to-84 relay team set a world record for the 4x200 meters. She became the first woman over 90 to even attempt the high jump. Now 94, she has set some 26 world records in sprints, throws, jumps, and the pentathlon.

By the end of the world masters event in 2009, Hepple and Taivassalo were determined to bring Olga to Montreal for a battery of tests. Keen to understand her own enduring longevity and do her bit for other seniors, Olga readily agreed. One result, the biopsy of a muscle sample plucked from Olga's thigh, would astound the researchers. Muscles, like rings in a tree, contain the biomarkers of biological aging: the cellular trash of metabolism, mitochondrial defects that can lead to cell death, muscular denervation (an unplugging of nerves firing muscle tissue). The biopsy results were mind-blowing: In her 90s, Olga had muscles comparable to those of someone 3 to 4 decades younger, and a resilience to the stress of aging and physical activity that shows no end point. When I spoke to Olga by phone before I arrived in Montreal, she told me she has no idea what being in her 90s should feel like—she claims to have the same energy level she had in her 50s. And she, too, has no intention of quitting any activity.

The researchers booked a return trip for Olga and hope to bring her back every 3 years to study how fast she is aging, or rather, in Olga's case, how slow, for it's clear she possesses some remarkable resistance to what was once deemed inevitable.

○   •   ○   •   ○   •   ○

ON BJ'S FIRST DAY OF TESTING, her results also blow a few mental gaskets. Like the other super seniors in the study, BJ has been age matched with a sedentary control who is able to live independently and considers herself healthy, but does not follow any exercise routine. By contrast, BJ runs for an hour 3 days a week and up to 2 hours or more on Saturday long runs. She follows up her midweek runs with yoga classes and also weight trains a couple of times a week. When she's injured, she does not stop, instead heading to the swimming pool, where she rehabs her way back with pool running. What BJ does for fun the rest of the time would be considered serious exercise for most: She cycles for transportation because she prefers it to driving, walks a mile up and down a very steep hill every day to fetch her groceries, and so avidly walks the dogs left in her care that friends joke that having BJ dog sit is like putting their pooches in doggie boot camp (one hefty woofer dropped 10 pounds during a 10-day stay). And until recently, once a week or more, BJ hiked to the peak of Vancouver's Grouse Mountain via the notorious Grouse Grind—nicknamed "Mother Nature's StairMaster" for its punishing 2,800-foot (853-meter) elevation gain over 1.8 miles (2.9 kilometers).

In Montreal, researchers are submitting BJ to a kind of lab-rat boot camp. Over the course of 3 days, technicians will take a functional MRI of her brain, draw blood, take urine samples, perform an echocardiogram, take muscle biopsies, measure muscle strength and electrical activity, test heart and lung function by having her ride a stationary bike to exhaustion, and give her a battery of written questions to test memory and cognitive ability as well as gauge mood, attitude, and motivation. It seems almost silly having BJ perform some of the functional aging tests such as balancing on one leg or timing how long it takes her to walk up a flight of stairs or to sit down and get back up. "These tests were mundane for all the athletes," Taivassalo tells me. "They were so much more fluid and smooth, more like fit people in their 40s and 50s taking them." Ditto for tests that measure brain function. "We're most amazed by their cognitive abilities. Just speaking to the athletes, it's clear they are cognitively superior to their age-matched controls."

In BJ's case, some of her results prove superior even to those of a fit person more than 3 decades younger—like me, for instance.

One of her first tests is a max VO2, that ultimate measure of cardiovascular fitness that I took at the beginning of my super-fit year. Riding a stationary bike, BJ cranks out a relative max VO2 of 46, twice as high as most women her age. But to my great shock, BJ's result is higher than the 39 I started my year at, and still higher than the 43 I would score after 9 months of working out like a fiend to get into the range of fit college-age women and running a marathon just 3 minutes off the Boston qualifying standard for women under 34! Of the women in the Montreal masters athletes study, only American Jeanne Daprano scored higher than BJ. Clearly, Daprano is no slouch, having set a whack of world records in middle distances from 400 meters to the mile. At age 75, she ran the mile in a world-record time of 7:13.5, which age-grades to 4:11.6; still, when Daprano registered a max VO2 of 49.5, she was 76, nearly a decade younger than BJ. The researchers consider BJ's 46 even more impressive than the highest max VO2 recorded in the study, the 50 posted by masters marathon legend Ed Whitlock, who, at age 73, became the oldest person ever to run a sub-3-hour marathon. He also holds the world marathon records for men 75-plus (3:04:54) and 80-plus (3:15:54). But given that men's lungs and hearts are about 10 percent larger, they typically have higher max VO2s. And Whitlock is also 4 years younger than BJ.

Later, BJ's impressive VO2 prompts considerable discussion between Hepple and Taivassalo. Not knowing what BJ's max VO2 was in her so-called athletic prime leaves the researchers with little more than questions and speculation at this point. Has BJ built and managed to retain her high VO2 with distance running and exercise? Is there some other protective factor at work? Or did she start out with the genetic advantage of a ridiculously high max VO2—in, say, the 80 range of Lance Armstrong or Joan Benoit Samuelson—that thereafter simply declined at a typical rate of 5 to 7 percent per decade to bring her into her current range, that of a fit 20-something female athlete?

Bolstering the retained-VO2 side of the argument is the 3:32 marathon BJ ran at age 55 that predicts a VO2 in the 44 range, which is in line with the 43 I registered after running 3:38. But if

BJ started out with a more modest VO2, she has not only managed to maintain it, but also actually *increased* it through her
senior years, which is perhaps even more remarkable. "BJ is not
aging at a normal rate," Hepple says. He believes there's something beyond exercise, something unique to her physiology, perhaps some special tolerance for high-intensity exercise, that's
helping her maintain her impressive cardiovascular fitness.

Considering how similar my body is to BJ's, I am less inclined
to believe BJ possesses any more physiological superpowers than
I do. And my own experience offers some proof that we can continue to improve fitness well beyond our so-called athletic prime.
After all, I boosted my absolute max VO2 by 13 percent in less
than a year, and that was after going through menopause. And I
believe I could rocket-boost my VO2 to BJ's level if I put in another
year or three of intense training. Could following BJ's routine help
me maintain that max VO2 into my 80s? I think that's also possible.
What seems less possible is mustering the mental fortitude to follow BJ's training routine *now,* let alone into my mid-80s.

After spending the better part of the day riding an exercise
bike for a series of tests to measure lung and heart function, BJ
wants to go for a run. Taivassalo laughs, then nixes the idea. The
lab will biopsy BJ's muscles the next day, and Taivassalo wants
them free of fatigue markers. At that, BJ's eyes practically bulge
from their sockets: She needs movement, fresh air, a walk at
least! Taivassalo finally consents to a walk, but shoots me a warning look.

So the task of reining in BJ falls to me—no easy thing. BJ has
never been to Montreal and is eager to explore. Because I went to
graduate school here, I know the city well and suggest jumping
on the subway and taking a stroll either through the artsy Plateau
area to the north *or* Old Montreal to the south. BJ suggests taking
in both—and talks me out of taking the subway.

While walking with BJ, I find myself looking out for her as I did my disabled mom. I grew up hypervigilant of Mom's labored walk, tried to think out the most efficient routes to save her steps, hurried ahead to open doors, tried to anticipate her needs so that I could be her legs and fetch the thing before she even asked because she never liked to ask for help. I was always on the lookout for any potential misstep or obstruction so I could warn her or catch her should she fall.

I can't help doing the same with BJ, can't help thinking about her age—*85*, just a few years younger than Mom. But BJ walks like no 85-year-old I have ever known. Her pace is more like a forward assault on space, brisk and unrelenting. From my hawkeyed perspective, the city hurls obstructions toward BJ's feet like cosmic debris in a meteor shower: uneven sidewalks, broken concrete, potholes, cobblestones, raised grates, suddenly narrowing sidewalks. Nothing slows or unsettles BJ's stride. She pays about as much attention to the urban dangers ready to trip her up as a typical 20-year-old would. And her feet land as surely as one's, too.

I can muster a pretty brisk pace myself, but it takes my top gear to keep up with BJ. I begin to worry about those fatigue markers in her muscles for her tests the next day. I point out highlights and try to slow BJ down with stories about them—St. Urbain Street, in the Jewish quarter of Montreal famously captured in Mordecai Richler's novels; the old Notre-Dame Basilica, site of singer Céline Dion's wedding and the funerals of the city's social elites. BJ barely slows down, as if to suggest that I try walking and talking at the same time. In a couple of hours, we cover nearly 10 miles (15 kilometers). The bottoms of my feet are scorched when we return to our hotel, just moments before Hepple and Taivassalo arrive to pick us up for dinner. BJ, showing no outward signs of having those fatigue markers, orders a five-course table d'hôte meal and polishes it off along with half of

Hepple's foie gras appetizer. She also downs a couple of glasses of red wine, all while regaling us with stories, usually inducing laughs at her own expense, such as her reaction to her high max VO2: "Maybe I should have gotten a longer warranty on my new roof." Or on shocking her running group by sparking up a cigarette after her first marathon: "I only smoked when I had fun, but I liked to have a lot of fun." Then, with the impish grin of a misbehaving child, BJ assures us that she quit smoking years ago.

○   ●   ○   ●   ○   ●   ○

FIGURING OUT WHAT ENABLES super seniors like BJ to seemingly stop aging in its tracks could be used to reinvigorate the lives of millions and, given that the ranks of seniors are growing faster than any other demographic group in North America, could also save billions of health care dollars. As things go now, growing old rarely kills anyone; what usually gets us first is a slew of lifestyle diseases such as type 2 diabetes, various cancers, heart disease, stroke, etc. Yet the bulk of research dollars flows to figuring out how to fix disease and dysfunction, especially if it involves costly pharmaceuticals.

Hepple and Taivassalo would love to attract funding to extend their pilot project, to study more masters athletes from a wider range of sports and perhaps determine if certain types of athletic activities are more beneficial to successful aging. Both are former competitive athletes—Taivassalo in cross-country running, Hepple in swimming—and they still try to keep up their training. Now pushing into their mid-40s, they are expecting their first child. Like many older parents, they have a vested interest in discovering strategies to live younger in their advanced years. They will be near retirement age when they see their child off to college, and they will need to retain some youthful vigor into their 70s and 80s if they want to ski, cycle, and hike with their young grandchildren, as BJ does with her adult grandchildren.

While we all yearn for the outward effects of slowing aging so we appear decades younger than we are, aging researchers increasingly are looking inward for antiaging clues, studying the very building blocks of our biology. Much of that early research has focused on mitochondria, the microscopic specks in every cell in the body except red blood cells. These sophisticated little organelles function as the lungs and stomach for a cell, using oxygen to convert glucose into energy that fuels the work of cells, and hence are ground zero for the body's metabolism, the production and breakdown of energy—or, to put it in other words, the rebirth and decay that are involved in aging.

In preparation for Montreal and my visit with BJ, I had versed myself in the minutiae of mitochondria by chatting again with world-leading neurometabolism researcher Mark Tarnopolsky, who was also an academic mentor to both Hepple and Taivassalo. He told me that I could "without a doubt" reach my goal of attaining the fitness of a 20-year-old, one big reason being that running builds mitochondria like crazy. He estimates that my marathon training has increased my mitochondrial mass by 60 to 70 percent. Doing high-intensity interval running during my speed-training segment could boost my mitochondrial mass by another 20 to 30 percent. Having more mitochondria will not only help me run faster and longer (they provide fuel to muscles, after all), but also enable me to replace those that die naturally. This process could play a key role in stalling aging.

These microscopic energy generators, as Tarnopolsky explained, are part of the "complex phenomena" of the aging process at the cellular level that also involves telomeres (caps on the ends of chromosomes, like a shoelace's plastic tips, that protect

DNA from fraying during cell division) and cytokines, a family of protein regulators that signal and respond to inflammation.

Tarnopolsky described that aging process as a continuous dance between renewal and decay. On the decay side, mitochondria damage themselves in their daily work of using oxygen to convert glucose to cellular energy. Oxygen molecules that break off during that process—called free radicals—ping destructively around the mitochondria until they find other rogue oxygen molecules to bond with. This oxidative stress leads to mitochondrial dysfunction and death. We can lose 40 to 50 percent of our mitochondrial mass over a lifetime as the mitochondria become less able to repair themselves and we become less able to generate new mitochondria to power the work of the cell, and therefore the work of the muscles, organs, and other tissues. That loss of power, Tarnopolsky said, makes aged bodies something like massive cars being powered by tiny, sputtering engines. Oxidative stress also activates inflammation pathways, which, over time, may spark aging-related diseases that are now understood to be inflammatory in nature, such as Alzheimer's, type 2 diabetes, arthritis, and cancer. In addition, during regular cellular reproduction, telomeres, those protective ends on chromosomes, get trimmed every time a cell divides until they are too short to protect chromosomes from fraying or fusing with other chromosomes, leaving the cell open to yet more dysfunction, disease, and, eventually, death. As enough cells go, so go we.

But occurring alongside this normal, ongoing process of cellular aging and decay is one of cellular regeneration and rebirth that, as researchers like Tarnopolsky, Hepple, and Taivassalo are discovering, is spurred by physical activity, in particular running. While exercise generates oxidative stress in mitochondria, it also stimulates the production of cytokines, antioxidants, and hormones (such as growth hormone) that flood into cells to clean up the damage, causing trained athletes to have less oxidative stress and inflammation than the sedentary. As well, exercise builds muscle and hence new mitochondria (energy-hungry muscles are packed with mitochondria) that replace dead or dysfunctional ones. Exercise also stimulates production of telomerase, a protein that protects telomeres from shortening and can even rebuild telomere length, which increases cells' regenerative power to divide and replace themselves.

Learning about telomeres sent me scurrying to a lunchtime lecture given by University of California, San Francisco, professor Elizabeth Blackburn, PhD, and Calvin Harley, PhD, a cofounder of Telome Diagnostics. Blackburn, along with two research colleagues, won a Nobel Prize in 2009 for discovering telomerase, since dubbed the "antiaging enzyme." Telomerase promotes the growth of telomeres, and long telomeres appear to be associated with better health and a longer life. In 2012, after measuring the telomeres of 100,000 people with an average age of 63, Blackburn's research team found that having shorter telomeres was associated with a significantly increased risk of diseases and mortality. Other researchers are finding the same thing: Shorter telomeres contribute to cellular aging and correlate with increased risks of developing aging-related diseases such as cancers, type 2 diabetes, heart disease, osteoporosis, and dementia. Recently, Harley launched Telome Diagnostics with a goal of making telomere measuring available to the masses. Combining this yardstick measure of longevity with research linking telomere length to mortality and disease risk, doctors could project where someone is on the aging continuum—not in terms of chronological age, but physiological age. Harley believes that in 10 years, telomere testing will be as commonplace as cholesterol testing, perhaps with folks tripping off to the doctor for annual checkups to monitor their aging process—and hopefully make lifestyle adjustments accordingly.

The banquet room for the presentation was packed with well-heeled 50- to 80-year-olds. Most were interested in finding a quick fix in a drug rather than being advised to exercise to lengthen telomeres and stall aging, although one woman told me she wanted to have her telomeres measured to determine her biological age for financial planning purposes. She wanted a measure of how much time she might have to live, so she could spend her fortune before checking out.

In this room, I stood out; perhaps not as dramatically as BJ would in a cohort of 80- to 100-year-olds, but enough that I saw two forks diverging in the road to aging, and I was on the path less travelled. Most people were carrying 20, 30, or more extra pounds and showing signs of inflammation, disability, and possibly disease—stressed joints, labored breathing, a certain gray pallor to the face. By contrast, I and a handful of others in the room looked as if our telomeres might be long enough to lasso a wild horse. "You look fit," my tablemates said when I introduced myself, and then they arrived at their own conclusion about what road I was on: "You must be a runner." Then as if I were some kind of fitness judge they might plead their cases to, they told me that they knew they should exercise more, but offered up a litany of excuses for why they did not.

Their loathing of exercise or unwillingness to make time for this crucial foundation of good health is, well, sad. A pharmaceutical solution promoting the growth of telomeres is unlikely to appear on the horizon anytime soon, as side effects could include promoting the growth of unwanted nasty things, such as cancers. And partying like you're 99 after a telomere test may not be such a hot idea either, because short telomeres correlate with old age and an increased risk of mortality, but do not predict it. Truthfully, I could not understand their desire to live longer when they did not seem to want to live stronger and more fully in their bodies now.

At present, as Blackburn admitted in her lecture, the only safe prescription for preserving telomere length is the exact same prescription we should follow for general good health: exercise, reduce stress, and improve nutrition. As for what type of exercise, I put that question to Harley after the lecture. His response? "Running is excellent." He referred me to a German study of young professional runners in their 20s and masters runners who kept up distance training into their 50s. The two groups had comparable telomere lengths, while a group of healthy, nonsmoking, but sedentary people age matched to the masters athletes had significantly shorter telomeres.

Tarnopolsky has conducted similar studies with mitochondria, comparing the muscle tissues of masters endurance athletes and sedentary people of the same age. The findings: The middle-aged athletes had more than double the mitochondrial mass. Mitochondria are not only more prevalent and larger in that group's energy-hungry muscles (they also help plump out muscles), but also 30 to 40 percent more prevalent in their cheek cells, and the face doesn't exactly include key muscles for powering running.

Tarnopolsky is fascinated by all the ways running appears to compress aging and extend life itself. During our interview, he chatted about the famous Stanford study published in 2008 that followed runners and their socioeconomically matched peers for 21 years after reaching age 51 and showed the death rate in non-runners was 30 percent compared to only 15 percent for runners. There was not only a lower risk of all-cause mortality, but also a lower rate of aging-related diseases such as cancers and neurological diseases such as dementia. "This gets at the systemic benefits of running, not just affecting our hearts and lowering cholesterol, but showing a lower rate of disease and cancers and overall death rate. And more and more studies are supporting this," he told me.

In one of Tarnopolsky's better-known studies, he tried to find out exactly how running seems to stall aging. Mice genetically engineered to have dysfunctional mitochondria that prematurely aged them were divided into two groups at the age of 3 months. Astonishingly, the group of mutant mice that was forced to run—at a brisk pace for 45 minutes three times a week for 5 months—remained youthful. By contrast, the sedentary group aged rapidly during those 5 months. By 8 months, these mice had reached the human equivalent of 60 years of age. They were frail, decrepit, graying, and balding. Their brains, muscles, and gonads were shriveled, their hearts enlarged. Within a year, all were dead. The running rodents, however, remained vibrant, fertile, and young looking. Somehow, running had "fixed" their dysfunctional mitochondria. It also spurred production of a protein that promotes the production of new mitochondria. In every tissue and body system the team studied, running had had a positive impact.

As with Tarnopolsky's running mice, the world-record-holding athletes in the Montreal masters athletes study, all over age 75, look healthier and younger than their sedentary controls, often by 2 decades or more. They certainly move like people decades younger and are also more mentally alert or "with it," as Hepple says. Other studies show that aerobic exercise is excellent for spurring neurogenesis, the growth of new brain cells and networks. Danielle Laurin, PhD, of Quebec's Laval University found that women over 65 who report higher levels of physical activity are 50 percent less likely than their inactive peers to develop dementia, reaffirming, as *Spark* author John Ratey writes, that "exercise is the single most powerful tool you have to optimize your brain function."

Catherine Sabiston, the exercise psychologist analyzing the cognitive side of the Montreal study, says that a higher level of fitness and more muscle strength are both associated with greater cognitive fitness. Compared to their sedentary controls, the masters athletes test higher on memory and verbal processing (the ability to take in information, process it, and react to it). However, there was no difference between the athletes and controls in their ability to focus on a task or in verbal fluency (say, to come up with a list of words starting with a certain letter). Both of these cognitive skills are strongly influenced by education level, and the masters athletes and sedentary controls were well matched in that regard. As Sabiston says, "We don't know what aspects of cognitive function are going to be affected by exercise. Are there structural differences in the brain? Are there differences in brain activity?" What she can conclude, she says, is that high-intensity training improves not only cognitive function, but also all measured quality-of-life dimensions: "[The masters athletes] report significantly less stress and more optimism. We see benefits emotionally, cognitively, physically, and even socially. We see lower levels of depression, higher levels of positivity, less pain, better sleep." In principle, she says, "higher-intensity exercise probably gives more benefits," but the trick is "to tax the body, but not overtax it."

BJ appears to have found that sweet spot. Still, she sometimes worries if exercising as hard as she does might have adverse effects. Her father and several of her siblings (all far less active than BJ) died of heart disease. The Montreal study, again, proves reassuring. Despite the stress of intense workouts, the hearts of the super seniors proved remarkably normal in function and structure. "We were looking for cardiac instability, but there was nothing," says Taivassalo, though she does point out that exercise did not prove to be completely protective of the heart—a couple of athletes studied did have stents inserted to treat narrow or weak arteries.

As for muscles, the difference between the masters athletes

and the controls "was striking," according to Hepple. Normally, the elderly become frail when their muscles atrophy, and they can lose more than 30 percent of overall muscle function. Hepple's research suggests that aging muscles stop working effectively as fibers come unplugged from motor neurons (the cells that tell them to fire). This could be the reason BJ has lost running speed, and why I can run considerably faster than she can now, even though she has a higher max VO2. But likely as a result of the "use it or lose it" rule, the masters athletes' muscles are still much better preserved and have less denervation than those of sedentary controls. Hepple believes the muscles of these world-record runners would be superior even to those of masters athletes finishing, say, 10th in the same event, as those at the back of the pack can be significantly slower. "The difference in [finishing] times is often dramatic," he says. The masters athletes in the Montreal study retained far more muscle mass than the controls did. That muscle also had less fat infiltration and better function. If the world-record holders possess a special resistance to aging or exceptional tolerance for exercise that has enabled them to retain their incredible fitness and youthful vigor, Hepple believes it will be found in their well-preserved muscles. He proffers this line of thinking: Our legs contain our largest muscles. Moving them increases bloodflow and improves circulation throughout the body. Stressing muscles with high-intensity exercise provokes the production of proteins and hormones that promote new cellular growth and renewal, good stuff like the growth hormone that repairs muscles and the brain-derived neurotrophic factor that sparks the growth of new brain cells and neural connections that support learning and memory. Whatever it is that is released to protect, repair, renew, and grow muscles "seems to be playing itself out throughout the brain and the body," says Hepple.

ON THE MORNING of her muscle testing, BJ declines the offer of a drive to the research lab, to nobody's surprise. Instead, the two of us power march the steep mile uphill from our hotel, chatting about our theories of aging during the tromp. BJ, a former nurse, is eager to discuss the test results and what they mean, but she doesn't think she possesses any antiaging superpowers. She attributes her youthfulness to this: having younger friends who keep her doing the things she loves, primarily running. "Quantity of life doesn't interest me much," BJ tells me. "But quality of life does. And I have a terrific quality of life." She has just returned from a hiking trip in Arizona with her adult children. She cycles and hikes with her grandchildren. In December, shortly after turning 85, she set a new world record with no particular intention of doing so. The real goal was to complete a three-generation marathon in Honolulu with her son and her granddaughter, who was in university at the time and running her first 26-miler. "She didn't have much time to train," BJ laughs, recalling the memory. "I half expected her to be in the ditch at the end gasping for breath, because I'm sure she was afraid I might pass her."

Most days, BJ trains with a lively circle of younger friends, her "entourage," as she calls the 40- to 60-year-old gal pals she meets for 5:00 a.m. trail runs. Along the way, there's a lot of storytelling, laughing, bonding, and plotting of the next girlfriend weekend getaway for a race. BJ used to lead the running pack and circle back to check on slower runners; now the front-runners return the favor. "They admire me," says BJ, "and I admire them for getting out there to run before getting their kids off to school and themselves off to work."

As BJ talks, I can't help thinking how similar her life has been to my mom's. Neither Mom nor BJ considers herself extraordinary, though their physical courage—how hard they push themselves—commands admiration from people. In addition to physical similarities, they both love having fun, love laughing, which also attracts people to them. The two even share uncannily similar biographies. Like Mom, BJ grew up on a farm in southern Ontario during the Great Depression, was a middle child among eight siblings, loved sports and played whatever game was going. Given the hardscrabble times, they also did their share of hard farmwork, which gave them each a strong base of muscle and cardiovascular fitness to carry into adulthood. Both had smarts and ambition, moving to Toronto to get what career training women could in the 1940s and 1950s, teaching in Mom's case and nursing in BJ's, which took BJ west to Vancouver, where she married. Both had good marriages, became stay-at-home moms in middle-class households, had two girls and two boys, stayed active, and nourished a large network of friends and family. Even more eerie, both watched their husbands descend into dementia in later years—and insisted on caring for them at home for as long as they could.

A defining difference in their life stories, of course, is their legs.

Mom has done extremely well maintaining her health into her late 80s, given that her leg muscles were wasted by polio. BJ's fitness, by comparison, is astonishing. She played tennis and skied as an adult—nothing very intense, she claims—and did not take up running until age 50. From her 50s to her 80s, Mom's legs grew weaker, as happens with many polio sufferers as they age, Mom says, and she went from walking with one cane to using two and then finally to a walker. BJ, meanwhile, was falling in love with a sport that she believes has given her a higher level of fitness in her 80s than she had in her 30s. At age 81, BJ was invited to run in the Rome Marathon as an elite—all expenses paid—to set an example for sedentary Italian ladies and get them "off of their stilettos," as BJ quips in her book, *My Road to Rome,* a charmingly chatty chronicle of her running life.

Mom's health story has taken a different path. Four years ago, her legs finally gave out and confined her to a wheelchair. She works at keeping her upper body strong by going to fitness classes in her retirement home and lifting small weights on her own. But the increased inactivity is taking a toll on her health, and her hearing and sight have declined dramatically, as well. Her feet and legs swell as her heart struggles to do its work. While she remains incredibly good-natured, some days she talks about being tired, about taking up space in her retirement home, like her young friend back in the rehab hospital so many years ago.

Whatever the results of all the testing being done on BJ, it's becoming crystal clear to me that the way to slow aging is pretty straightforward: If you have use of your legs, use them.

○　　●　　○　　●　　○　　●　　○

ON THIS FINAL DAY in Montreal, I get yet another unexpected present, though I still haven't fessed up that it's my birthday. BJ is to undergo a DXA scan, the most accurate way to measure body fat, bone density, and muscle mass. On the way there, Taivassalo asks if I want to be scanned too. Given how obsessed I've been with the physical similarities between BJ and me, I leap at the opportunity to peel back the skin, so to speak, and compare the actual composition of our bodies—and get an even more accurate peek into the future and what my body might look like at age 85.

BJ goes first, stretching out on what looks like a bed-length photocopier, her feet strapped together to keep her body in alignment. After the technician leaves the room, she activates a low-dose radiation scanner that slowly passes over BJ's body from head to toes, emitting x-rays that measure the percentages and weights of BJ's bones, fat tissue, and muscles throughout her body, even breaking down those measurements by body part to give the weights of bone, fat, and muscle in BJ's left leg, for instance. The scan takes all of 6 minutes to produce a whack of measurements that can be compared to the general population of 30-year-old women (a T-score) and the general population of age-matched women (a Z-score).

As we watch from the doorway, the technician tells me that DXA scans are primarily used by doctors to track bone mineral loss and diagnose osteoporosis, but increasingly fitness professionals are using them as another way to gauge fitness. While a max VO2 test measures cardiovascular fitness, a DXA scan measures body composition, pinpointing where—and how much—fat is distributed throughout the body. Too much visceral fat packed in the torso around the organs—giving someone the swallowed–beach ball look—is associated with increased risks of heart disease and type 2 diabetes. Subcutaneous fat, which is the kind stored under the skin, is less dangerous, but losing a layer of lard and building up muscle will yield a higher level of fitness. McGill University varsity athletes undergo scans to get an under-the-skin look at fat and muscle distribution so they can fine-tune their training to build leaner, stronger bodies.

When it's my turn to be scanned, I have to give the technician my birth date. The surprise is finally out of the bag. "You didn't say!" BJ exclaims with a slightly accusatory edge as if I was holding back on a perfectly good reason to party. When we sit down after my test to discuss our results with the technician, I tease BJ that I didn't want her to know my age because, on yet another comparison of our fitness, this 51-year-old marathoner who thinks she's in pretty great shape is getting her butt kicked yet again by an 85-year-old.

We turn out to be exactly the same height—5 feet, not the 5 foot 1 we both boast of. But on that day, nearly a month before that spring marathon when I am at 113, I weigh in at 116 pounds. That is 5 pounds heavier than BJ at 111 pounds and, as the scan shows, those 5 extra pounds *plus another 2 pounds* are all fat. That slight edge of strength or sturdiness I felt when standing next to BJ is clearly an illusion—or rather, *fat*. BJ has a much lower percentage of body fat: She is a buff 22.7 percent compared to my puffier 28.7 percent. While our weights and body fat percentages fall well within the normal ranges for our age groups, mine is in the upper range for a runner. I'm surprised by that because of the weight I've shed and the muscle I've built pumping iron twice a week. Apparently, I have more work to do. At least now, by comparing my scan to BJ's, I can see exactly where I can trim the extra fat I carry; it's all on my legs, hips, and arms! But what really leaves me sputtering with shock is that BJ, despite weighing less than I, has more muscle mass, a whopping 4.5 pounds more muscle! I think back to all the times during our walks when I raced ahead to open doors for BJ, as if she were the frailer one.

"BJ," I say, "I swear I'm going to stop holding doors for you."

The one area where I come out ahead of BJ is in bone mineral density. Compared to fat and muscle, our bones weigh almost nothing. BJ's entire skeleton weighs just 3.78 pounds, while mine weighs almost a pound more at 4.62. In her vertebrae, BJ finally shows traces of her advanced age. Her spine is slightly twisted and has lost considerable density, even more than the average in the general population of 85-year-olds. Clearly, the muscle mass that she built up and has retained is helping her maintain her extremely straight, strong, and upright posture. Several of BJ's siblings have osteoporosis, and the technician says that without all the pounding of running that builds bone density, BJ likely would have it too. Due to BJ's regimen of running, yoga, and weight lifting, the bones in the rest of her body—her arms, legs, neck, and torso—have fared much better. While she has lost some bone density in these areas compared to 30-year-olds, she has retained far more density than the general population of 85-year-old women. As for the common belief that running is hard on the joints, BJ's scan suggests otherwise. In her hips, which are particularly susceptible to fracture in frail seniors, BJ has retained the bone density of a 30-year-old.

Running has clearly been helpful to me as well. My bone density scores are not only higher than those of most women my own age, but also, in six of seven regions, I have greater bone density than the general population of 30-year-olds. The straightness of my spine actually provokes a "Wow" from the technician, wonderful news for me as my father and my three siblings have all been plagued by back troubles. Interestingly, though, like BJ's, my spine shows the greatest loss of density. Not enough to signal osteoporosis, but in some sections of my spine, my bone density scores are slightly lower than those of the general population of women my age. There's not much more I can do other than to keep doing what I'm doing—studies show that high-impact activities like running and weight lifting are best for building bone strength, especially in the back, while cycling, swimming, and walking are too low impact to provide much benefit in that regard. But looking over BJ's scan and considering her amazingly sturdy and straight posture, I realize there is one thing I can do to protect my somewhat vulnerable spine and hold me upright into my 80s: work on shedding my extra pounds of fat and building muscle, as BJ has.

○   ●   ○   ●   ○   ●   ○

I DON'T GET A CHANCE to say good-bye to BJ because she is still undergoing a brain fMRI when I have to leave to catch my train (since exercise grows brain cells, I know there is probably quite a lot to scan). Even though my bulging knapsack feels like it weighs as much as my body fat and my rolling suitcase tips frequently on the uneven sidewalks, I persist in walking the hour to the station. What else could I do after coming under BJ's influence? She would always choose exercise. That, I am sure of. It's that choice, I believe, that has enabled her to retain her incredible fitness into her late 80s. The Montreal study may well show that she and her cohort of world-record-holding seniors possess screamingly high levels of this growth hormone or that antiaging protein that enables them to tolerate high levels of exercise into their advanced years, but these are surely the hard-earned results of training for the past 35 years almost like 20-something Olympians. In constantly comparing myself to BJ, I can't fathom setting any world records in my 80s, but I can imagine hitting 85 in a shape as good as BJ's *if* I can keep up a similar training regimen. I have another 34 years, after all, to nudge my 43 max VO2 up to her 46, trim my extra fat and build 5 more pounds of muscle (I will attribute the 3 pounds that fall off over the next 3 weeks to the shock of seeing my DXA results next to BJ's). BJ, who did not start her extreme fitness kick until she was 50, surely proves that it's possible to achieve superior fitness at any age. Yet trying to maintain BJ's level into my 80s will mean that this super-fit year can never end. Can I continue running marathons and striving for super fitness for the rest of my life? Today, on my birthday and with a glorious spring sun shining, that seems entirely possible, and I'm even jazzed by the challenge. But tomorrow?

I put that question to Catherine Sabiston, who analyzed the motivation and cognition side of the Montreal study: How can I muster the motivation to keep training beyond the World Masters in Italy, beyond my super-fit year, so that I might have BJ's fitness when I'm 85? Her response? Laughter. She told me that I can't just put a picture of BJ on my fridge and stick my head over hers like I might some supermodel and expect that inspiration will get me out the door to train. That extrinsic motivation, she said, will soon wear out. I will have to muster up some deeper passion to drive me.

And that scares me, because during my next and final training segment heading into Italy—building speed—I begin to suffer some mental burnout.

So my questions remain: What keeps BJ training so hard? And how can I find that for myself?

Until a brain fMRI can capture thoughts, motivation, attitude, and drive, I am pretty certain that the scan of BJ's gray matter will not reveal the secret to how she keeps mustering up the motivation to run and train so intensely, day after day, year after year, decade after decade. But I am determined to find out. Before leaving Montreal, I made arrangements with BJ to travel to Vancouver to run an upcoming half-marathon with her. While there, I will also meet other world-record-holding women runners who were invited to participate in the Montreal study.

My goal is this: go for a run with them, then get them together over lunch to chat about their fitness journeys and, hopefully, find out what makes them run and keep running and running and running.

CHAPTER 9

LEGACY

THREE WORLD-RECORD HOLDERS arrive at a luncheon in their honor in a sleek silver sports car as flashy as their running résumés. Behind the wheel and looking Hollywood glam—a primrose yellow scarf flowing from her neck—is sprinter Christa Bortignon, 76. Riding shotgun is another sprinter, styling in a cream-colored jean jacket and jeans ensemble, Olga Kotelko, 94. And in the backseat, cracking jokes and laughing as usual, her auburn hair glinting on this sun-drenched day, is my running soul mother, marathoner BJ McHugh, 85. They revel in their youthful vigor as much as 20-something world-record holders might, but the triumph of these senior athletes may be more meaningful, for they are exploding the limits of human performance not only in sports, but also in the human life cycle, showing us vast new potential. Each looks 2 decades younger than she is and moves like someone even younger as they all pop out of the car to greet a fourth world-record holder, marathoner Gwen McFarlan, 79, a tall, lithe strawberry blonde who, as if inspiring lyrics to some pop tune, travelled downtown on the SkyTrain.

The four live in Vancouver, on Canada's west coast, but this is the first time the world's fastest women in their respective age-group events have gathered together. (This area is surely a hot spot for super-achieving seniors, with two more world-record holders—Diane Palmason and sprinter Lenore Montgomery—also having been on my guest list, but unable to make it.) I orchestrated this luncheon with the help of two of my running pals, Mary and Phyllis, who leapt at the opportunity to get this rarified glimpse into our likely futures, if we continue running as strong and for as long as these extraordinary women have.

The three of us flew west, Mary offered up her parents' home for the occasion, and my two running pals pitched in to help me prepare a gourmet spread of wild Pacific salmon, local vegetables, and British Columbia wines and cheeses. My goal in bringing together these pioneers of the women's running boom is to find out what has motivated them to train so intensely into such advanced years, but I also want to honor them for the extraordinary legacy they are gifting us—showing us that it is possible to live younger much longer than we ever imagined. And as my super-fit year draws to a close, with the World Masters in Italy just 2 months away, I can't help but look beyond. I am a little afraid I won't have the stuff to continue training as long as these super seniors, yet I desperately want what they have, this chance at an entire second act to our adult lives.

Within minutes of arriving, our guests become fast friends. They discover much in common besides their world records. The four all had extremely active childhoods that likely fueled their desire to stay active: Olga, BJ, and Gwen grew up on farms, while Christa, who grew up in Germany at the end of the Second World War, walked 40 minutes to school and delivered newspapers to help support her family. All four married and had professional careers—Olga and Gwen as teachers, BJ as a nurse, and Christa as an accountant. They also raised children, and Olga and Christa were trailblazers in that area too, as working single moms after divorces. The four did not start running until later in life—BJ at 50, Olga and Christa in their 70s, and Gwen at 60 after developing breast cancer. But all credit exercise with enabling them to live younger long into their senior years, Gwen most emphatically. "Without running, I may not be here," she says, explaining that as a working mom, she put family and career before her own health and believes stress, lack of exercise, and poor nutrition contributed to her cancer. After her diagnosis, she took up running, which led her to take much better care of her overall health. "It extended my life by 20 years," she says, but the 79-year-old could have instead said "by *at least* 20 years," as she shows no sign of slowing down anytime soon.

Beyond all their similarities, what bonds the women immediately is their attitude, which seems also to be shaped by sport: They are relentlessly positive, confident, curious about each other's life experiences, and very serious about their athletics, yet they are quick to tease each other and even quicker to make hilarious self-deprecating remarks. They laugh boisterously and often. And while they can't deny their achievements are extraordinary, they are remarkably humble; in fact, they still seem a little stunned to find themselves in the pantheon of the world's best. They tell us that anyone, if he or she puts in the training, can achieve their level of fitness, if not their world-record times.

For Phyllis at 61 and Mary and me at 51, it is profoundly moving to get this look at the next stages of our lives and see such happiness, youthful vigor, exuberance, and passion for life. We keep throwing each other amazed looks as we take in their version of aging and realize it can be pretty fantastic. It's not that the women are in denial of their years—they crack jokes about that too—but they behave more as if old age is just another opponent on the track, something that has yet to catch up to them, for they're certainly not going to slow down for it.

During lunch, which is punctuated with more teasing, more laughter, and quite a few glasses of wine, we pepper these trail-blazers with questions: What motivates them to keep training like college kids? What does it feel like to set a world record, to be the fastest woman her age in the world? And the question I've been asking myself throughout my super-fit year: How is it even possible that older women—well beyond their childbearing years—can acquire and maintain such superior fitness and life vitality?

Really, how is it that Olga, at 94, can still be travelling to inter-national track meets and laying down new world records in sprints and jumping and throwing events when most women her age wouldn't even step on a plane? Or that Christa, at 76, can run 100 meters in under 16 seconds, barely 4 seconds off the Ameri-can high-school girls' record? Or that BJ McHugh, at age 85, can even run a marathon, let alone do it in 5:14, nearly 20 minutes faster than the previous world record set by the extraordinary mar-athoner and ultramarathoner Helen Klein. Or that Gwen McFarlan could run a 3:57 marathon at age 75, which is faster than the aver-age finishing time of *every age group* in the NYC Marathon, includ-ing 20- to 40-year-old men in their so-called prime? At 80, BJ ran a 4:36, better than the average finishing time of 30- to 34-year-old women in the NYC Marathon. According to a look at distance-running veterans, "Aging and the Marathon," one of a series of lectures presented at a British Heart Foundation symposium, the decline with aging in trained men and women is very gradual—just 1 to 2 percent in speed per year—until the age of 80. After that, the decline can become more dramatic. Yet, 2 days after our luncheon, BJ and Gwen will run the Vancouver half-marathon in new world-record times for their respective ages.

That these women don't consider themselves genetic outliers, that they think many women their age could be doing what they do, seems even more extraordinary, for it would appear to be a deeply puzzling quirk of nature that women are able to live this long, let alone run such phenomenal distances and speeds. After all, in nearly every other mammal species (with the exceptions of killer and pilot whales), females rarely survive beyond their reproductive years. Even our closest evolutionary relatives—great apes—grow old and decrepit while still cycling and usually die while still fertile, whereas humans can live and thrive for many decades after menopause. From a biological, evolutionary standpoint, logic would suggest that our work on this earth—and, hence, our usefulness—is done. And yet Gwen, a well-trained 79-year-old woman, can still leave 20- and 30-year-old male marathoners huffing in her dust. Why?

○   ●   ○   ●   ○   ●   ○

BEFORE MY TRIP WEST, I put in a call to University of Utah evolutionary anthropologist Kristen Hawkes, PhD, who had her own inspirational encounter with a group of older female super athletes when she travelled to Tanzania in the late 1980s to study the foraging techniques of the hunter–gatherer Hadza tribe. Seeing them at work prompted Hawkes to ask a more complex version of my question: Why is it that women can retain such fitness and vigor well past menopause, and could a few super-fit, long-lived females have been the "defining signature of our species," the very spark that caused humans to evolve from primates and develop that distinctly human characteristic of a long postreproductive life span, permitting the evolution of an extended childhood, late maturation, longer life spans for both women and men, bigger brains capable of complex language and thinking, communal child rearing, and cooperative communities? When Hawkes and her team landed in the Hadza community, the answer to what set us on the path to humanity, she said, "was right before our eyes."

While the men of the tribe hunted for game and young mothers nursed and looked after infants, women past childbearing age foraged for the starchy food staple that nourished the nursing mothers, fed their weaned children, and sustained the tribe through the boom-and-bust cycles of the hunt. "The starchy tubers grow underground in very rocky soil and digging them out requires a lot of strength," Hawkes told me in a phone interview from her office at the University of Utah. "By all conventional measures of strength [such as grip strength and ability to carry a load], these old ladies were amazing athletes." In addition to marathon feats of foraging, these long-lived women also cared for young children, which allowed mothers to have more babies before their oldest children were independent, another distinctly human trait. Of the reams of tests and measures Hawkes's team performed, one in particular highlighted the influence these helpful older women had on the future well-being of the tribe: There was a direct correlation between a baby's birth weight and how much foraging his or her grandmother did.

Earlier evolutionary theorists had proposed that natural selection of grandmothering *alone* could have propelled the evolution of our unique postmenopausal longevity, and Hawkes expanded on that work to develop a "grandmother hypothesis" of human evolution. She argues that at the dawn of *Homo erectus* nearly 2 million years ago in Africa, a change in climate creating a drying continent presented older females with a fitness opportunity to survive, likely by learning to forage for new food sources such as nuts, hard-cased seeds, and underground tubers. The helpful ones, relieved of their reproductive duties, opted to help their daughters raise children, which increased the survival rates of both their daughters and grandchildren and so ensured that the helpful grandmothers' genes—with the "inclusive fitness benefits" of longevity, strength, vigor, and compassion—would be passed on. As Hawkes said of the mathematical modeling of population growth her team did to test her hypothesis, "Even if very few individuals are eligible to grandmother, way less than 1 percent of caregivers, that's enough [for a population to take off], and selection pushes life history into one that looks like ours today." In other words, a few strong, helpful grandmothers propelled selection for a long postreproductive life span, from which gushed a cascade of genetic changes—longer lives for both sexes, later maturation, larger brains, as well as traits for empathy and cooperation—that set our ancestors on the path to becoming human.

Competing with Hawkes's grandmother hypothesis are a myriad of other theories of evolution, most notably the running man theory championed by Harvard professor Daniel Lieberman, PhD. He proposes that the evolutionary catalyst leading to *H. erectus* was another adaptive trait—our unique ability to run at low speeds for very long distances. Although *H. erectus* emerged some 2 million years ago and tools for hunting and carving up animals arrived a mere 200,000 years ago, Lieberman makes up for that massive gap in time by arguing that our earliest ancestors used their endurance running ability to persistence hunt: essentially, to run animals to exhaustion, particularly the antelope, which can trot only as fast as a man can jog, yet tires easily when forced to run faster. Persistence hunting, still practiced in some hunter–gatherer tribes, is, according to Lieberman, what enabled our earliest ancestors to gain access to a protein source, which sparked the human brain to grow, speeding up the myriad of selective adaptations that make us uniquely human. Not surprisingly, Lieberman's theory received an enthusiastic audience in running communities and gained even more traction with Christopher McDougall's tales of the ultrarunning feats of the Mexican Tarahumara tribe recounted in his massively popular book, *Born to Run*.

On the battleground of competing evolutionary theories, both the grandmother and running man hypotheses have their share of critics, and yet another evolutionary theorist, John Hawks, PhD, of the University of Wisconsin, uses Lieberman's own arguments to critique the running man theory. Lieberman, in marshaling scientific evidence to support his thesis, had 15 subjects with varying toe lengths run on a treadmill. He found that an increase in toe length of just 20 percent doubled the mechanical work of running. And he points out that pre–*H. erectus* hominids—Lucy being a prime example—would have found it difficult to run long distances due to the length of their toes. Hawks argues that Lieberman's so-called short-toe revelation is actually evidence that humans are optimally designed for walking rather than running, as toe-length variation, which endures in these modern times, is "relatively good evidence that toe length *wasn't* selected for" in the set of traits that would make endurance running the defining signature of our species.

While humans have evolved into amazing endurance walkers and runners, Kristen Hawkes suggests the fact that well-trained 60-year-olds can compete with 20-year-olds in marathons is evidence that it is our design for longevity that set us on the course to becoming uniquely human. At some point, it became advantageous to the emergence of our species to pour energy into supporting existing offspring, suppressing adult mortality, and selecting traits for maintaining bodies into old age, particularly those of women, who, on average, live 4 years longer than men. As Hawkes points out, apes are still cycling when they become frail and weakened old women; however, human females can remain fit and strong long after menopause, when the ovaries stop producing estrogen. As a result of a complex set of adaptations on our path to becoming human, our bodies have found ways to maintain and renew physiological systems without that all-important hormone. The human body, she pointed out to me, is able to produce dehydroepiandrosterone (DHEA), a precursor for most sex steroids that I wrote about in Chapter 5. In response to biological stress—such as exercise, whether running or yanking tubers from rocky soil—the adrenal glands and brain secrete DHEA, which can be taken up by tissues and metabolized into androgens and estrogen. Also, mitochondria have their own DNA, which is different from the DNA of the cells they inhabit: Only mothers pass on that mitochondrial DNA to their offspring, and natural selection appears to weed out mutations in mitochondria that might adversely affect women's life spans. Women's T-cells also age slower, allowing for more robust immunity. The XX female chromosome provides protection as well: Its telomeres stay longer over a life span than those of the male Y chromosome, and the second X provides backup protection should disease or mutation affect the other X. Another key to healthy aging, as modern researchers are discovering, is maintaining a rich social network of family and friends, which requires psychosocial skills that our ancient grandmothers may have encoded into our very DNA.

Evidence swaying me toward supporting Hawkes's grandmother hypothesis came at me from all directions during my own trip to Africa at age 49, just 3 weeks after completing my second marathon. One morning seemed like a dream: I was running with a group of Kenyans along a country road in the Great Rift Valley, the cradle of civilization and birthplace of the best marathoners in the world. Astonishingly, I was in the lead, leisurely loping along while the Kenyans struggled to keep up. Okay, admittedly, the Kenyans were schoolchildren I had happened upon during a morning run, but some of them seemed as old as 12 or 13 and I was staring down 50. How was it possible that I could be faster?

More astonishment followed on a climb up Mount Kilimanjaro, which I did with a group of women ranging in age from 45 to 55, most of us meeting each other for the first time upon arriving in

Nairobi. We took the toughest, steepest route with the lowest success rate, yet every woman reached the summit, amazing our African guides, who hailed us as "strong, strong like Simba." Everyone had trained to achieve a decent level of fitness, but not one of us felt that our success came from our individual physical strengths. Facing the emotional stress of the challenge as well as the physiological stress of starting the climb at significant altitude, our group responded by forming an immediate and intense bond. Encouraging and supporting each other during the climb made us strong as a whole. Evidence: me. Arguably the fittest in the group after completing a Boston-qualifying marathon 3 weeks earlier, I was the first to struggle on the final push to the summit, bonking just 2 hours into a 6-hour climb up 4,000 feet to the peak at 19,336 feet. Battling altitude sickness and hypothermia from the icy temperature, I became delirious and imagined that curling up beside the trail to sleep would actually be a good idea, even though, rationally, I knew that guides and porters have died on the mountain this way. I also convinced myself that I already had the accomplishment of having finished a couple of marathons, so did I even need the finish line of summiting Kilimanjaro? No, I did not. I longed to turn back, yet I knew that quitting would dishearten my climbing sisters by sowing seeds of self-doubt—if marathon girl couldn't make it, could they? So I sounded the alarm. I admitted my weakness, let a guide take my backpack, had some food and hot tea, did some pressure breathing to get oxygen to my brain and push back the fatigue. And then I persisted, not so much for me, but for my climbing sisters. Over copious beers after the climb, each one of us told stories of similar dark moments—many more extreme than mine—and of drawing on the deep connection of the group. On the climb, that sort of bond inspired us to push on to the rooftop of Africa, which we reached at dawn, just as the sun broke over the horizon and sprayed the world with light. It was spine-tingling, the gratitude we felt for what seemed like a gift, this apparently inherent ability for a group of women meeting each other for the first time to bond as sisters, giving us an unfathomable strength to persevere. My running sisters also know that strength. It's the fuel we draw on at the end of our toughest runs.

My last adventure in Africa was the Safaricom Marathon and Half Marathon, the only footrace in the world held in a game park. Local and international runners flock to the Lewa Wildlife Conservancy at the base of Mount Kenya to raise money for conservation and community development projects in exchange for the unique experience of running through the African grasslands among lions, elephants, rhinos, zebras, and giraffes just as our ancestors did (though rangers and a plane buzzing overhead kept the most ferocious beasts at bay during the race). Of course, I posed no challenge to the top Kenyans competing for prize money. Yet, at age 49 and still recovering from climbing Kilimanjaro, I could easily outrun the majority of African runners, who were much younger than I, the 20- and 30-something white-collar workers from Nairobi. How was that possible? While they may be more closely related to the fastest marathoners on earth—the Ethiopians and Kenyans from the Great Rift Valley—their waistlines are expanding as fast as their country is urbanizing. Meanwhile, just a year earlier, I had been a short, stocky, flat-footed, still-smoking premenopausal woman so rocked by a primeval fear of aging that I subjected my body to a dose of extreme stress similar to what our ancestral grandmothers may have faced when searching for new food sources on a drying continent, but mine was from training for a marathon. And my body, as if following the script of Hawkes's grandmother hypothesis, responded to that encoded fitness opportunity and thrived.

○   ●   ○   ●   ○   ●   ○

FLASH FORWARD 2 MILLION YEARS from the dawn of *H. erectus* to this great women's running boom, and millions and millions of women are *suddenly, consciously,* choosing to get strong. And perhaps in the process, we are realizing that *we are meant to be strong.* Why "suddenly"? In the vastness of evolutionary time, the 3 or 4 decades of the women's running boom are sudden. Why now? Could becoming physically strong—which typically confers psychological strength—be key to women taking control over their lives, taking on leadership roles, claiming a full and equal place in the world? After struggles for rights in the legal, workplace, and domestic spheres, could the women's running boom usher in the next wave of feminism, in which we claim the right to be physically strong? And, presuming that older women will not have to dig for starchy tubers, what will we make of this glorious fitness opportunity, this chance to live for several decades after 50 with the wisdom of our years *and* the energy and strength of 20-year-olds? What will we do with this entire second act to our lives? If our ancient grandmothers, by seizing their fitness opportunity to be strong and helpful, set us on the course to being fully human, where might our fitness boom lead?

I found myself discussing these big questions with the Iron Nun, Sister Madonna Buder, 83, whom I dropped by to visit in her hometown of Spokane, Washington, on my trip to the West Coast. A Catholic nun, she earned her nickname for the roughly 300 triathlons and 45 Ironmans she has tackled since taking up running at age 48 (she qualified for Boston on her first marathon, with a 3:29 at age 52) and triathlons at 55. At age 82, she became the oldest person in the world to complete an Ironman. She held that world record until Lew Hollander completed the World Ironman in Hawaii 6 weeks later. But she retains the record as the world's oldest woman to complete an Ironman—a record many believe will not be broken, unless Sister Madonna breaks it herself.

And that she is trying to do, though this time she wants to complete the ultra triathlon distance at the World Ironman, which would make her the first 80-plus woman to do so, thereby proving to other women that such a feat is possible. Opening that age category at the World Ironman Championships, as she did for women 75-plus, is "the motivation that's keeping me going," she told me. "Get the thing done, so it's there for women." For decades, Sister Madonna has been smashing through the limits our imaginations have imposed on physical activity as we age. "Men will pass me on the bike and say, 'I hope I can still be doing this at your age,' and then I'll pass them later," she laughed, acknowledging how she's turned heads in competitions. When she actually has competition in her age group, she often beats not only her female rivals, but the fastest men as well. Still, she admitted to me that "it's getting harder and harder" to keep up a pace that has her competing nearly every weekend throughout the summer, and she would likely give up the Ironman competitions and focus on shorter triathlons if people weren't looking to her for inspiration. "If it weren't for my age, I probably wouldn't be doing this," she said bluntly. Then, realizing the odd logic of that, she threw her head back and howled with laughter.

I wanted to spend a day with Sister Madonna doing what I nickname the "Iron Nun Triathlon" and what she calls "not training." Calling herself the most untrained triathlete ever, she incorporates training into her daily life and tries to "make it joyful," the great advice for exercise adherence that she offers in her memoir, *The Grace to Race*. She uses her legs as transportation, running several miles to morning Mass and then to various volunteer commitments around town, such as giving spiritual counsel to jail inmates or communion to the sick in hospitals. She squeezes in swims at the Y or, in the summer, cycles to a lake to swim, a 40-mile round trip. During daylight hours, she says she moves constantly, gardening, puttering around her house, doing chores.

So, after flying in late the previous night, I ran to meet her at morning Mass, at 6:00 a.m. As her "habit," she wore a gold cross necklace and an all-black ensemble, albeit a long-sleeve running shirt and capri tights. After the service, she looked weary. It may have to do with the recent competition woes she spoke about nonstop on our jog to breakfast at my hotel. She was supposed to compete in the New York City Marathon that was cancelled by Hurricane Sandy, was diverted from the finish line of the Boston Marathon by the bombings, had a flat tire that blew a World Iron-man qualifying event, and was blown off course by high winds (and unnerved by alligators) during the swim at a Florida triathlon. She admitted that it's becoming a struggle just getting her bike, her gear, and herself to events; a recent travel glitch had her sleeping on the floor of the Denver airport one night.

Our next stop was the Spokane County Jail, where she visits inmates as part of her ministry. After an hour of offering spiritual counsel, she staggered out "in a fog," as she described it. But she pushed on to the Y for a swim. She does an awkward scissors kick with her front crawl, yet she swims far faster than I do, and the hour doing lengths seemed to revitalize her. She ran home to get her prized Cannondale while I rented a bike, then we set out on a path along the roiling Spokane River. Though I don't cycle this kind of distance or speed (I have never even ridden a road bike), my marathon base helped me keep up, sort of. More impressive, though, was that the more exercise Sister Madonna did, the more Iron Nun she became: Her fatigue faded and an exuberant glow came over her face. With her still-brown hair tucked under her helmet and wearing a grin like a kid, she looked closer to 60 than 80. After cycling for nearly 2 hours, almost to the border of Montana, she suggested that a drink would be a perfect end to our training day, and I readily agreed. We sped back into town in time for happy hour at her favorite restaurant, an outdoor patio high above the raging waterfalls of the Spokane River.

As we worked our way through the sunset martini specials, Sister Madonna asked me if I felt stronger in any way after doing the Iron Nun Triathlon.

That "in any way" caught my attention. I imagine she uses little catchphrases like that to get inmates to open up, for suddenly I was coming out to her about not believing in God, about being gay, about my antipathy for religions that don't respect my life partnership or allow women to take leadership roles.

Sister Madonna is unfazed by my happy-hour confession. She has been somewhat of an Iron Nun trailblazer in her career as well. After she started running, she left a traditional order to join the recently formed Sisters for Christian Community, comprised of "liberated gutsy women" (as one sister blogger put it) called on a journey to be cofounders, coequals, and co-responsible in religious life. She moved into her own house and developed her own ministry. "I believe what a man can do, a woman can do," Sister Madonna responded. "Why not? We're both human. We have equivalent abilities."

She thinks the women's running boom has been instrumental in advancing more gender equity in society and within families. While most sports segregate the sexes, men and women compete side by side in triathlons and running events. Initially, men did so grudgingly, Sister Madonna said of her early days in the sport. Still, men knew how difficult it is to complete a marathon or triathlon and grew to respect women who trained hard enough to accomplish the feat. They also learned to deal with women finishing ahead of them. "Men were a bit jealous of their spot and didn't want to be surpassed by a woman. Now there are so many women, [men] can't help but be surpassed," laughed Sister Madonna, as she often does. "Instead of being a threat, I began to be recognized by men. They want to compliment me. They want to be around me." Acceptance for women athletes gradually morphed into respect, support, encouragement, and even celebration.

In her 35-plus years of competition, Sister Madonna has seen families transformed by the sport. A study of marathoners in Utah backs her up: It found that families with marathon moms or two running parents have "more egalitarian relationships," as supporting each other through training led them to develop a more flexible and equitable division of household chores and child care. Todd Goodsell, PhD, and research assistant Brian Harris of Brigham Young University chose Utah for the study in the belief that what they discovered in a state known for its strong conservative family values would be even more likely elsewhere.

As for where all these changes will lead (besides more drinks and another hour of discussion), Sister Madonna was certain: "We used to be a matriarchal society. I think it's going gradually to come full circle."

We made a toast to that and wobbled outside, which was when we realized that maybe rehydrating with martinis was not such a good idea after doing an Iron Nun Triathlon: Today's workout was some 8 miles of running, a mile of swimming, and about 40 miles of cycling—longer than an Olympic-distance triathlon.

○   ●   ○   ●   ○   ●   ○

ON ANOTHER DAY with another running hero, Kathrine Switzer, I get yet more insight into the legacy of this women's running boom. Not long before my trip west to host the world-record holders, Switzer flew into my hometown of Toronto for a speaking engagement and a star appearance at the nearby Niagara Falls Women's Half Marathon. She agreed to an interview "on the run," and from our first steps we started yakking away, as running sisters do, about sports bras and empowerment. At 66, she's funny, intelligent, vivacious, and still as fiercely passionate as the day she crossed the finish line of the Boston Marathon in 1967, the first woman to officially do so. "I often say I started the Boston Marathon as a girl who just wanted to run," Kathrine explained as we trotted over the brick streets of Toronto's Victorian-era Distillery District. After the race director, Jock Semple, tried to rip off her bib numbers and throw her out of the race, she said she got radicalized. "I got mad, then determined. When I finished the race I was a grown-up woman." One with an idea that would set the pattern for her life and change the lives of millions: She would dedicate her life to creating opportunities for women.

We know how that unfolded from her book, *Marathon Woman*: She threw herself into running activism; helped organize the New York Mini 10K as the first women-only race in North America; pressed for rule changes to admit women into marathons; used her position as a public relations executive with cosmetics giant Avon to sponsor an international women's race series; and worked furiously to launch some 400 races in more than 27 countries, which attracted hundreds of thousands of women to the sport, all strategically planned to convince the International Olympic Committee to include the first-ever women's marathon in the 1984 Olympics.

And she's still at it. As my running tour of historic Toronto took us into a downtown park, she told me that, this time, the revolution seems to be coming to her: Women at book signings tell her they saw the number on her historic Boston bib—261—as a symbol of fearlessness. First-time marathoners speak of how they made homemade "261" bibs to wear alongside their official race bibs. Other runners say they had the number engraved on jewelry, even on their skin in the form of tattoos. Kathrine told me that the women are urging her to give voice to this movement that is stirring, this desire to use the fearlessness they have gained through running to reach out and make change, to empower other women around the world with the sense of fearlessness.

Initially, the hugeness of the idea terrified her. "I went to a counselor to get advice. I thought I was too old for another revolution." Two blocks ago, she told me she had felt "a loss of magic" when she went through menopause. On this block, she said it's flowing back stronger than ever in her 60s. "Most people who get older, their careers and aspirations diminish. The exact opposite is happening to me. It's getting bigger and bigger." And the counselor reminded her that she doesn't have to pull off this revolution alone, that there are millions of running sisters who want to travel this road with her. "I've learned I'm more powerful, yeah," she admitted. "I have more confidence in my abilities. You put a proposal out there, and people come to you."

She has no idea what shape this "fitness and empowerment revolution" will take, but she imagines a global network of women runners reaching out to less-empowered women to encourage them to run and support them on the path to change. She spoke of creating safe portals on the Internet to connect through, communicating over social media, organizing events that promote running to women around the world. As for how women runners can make change, she talked about female marathon stars in Africa who funnel their earnings to rural villages to build schools, community centers, and wells for fresh water—development initiatives that elevate the status of all women and girls in those communities. "What's going to happen when they retire [from professional running] and take up leadership roles?"

Having observed the river of change that flowed from the first fledgling decades of the women's running boom, she said she senses a tidal wave coming. "Running is all about fearlessness. That's why it's so empowering for women." Then, in another stride or two, she added this: "Running is changing the world. Men and women running together have come to accept each other on other terms, on an equal playing field."

She wants that message, that sea change in attitudes, to spread around the globe and believes the women's running boom is the perfect messenger. Some time after our talk, the first baby of this "fitness and empowerment revolution" is born: The inaugural 261 Marathon and 10K is held in Palma de Mallorca, Spain, on March 30, 2014, the first women-only marathon ever held in southern Europe and one of many 261 women's races that may crop up around the world.

As we came to the end of our run, Kathrine Switzer told me her dream for the movement: that girls around the world can grow up without a sense of limitation, to realize they can do anything. "This is way bigger than anything I've ever done," she said. Then, as if to bolster her own confidence, she added this: "We can do so much more than we ever believe. We sell ourselves short. We can do much more."

○ ● ○ ● ○ ● ○

WE ARE ALREADY DOING quite a lot, according to two male observers of the women's running boom, Running USA media director Ryan Lamppa and John Stanton, founder and CEO of the Running Room retail stores, which have trained thousands of women and men in their running clinics. The two say that the influx of women has fundamentally transformed the culture of running, making it more accessible, inclusive, and fun.

The self-doubt and fear women brought to the sport likely had the biggest impact because we did what women do: We looked for support. "Women have been smarter than men in how to start [running]," says Lamppa. "They say, 'I don't know.' They take a training program or join a clinic." That led to a professionalization and proliferation of training clinics as women flocked to them to learn how to train effectively—and invited friends and partners to join us on the journey. "It's encouraged a lot of guys sitting on the sidelines who wake up in their 30s and realize they're out of shape," adds Stanton. Our willingness to seek out knowledge and support, both men say, has transformed running from a solitary, competitive endeavor to one with a strong social dynamic, with an emphasis on enjoyment, participation, and health. "It's not about running hard, breathing hard, and spitting," says Stanton. "It's about enjoying a run and having a conversation and coming back with more energy for business and family." Lamppa notes, with some chagrin, that he's never had a male running buddy call him up and say, "Let's do a running weekend away with our running buddies." "But women say, 'Let's get our friends together and make it a long weekend and do a race and have fun.'" That impulse to celebrate our participation in the sport, he says, has inspired race directors to create a whole slew of new events that have a greater emphasis on having a blast than on blasting out a personal best, such as women-only half-marathons in destination spots, color runs, tough mudders, warrior dashes, zombie runs, holiday 5-Ks and 10-Ks. The permutations seem endless.

Echoing Kathrine Switzer, both men believe that women have imbued the sport with a higher purpose, a sense that one runs not only for oneself, but also to be stronger for family, friends, career, community, a life calling. That originated, Lamppa believes, with breast cancer runs in North America, which have raised millions.

In Ireland, the Flora Women's Mini Marathon is that country's largest single-day fund-raiser, with some 40,000 participants running to raise $20 million for more than 700 charities. It's little wonder that charity fund-raising has become a major component of big road races. "Race directors have added charity programs because they will bring in guaranteed registrations from women," says Lamppa.

Stanton also thinks that the women's running boom is igniting a fitness revolution with far-ranging impacts and will be "the salvation for rising childhood obesity." As women become "born-again athletes," as Stanton says, we tend to take charge of our health, improving our nutrition and overall fitness—and usually hauling our families along on that journey. Early research from the Melpomene Institute for Women's Health Research backs that up: A 1987 survey, on the cusp of the running boom, tracked the physical activity of children into their teens and found that those who were most active had physically active mothers. The next-highest-ranking influences were both parents modeling physical activity as well as participating in and facilitating their children's activities. Says Stanton, "It's often Mom who leads the lifestyle of the family, so it will likely be Mom solving this thing, getting kids active, and making the right nutritional choices."

From his post at Running USA, Lamppa sees that next big running boom building. The children of the baby boomers who run are now adults—and many are taking up the sport themselves. Thanks to the women's running boom, they see running "less as punishment and more as a lifestyle" and even "cool." And as people tune in to health care costs and the fitness benefits of running, Lamppa believes still more will join the echo-boom children in this third running wave. "With more women in the sport, there's more talk of the sport, there's more social reaction."

SPORTS PSYCHOLOGIST KIM DAWSON, PhD, is also vocal on this topic, believing there is something about running that is particularly empowering for women. The Wilfred Laurier University professor, who teaches high-performance thinking to both Olympic and recreational runners at clinics, says women often have more barriers to overcome when they first take up running: low self-confidence due to lack of athletic experience or years away from being active, poor self-esteem linked to body weight, sometimes little support from partners, even their own nurturing instinct that tells them to devote time to family rather than themselves. "The other side of all that thinking [to overcome obstacles] is it makes them stronger," says Dawson. And for women, confidence builds from the process of running: getting support from running sisters, conquering fears, seeing results, having success, all of which creates positive psychological momentum. "In every clinic I do with recreational runners, there is usually one woman who will do something big in her life: She leaves her husband, changes her career, goes back to school. Women get that universally empowering thing that men don't usually get because men compartmentalize. Women are more likely to leave behind some unsatisfying aspect of life because completing a marathon means so much more to them."

So much so that women are often driven to replicate the empowered-through-running model to help others, as Switzer and her 261 revolution are doing. US-based charity Girls Gotta Run funds a network of girls' running camps across Ethiopia. The teens in them may have fled extreme poverty or a marriage to an older man that parents force daughters into in exchange for a dowry. In a country where a girl is more likely to die in childbirth than reach grade six, these camps provide young runners with shelter, food, and education alongside training, coaching, and opportunities to race internationally. While the girls may dream of becoming professional runners, the primary goal of Girls Gotta Run is to help them, through the discipline of running, stay in school, develop leadership skills, go to college, secure good jobs or start businesses, and ultimately achieve economic independence. And when they do, they are expected to pay that help forward by helping the next generation of Ethiopian girls.

Here in North America, Girls on the Run is using the running-to-empowerment model to help preteen girls build life skills, boost self-esteem, and realize their individual strengths. The program launched in 1996 with 13 girls meeting after school with volunteer coaches to work through the life-skills curriculum and practice those skills during running games. The program has since grown to serve 130,000 young runners in 200 North American cities.

In my city, I am a volunteer coach with a similar program, the Start2Finish after-school running and reading club that helps underprivileged boys and girls build confidence, fitness, literacy, and life skills. I got involved after the national director, Sylvia Ruegger, spoke to my running club about the drive, discipline, and dreaming required for her to get to the start line of the first-ever women's marathon in the Olympics, where she finished eighth at just 23 years old. Now 52 and still an avid runner, she works to give less-fortunate kids a similar opportunity to dream big and learn the life skills required to realize those goals. The program combines two of my favorite things—running and reading—and a school in need of coaches is practically in my backyard, in a community just south of my neighborhood. It is one of the most diverse in all of Canada, and the kids, most new Canadians, face challenges adapting to a new culture, learning English, and building self-confidence. One day a week for 2 hours after school, volunteer coaches run and read with the kids, preparing them for a grand finale 5K Run for Change and Reading Challenge, where schools compete against each other. I'm shameless about telling friends this story: I have paced an Ethiopian runner to a first-place finish. After she claimed her trophy, she leapt off the podium and rushed to thank me, exclaiming that she could not have won without me running alongside, urging her to go faster. Then I fess up that the grateful Ethiopian 5-K star was, well, only in grade five.

The first time I participated in that 5-K challenge, I woke up the next day, my muscles stiff and aching. I wondered why, because a 5-K is but a spin around the block in my usual 70-plus-kilometer weeks. Then I remembered: After pacing the young Ethiopian, I ran back to sprint another child to the finish line, then another and another and another, cheering and urging all of them to run harder, to give it their best in front of their wildly cheering parents and teammates, until all 50 of our kids had crossed the line, triumphantly, proudly.

How many 100-meter dashes did I do? I didn't keep count. That's when the question began to percolate in my mind: How is it that I could get this strong at age 49, after just a year and a half of marathon training? I remember looking to the stands of cheering parents and thinking that so very few of them were fit enough to run with their own kids, while I was so fit I didn't even think about what I was doing, which was something even Usain Bolt doesn't do—complete multiple 100-meter races back-to-back.

Sure, fine, I was sprinting with kids. But just try it.

○　●　○　●　○　●　○

HOW MIGHT THE FUTURE unfold for my Ethiopian sprinting star and all these girl runners when they grow up? Penny Werthner, an Olympic track runner in the 1970s, went on to a distinguished career as a sports psychologist and is now dean of the kinesiology faculty at the University of Calgary. Throughout her career, she has worked to advance gender equity in sports, academia, and business and has observed that many women who achieve success in business also have strong backgrounds in athletics. Becoming strong physically "is a huge piece" in that success, she says. While at a conference in Qatar, a Middle Eastern country where Muslim women are not allowed to leave the house without a male escort, she was reminded of how much restriction of women's physical movement is tied to keeping them passive and powerless. But let's not kid ourselves—not so long ago in North America, women had few athletic opportunities and were told that their uteruses might fall out if they did anything too strenuous. In the 1970s, Werthner competed in the 1,500 meters—the longest distance women were allowed to run in the Olympics at that time. In the United States, Title IX legislation passed in 1972, forcing schools receiving federal funds to support girls' and women's athletic opportunities to a degree similar to boys' and men's programs. For the first time, girls there had the opportunity, as Werthner describes it, "to learn through sport how to stand up for yourself and get strong." And the sports skills they learned were directly transferable to business and career. "You learn from competing," says Werthner. "You learn a sense of focused excellence, what it feels like to excel and fail and pick yourself up. Sport is immediate in its feedback. And it teaches you a lot about that process of trying to be really good at something. It teaches you to pay attention to singular things. It teaches you how hard it is to do something and also how rewarding it is when you do it."

After that conversation, I put in phone calls to some of the highest political offices in my country. In the past few years, Canadians have elected women to lead 5 out of their 10 provinces and, perhaps not so coincidentally, three of these five female political leaders are runners and another starts her day power walking on a tread-mill. The United States also has its share of female politicians who run, Illinois lieutenant governor Sheila Simon, US senator for New Hampshire Kelly Ayotte, and former Alaska governor and vice presidential candidate Sarah Palin among them. The leader of Canada's most populous province, Ontario premier Kathleen Wynne, told me that running was her training for politics. A lifelong runner, she did track in high school and took up distance running after her third child was born. She completed two marathons and numerous halves and 10-Ks, got involved in politics, and earned a reputation as a giant slayer for winning against a number of political heavyweights en route to her current position: At age 60, she became the first female premier of the province as well as the first openly gay premier in Canada. The TV advertisement intro-ducing her to voters featured her in running gear, out on a long-distance run, talking about her willingness to take on big problems. Between working on those, she took time to return my call to talk about this hunch I have that the women's running boom may well usher in the next wave of feminism. She believes that the wom-en's running boom "speaks to a huge part of our future" and that running has given her the stamina and confidence to withstand withering attacks from political opponents. "You look at women over the past centuries, they were told to stay still, not move around. It's very disempowering. Being strong is part of taking your place in the world. If you're not physically afraid, you're less likely to feel mentally and emotionally afraid. It takes strength to take your place in the world."

○　●　○　●　○　●　○

BACK IN VANCOUVER, over lunch with the four world-record-holding runners, I share some of these stories, and the dining room buzzes with conversation about how these pioneers got their own starts as legacy builders. Their stories are hilarious. Most of them didn't realize they had even set a new world record, at least not with the first one. "There was no certificate, no recognition, nothing," says Gwen. Indeed, it took years for someone to even notify her that she had eclipsed BJ's record ("Which one?" BJ shoots back. "You've broken so many of them"). And then came Gwen's shock when she finally found out she had the women's 75-plus marathon world record: "It's something I can't believe: I'm the fastest woman in the world in that age group."

Olga admits she didn't even know "there was such a thing" as an age-group world record when she went to her first track meet at age 77. After hurling the javelin 15 feet farther than the women's 75-plus world record, she was swarmed by her fellow competitors. She recalls feeling stunned. In the years since, she has broken or set many more and still holds more than 20 world records, most in the 90-plus age group. But she had no idea what to think about that first one, or whether it was even important. "I got my gold medal, and I stood on the top level of the podium. People thought, 'Isn't this great.' And I thought, 'Okay, maybe it is great. Hey, I should try to feel very good about this.' So I went shopping."

We erupt in gales of laughter because Olga, in two-tone leather pumps that coordinate perfectly with her outfit, clearly still loves to shop.

Christa, who started in track just 5 years ago but would be named Best Women's Masters Athlete for 2013 for breaking 14 world records over the past 2 years, credits Olga for introducing her to masters sports.

"Don't blame me," Olga chirps.

"Seriously," Christa laughs. "How [else] is anyone to know about it?" She has been advocating to get more recognition and funding for masters athletes because she knows well what a powerful and inspiring example they can be for an aging and sedentary society.

But challenges abound. Their pursuit of world records, which blows open the possibilities of human performance well into the advanced years, does not come cheap, and most seniors live on modest incomes. Many local road races—even big city races—are not certified to recognize a world record, forcing seniors pursuing one to travel to races with certified courses. Competing against the world's best in track also involves costly trips to international masters track-and-field meets, and in most countries, there is zero government funding for masters athletes representing their nations like young Olympians do. At 76, Christa still works part-time and is also dipping into her retirement savings to fund her athletics. "The media is totally ignoring us," she says. "Last year, Olga and I were in Finland for the indoor world championships. Canada won 22 medals and Olga and I won 19 of those and there is nothing in the papers. Some local boys go to some small little meet and get a third and there's a story in the paper." She's not looking for attention for herself, but rather for the movement, in order to attract more seniors to sports and garner more financial support. "If [seniors] are active, what impact does that have on medical costs? There should be research on that, and help to increase participation. Governments should put money there to encourage seniors."

A recent study led by the University of Southern California's Schaeffer Center for Health Policy and Economics agrees. Researchers found that investing in delayed aging or healthy aging would be more cost-effective—delivering some $7.1 trillion in economic benefits over the next 50 years—and also more effective at both extending and improving quality of life than the current "disease model" of research investment that targets individual diseases such as cancer and heart disease. Currently, 28 percent of the population over 65 is disabled, a prime cause of which is age-related conditions and diseases, and the population of seniors is expected to double in the next 50 years, compounding the cost and misery. The study found that conservative estimates of even modest investments in research to slow aging by attacking the underlying risk for all disabling diseases would result in 11.7 million more healthy people over the age of 65 and increase overall life expectancy in the United States by 2.2 years; by comparison, major and vastly more costly advances in cancer treatment and heart disease would extend life by only 1 year and still leave many elderly disabled by those diseases.

No doubt the health industry will look for miracle drug interventions to slow aging, but the four world-record holders are shining examples that the key to staying healthy into your advanced years is staying physically active. Each has been invited to participate in the Montreal masters athletes study of world-record holders (see Chapter 8), to be tested, probed, and analyzed for some underlying clue to her seemingly bulletproof resistance to aging. Yet the women shrug off any notion that they are in any way special. They believe that most people can enjoy a high level of good health into their advanced years if they simply keep moving. And they hope their exploits inspire other seniors—as well as younger people—to be physically active.

They do admit that chasing world records and being role models give them extra motivation to train hard. They also enjoy being fit and having the active lifestyle that it allows. But they maintain that they continue to train intensely and compete for a very simple reason: They love it. They love the training, the camaraderie of running with friends, the challenge and thrill of competition. At track meets, Olga is as much a coach as a competitor, sharing tips with her fellow competitors to help them improve their skills—and increase the competition for her. The first time I saw Christa compete, she pulled out a spreadsheet she keeps to track her national-record and world-record times—and there are a lot to track since she not only sprints, but also hurdles, jumps, and throws. Based on how she's performing on a particular day, she might ditch one event to conserve her energy for an attempt at a record in another. But if a record is out of reach, she wants to participate in everything, often to the chagrin of her coach. "I love challenging myself," she says. "I like learning new things." (Indeed, after she turned 77 some months after the luncheon, she told me she wants to learn how to pole-vault!) BJ tells us that she plays bridge with women her own age, but all the talk of medication and aches and pains bores her. She would much rather be yakking away with running friends 3 decades younger, travelling with them on gal-pal weekend getaways for road races, or doing destination races with her adult children and grandchildren. Gwen, the quietest and perhaps shyest of the foursome, regrets that her husband no longer runs, but that hasn't stopped her. She meets up with her two out-of-town adult children to run destination races, and they stay connected over the phone, trading training stories. At a time in life when other seniors meet up for crafts or cards, she does speedwork with a track club 1 night a week and runs 4 mornings a week with two other running clubs, one a seniors' running group called the Forever Young. "We run for 1 hour and drink coffee for 2," laughs Gwen. "I have more friends in the running community than I could ever think of, and they are so caring. You're not judged at all when you're running. It doesn't matter what you do for a living or how old you are. People accept you."

○　●　○　●　○　●　○

I'M NOT SO SURE I'm feeling that acceptance just 2 days later at the Vancouver Half Marathon. I had planned to run with BJ to see firsthand how an 85-year-old conquers that distance, to see her passion for running in action, but when I call the night before to confirm, I sense that she really does not want the pressure of playing research specimen during a race, although she uses the excuse that she doesn't want to slow me down. "I just really like to run my own race," she admits finally. Gwen had already thrown up a preemptive block at the lunch, claiming she's recovering from an injury and will walk–run the course, though her finish time will suggest she did not do a whole lot of walking. At 85 and 79, these women aren't out for a fun run. They are *racing*. And with loads of experience, they don't want or need pacing support or cheerleading.

The change in plans spins me into a state of existential angst. I flew here to race with my running soul mother. If I'm not doing that, then what am I doing? I can't actually race this one for a fast time, as I have not properly tapered, having put in way too much mileage over the past week. Yet, if I'm not shooting for a time goal, then what? Could I actually run a race leisurely, *for fun*? Isn't that called a 'long run'? All those questions pounding in my head start to make me question who I even am as a runner. I started on this journey to run myself out of a midlife depression, a smoking habit, and 25 excess pounds and into glorious good health. Bizarrely, I never imagined I would get faster. Becoming competitive was never my goal. But there it is, and I fear I may have become entirely performance obsessed, incapable of striving for anything other than a fast time. Is that *my legacy*?

Perhaps only close running pals can understand how even a slight change in race plans (and this is not slight!) can whip a runner into a writhing heap of self-pitying, nihilistic whining. And so before I can drink myself silly on the wine left over from lunch, Mary and Phyllis leap into the void with a plan: I will pace Mary for the first 10 kilometers to set her on course for a personal best and possibly even a top three finish in her age group, then I will drop back a few minutes and pace Phyllis over the next 10 kilometers to a podium finish for her age group, and then I can hang at the 20-kilometer mark and run in the final kilometer with BJ, which she had proposed on the phone as consolation for dumping me.

Their offer is entirely altruistic, I'm sure, though I do wonder about another possible legacy of this women's running boom—that women are learning to ask for what they want and in damn clear terms. And what my running pals want from me is no walk to Stanley Park at the finish line. Mary will be trying to run at close to our World Masters Games race pace in Italy. And Phyllis, who has been training like a professional while on a work sabbatical for the past 4 months, has been laying down personal bests in every race distance she's entered and has become the fastest half-marathoner in the women's 60-plus age group in our province.

My angst quickly shifts to race-day terror, only now it's freighted with responsibility: not just *Can I do this?* but also *What if I let everyone down?* Oh, but I love what running can teach us about ourselves. At the start line, the duty of leading fills me with a determined calm. Mary and I set out, and the pace is not easy, nor is she at ease. Living in Toronto for the past few decades, she has never had a chance to race in her hometown of Vancouver with family watching. She wants to do well, but she's also feeling the heat on this sultry June day. And Mary is not a hot-weather runner.

Weirdly, I gain a crazy strength from taking charge of our pace, and I do it in meticulous fashion, keeping a hawk eye on two critical windows that I open on my Garmin race watch: our pace at the moment and our pace averaged since the start of the race. Then I run at a speed to make the two line up to the target pace that will give Mary her personal-best finish. Perhaps I rely too much (or completely, as some tease me) on my watch, but the strategy has enabled me to run smack on target pace through entire marathons and made me one of those exceptionally steady pacers that researchers rave about.

But I'm not all about technology. When I'm pacing, I also do a fair amount of coaching, reaching into a big bag of sports psychology tricks I have learned over this year to calm Mary's nerves and make her believe that there is no failing in this race, only triumph. The two of us have become so close in pace and in life that we plan to team race the half-marathon at the World Masters Games, as we have at so many events, pooling our strengths to be stronger together. This is yet another experiment on our road to Italy, I tell her, to test our race pace. She will see how long she can hold it after 10 kilometers. If that's to the end, then we are ahead of our training. If not, we still have weeks to get faster. When I let her go on alone at 10 kilometers, Mary is on track for her personal-best time, and in the head space she should be in to race: focused on giving her all but prepared to accept what her body can do on this day.

Phyllis is farther behind than I expect. She's a brilliant pacer, as many older women are, and likely started the first 2 kilometers a little slower than race pace to warm up, a great strategy. And sure enough, after a few minutes, she catches up to me where I am waiting, halfway up the wickedest hill on the course. Seeing her close running buddy gives her a huge psychological boost, which translates into energy, and she attacks the hill. As we crest it, I get her back on her race pace, freeing her to focus on good form, keeping her shoulders and arms relaxed. In the second half, she holds a rock-steady pace that is slightly faster than what she started at, which means we have to start passing runners, usually less experienced and younger, the hundreds who started out way too fast and are now slowing down and clogging up the course. I chart a straight path through the maze so that Phyllis can follow without dodging and weaving and adding on mileage. "Age-group winner coming through," I shout as a warning, then point back to Phyllis lest they think I'm cheering myself on. And the astonishing, wonderful thing is that men and women decades younger cede

Phyllis a clear path, even cheer her as she blazes past them. That gives her a boost too, though I know from running at least a thousand kilometers with Phyllis over these past few years that she doesn't want the constant, inane chatter of "You go, girl" coming from me to break her focus. Periodically, I offer reminders about form—relax, drop the shoulders, get control of your breathing, shorten your stride going uphill, lean forward and let the brakes off going downhill, and shake loose those arms—all stuff Phyllis has taught me, but we can forget as fatigue builds. I also give her some sense of what's ahead of us—the route I'll take through a water station or a curve in the road or a crowd of runners. At kilometer markers, I'll tell her how strong she's looking. Mostly, though, I reassure her that we're bang on pace or even doing better, but if I feel her lagging back, I point emphatically to the pavement beside me, to give her a short-term goal to work toward, until we're back on pace.

The revelation of this race for me is that I have been so focused on helping my running pals achieve their best that I don't feel the extreme effort I have put out—at least not until we near the 20-kilometer mark, where my pacing duties will be over. Suddenly, I hit a wall of exhaustion, and Phyllis blazes on without me, leaving me to stagger to the sidelines. My heart is doing crazy leaps and yelps, but it's from exhilaration more than fatigue because I have found this thing I came west looking for, this thing I wanted to learn from these extraordinary senior runners. As I wait for BJ, I feel an overwhelming, endorphin-spiked joy swelling up inside me, and I don't know how to describe it other than to call it love—for this running journey I am on and all that it has given me, my running pals, my new running mentors, my running body and my running mind. And today, my running journey has shown me yet another way to love my sport, through pacing to help others achieve their best. And my pals will tell me later over beers and a pub lunch that I'm damn good at it.

While I am busy reveling in all that love and patting myself on the back for staying so strong for my pals, I miss Gwen charging past at a torrid pace, to finish first in her age group in a time of 1:58:24. That turns out to be the fastest half-marathon ever for a 79-year-old. Out of 4,077 runners in the race, she finishes 1,585th, easily in the top half and faster than 2,492 others.

Not wanting to "stand out," as she says, Gwen will head home before the awards ceremony, where Phyllis will pick up a medal for finishing second in her age group. The heat caught up to Mary and her pace fell off badly in the second half, but she still finished seventh in our age group and less than 2 minutes out of first place. She knows that on another day, with a little more speed-work and a longer taper, the top spot might be hers. I am thrilled by her performance and also by this field of competitive 50-plus women runners! The course was far hillier than we expected, yet Mary held our World Masters pace for half the race, and we still have more training time before leaving for Italy. I can feel excitement for the World Masters surging up inside me, and I can hardly wait to get there.

Finally, BJ comes along. I almost miss her beaming smile as she reaches the 20-kilometer mark, but a roar of "BJ, BJ, BJ!" rises from the crowd. The race committee gave her a bib with her age as her number—85—and her trailblazing career in the Vancouver running community has clearly won her hordes of fans.

I leap into the race beside her. BJ has a rock-steady pace, though it has slowed considerably over the last 15 years. While she's fantastically fit, aged muscle tends to fire slower and there's nothing much she can do about that, though it irritates her. Still, she doesn't push herself beyond what she can do. She protects the fun in her running. Her goal in any race is to finish feeling good (rather than in the ditch or throwing up, she jokes) and with a smile on her face, and that she will do today. To my surprise, she immediately starts yakking to me about details of her race, how good she's feeling, the cheering fans. I want to suggest she save her breath and focus on the finish, but who am I to tell an 85-year-old world-record holder anything?

Instead, as we trot through those last 500 meters, I gesture to BJ while shouting out to the crowd so that they can share in this amazing moment: the oldest woman in the race finishing in a time of 2:31:09, which also turns out to be the fastest that a woman her age has ever completed a half-marathon. My time in that half, I am inspired to say, is 2 seconds slower than BJ's, placing me among the 475 other runners who were bested that day by an 85-year-old.

CHAPTER 10

THE ULTIMATE TEST

I AWAKE IN A STATE OF prerace anxiety at the World Masters Games in Turin, Italy. There is a lukewarm shower to beg from the four or five rivulets of water offered up by the showerhead in our generously three-starred hotel; race gear to gather up in the still-dark early morning, especially the race watch that I rely on so heavily; then somehow breakfast to scrounge together in a hotel dining room that will not officially open for another hour.

My closest running buddies wander into the dining room at various stages of their own prerace constitutionals. My partner, Nancy, teasingly calls them my "running wives," and it is apt. Almost from the moment I broached the idea of competing at the World Masters a year ago, Phyllis, Danielle, Mary, and Katherine committed to joining me on this momentous life journey, to put themselves through a year of dedicated training leading up to these games. I could not have done this without them, mainly because I did not *want* to do it without them. The five of us have turned the so-called loneliest of sports into a team sport and made it so much fun. I remember Phyllis cracking me up during one particularly tough interval-training session: "Just think," she said, "there's probably some 50-year-old in Italy training harder than you are right now, so pick it up." Training together through winter snowstorms, April rain, and summer heat, we made the World Masters into A VERY BIG DEAL, intensifying both our motivation and our friendship. On top of running together 4 or 5 hours each week, we blasted out a daily flurry of e-mails to one another, sharing tips on training, nutrition, and mental strategies; relating discoveries of five-star bathrooms along training routes; organizing the trip to the Games and the vacations we would take after; and supporting and teasing each other through the emotional highs and lows of the thousands of kilometers we each put in over the year.

Now the year of intense training has all come to this one race.

It all seems so weirdly, unbearably light.

Our spouses soon trickle into the dining room, a little nervous for us and maybe also about their own duties in this grand finale to our year. Phyllis's husband, Bruce Kidd, who garnered international fame by capturing 18 national running titles in Canada, the United States, and Britain in the 1960s, had met with us earlier to give us racing tips. His eyes twinkle now when we ask him for last-minute advice. What can he tell us at this late stage? "You're ready," he assures us.

We conscripted the rest of our spouses into setting up impromptu water stations during the race, as the Games' official communiqués were annoyingly vague about whether there would even be any water on the course. Hilariously, Danielle tells us that she "trained" her husband, Alan, by making him stand on the street in front of their house and practice handing her cups of water as she raced past him. Apparently, he required a lot of training, to the amusement of neighbors watching. We assure Katherine's fiancé, Tim, a newbie to the racing scene, that Mary's husband, Ed, and their 11-year-old daughter, Anna, can show him the ropes.

They have jumped in to help out at understaffed water stations while cheering us at previous races. And Nancy, an amateur photographer, will take our "official" race-day photos, no small pressure there.

Nearly 2 hours before the start, we five runners cram into one taxi and head to the race in Valentino Park. Later, our fans will make their way to the two cheering-and-water stations that we scouted out on a trial run of the course, one on the front side, one on the back. Unlike most other distance races, this one is spectacularly laid out for fans, if not the runners. We will start 1.1 kilometers behind the finish line, then complete four loops around a 5-kilometer oval course that runs along both sides of the Po River and crosses bridges at both ends. If our fans hurry back to the finish line, they will see us pass by five times, witnessing every stage of racing—or every state of physiological deterioration, as we forewarn them, for this course is tough, far from conducive to setting a personal best, let alone a world record if anyone came here trying for one. There are one monster hill and two thigh-busting uphill grades, all of which we must slog up four times. And the temperature will spike to a stifling 80°F or more, far above the mid-50s that is ideal for distance racing.

On the taxi ride to the start line, we talk out our race strategies, expectations, fears.

For Katherine, who just met the minimum age requirement for these games when she turned 30, this is her first race back from an Achilles injury that has derailed her training for much of the winter. She jokes that her injury downtime has been good for her relationship—she and Tim recently got engaged—and she's not going to push things too hard in this race and risk reinjuring herself before their postrace hiking vacation in the Alps. Of course, we tease her mercilessly about misplaced priorities and threaten to crash their upcoming wedding in our running gear.

Danielle has had her own battles with injuries through the year, suffering plantar fasciitis in both feet. She admits the excruciating pain would have kept her out of any other race, but not this one. Born in France, she became a dual citizen of Canada when she moved there and now, at age 55, sees this as an opportunity to race for her adopted country. She is thrilled. Her eyes gleam. "I've never represented my country before," she will tell me later. "I had an injury, but I still trained. I was still going to the Worlds. I might not be able to run as fast as usual, but I wanted to get that flag on the podium. I've learned I'm pretty competitive!"

Phyllis, who has just turned 62, took full advantage of a half year's sabbatical from work to train for the event as an elite athlete would. Much like I did, she gathered a small support team around her—physiotherapists, personal trainer, coach—who took her seriously as an older athlete. She also took herself seriously, becoming supremely disciplined about every detail of training, from nutrition to strength work to recovery. "Strangely enough, being disciplined makes me happy," she will tell me later. "I realized that while I love my training partners (and I mean that), I can run well on my own." Already a strong runner, she got even faster after 60 and emerged as one of the top distance runners in her age group in Canada. We teasingly heap pressure on her, saying that she's within minutes of breaking a national record, that she's our best bet to finish on the podium. She laughs it all off. But she did two trial runs of the 5-kilometer-loop course and conspired with her hubby, Bruce, about how she will run every inch of it.

As for Mary and me, we should be bubbling with confidence after setting massive personal bests in every distance we attempted this year, from the 5-K to the marathon. But we haven't had any real break in training through the long, intense year (lesson learned here), and we have both been struggling with mental burnout these past few weeks. Also, improving our half-marathon speed has proven to be a lot harder than getting faster in the full. We needed more time in this training segment to work on speed, but we didn't have it (another lesson learned). Still, with the taper leading up to the Games, we have fresh legs to run on. And looking forward to a long holiday in Italy after has gone a long way toward rejuvenating our spirits.

We would rather be more ready, but we're as ready as we can be and intend to give this race our all.

Mary and I plan to run together as we usually do, using each other to set a pace that is faster than we could likely run on our own. If we're still together heading into the last 500 meters, there will be no crossing the line holding hands. We have worked it all out in hilarious e-mails, how we're going to sprint each other into the ground, how we're going to make each other suffer, how we're going to beat the others to finish first in the World Masters. Given the competition here, winning is a very remote prospect, and our ruthlessness is a charade. The journey over this past year has made us the best of friends and training partners: We want the best for each other and we also want to get the best out of each other. Throughout the year, I set ridiculously high expectations, like getting down to a 1:36 in the half. Mary poked all kinds of witty holes in that balloon, but still gamely went for it with me. Though we have gotten nowhere nearly that fast, our training and race times over the year project a 1:38 or 1:39 finish, a whopping improvement from the 1:46 half I ran before this super-fit year.

Today, on this course and in this heat, getting below 1:40 may be impossible. But this race isn't so much about time. It's about racing against a cohort of super-fit 50-year-olds from around the world to see where we might place among them. On that, my confidence has soared. I started this year hoping I could finish in the top 10 at the World Masters. I haven't even admitted this to Mary, but now I am hopeful of making the top 5.

As the taxi deposits us at the park, I remind my pals to expect the worst and stay focused. This isn't my old negativity cropping up. While competitors say previous World Masters Games in Edmonton and Sydney were very well organized, this one, at times, has teetered on the chaotic. Earlier in the week, the start of the 10-K was delayed for an hour—and in this sweltering heat!—because an overwhelmed race official could not distribute timing chips fast enough. He finally gave up and, with a grand Italian flourish, threw them in the air. Soon after, the balloon arch over the start line collapsed. And in yet another logistical lapse, these Games have failed to denote 5-year age groups on our bibs, as masters events usually do. That means I can't pick out my age-group competition from the 400 racers at the start line of the half, making the task of racing to place even more difficult.

Of all events, the World Masters Games should provide the conditions for elite masters athletes to chase world records and the rest of us to try for personal bests, as a way to measure ourselves against the top athletes in our age groups. Distance courses, for instance, should be laid out for speed and properly certified to attract the world's best age groupers and give them fair shots at setting records that could stand. Sadly, the local committee of this Games fell far short of providing these conditions, but what can we do now but stay positive in the face of whatever might happen?

It takes everything I have in me to do just that when we reach the start line. I have developed a few strengths as a runner, one being that I have become a rock-solid pacer—with the help of my running watch, that is. But just before this start, when I turn on my race watch, there's nothing. I frantically push every button on the thing, but the battery is dead. I can't even blame my beloved Garmin. I didn't check it the night before and somehow the battery had drained down. It's a devastating moment. My running pals know it. They realize that without my watch, I'll feel like I'm running blind, with no way to check my pace. They sympathize, but they also don't let me turn this into a catastrophe, thanks to all our sports psychology training. My pals reassure me that I *know* my pace, that I'm an excellent pacer. It's who I am as a runner.

It's all very flattering, and I have no better option than to believe them—and to believe in myself.

In this ultimate race of my super-fit year, I will have to run entirely by feel.

○　　●　　○　　●　　○　　●　　○

THE NIGHT BEFORE, I pored over my race strategy. I broke the race down into sections, and the four loops are perfect for this. Bruce had suggested we run the first loop a bit slower than our target pace and figure out the fastest line through it, then build speed on each subsequent loop. It's a great strategy, and I likely should have followed it, but I've had success running my way, which is holding an even pace from start to finish. I don't know if not following the advice of a former Olympian is evidence of the self-confidence I have developed over this super-fit year, or of an enduring stupidity.

In my race plan, I tried to foresee every detail: when I will fuel with gels and sports drinks, what I will visualize on each loop to keep me relaxed and focused, even thinking out the positive self-talk I will use to keep me confident and surging forward when fatigue sets in. I had written out a page and a half or more. And then four words rushed into my mind, one to guide me through each loop: "fun," "stronger," "faster," "fearless."

I conjure up that word "fun" as we step up to the start line and exchange good-luck hugs, as we usually do. For women, this prerace hug fest may be a potent secret weapon, as social bonding can release the hormone oxytocin, which has been credited with reducing fear, anxiety, and even inflammation. All useful for racing, and particularly for this race, as the glitch we had been expecting finally happens: The inept committee allows the front-runners to push over the start line by 25 meters.

"What if our age-group competition has pushed ahead?" one of us jokes.

We expect the race officials to push the runners back behind the start line, but, incredibly, they do not, and the horn blasts, and the race is on.

Fun, I tell myself as some 400 runners surge forward, *fun, fun.* Soak up every moment of this incredible experience and savor it all, for it will all be over, and all too fast.

     ○   ●   ○   ●   ○   ●   ○

TRYING TO WRING PLEASURE from every moment is an entirely new outlook for me. And the shift in perspective tells me how far I have come since my teenage years when my father started losing his mind, and I started losing the joy that had gushed through me as a kid. But stepping up my running intensity these past few years has rewired my brain from that negative bent. A close non-running friend who has seen me in my darkest, most harshly self-critical days recently joked that I have become something of a bon vivant, a hedonist who revels in extremes—in my case, extreme exercise that is balanced with extreme enjoyment of good friends, good food, good wine. She would be chortling if she saw me this week.

Nancy and I arrived at the World Masters Games before the rest of my running pals to take in the opening ceremonies and exceptional athletic performances, but we also got caught up in having an exceptionally good time. These multievent World Masters Games are bigger than the Olympics in terms of the number of athletes, and they feature nearly as many events. Some 15,000 came here to participate in some 30 sports, down from the 28,600 who competed in Sydney in 2009. But that drop, ironically, may be due to the increasing popularity of masters competitions. A competing event just 4 months after this one—the World Masters Athletics outdoor games, which features track-and-field and road races—likely siphoned off a number of athletes. Still, the ones who made the trip here managed to take over the bars and restaurants in the old town of Turin, celebrating the youthfulness that sport has given them by partying like teenagers.

Even with the organizational gaffes at these World Masters Games, there is still something truly alluring about Olympic-style events, which bring together athletes from a broad spectrum of sports, from around the world, ranging from 30 to more than 100 years old. To open the Games, the athletes marched through a downtown street to the opening ceremonies in a massive square in the center of the old town. Many wore fun-loving riffs on national uniforms, such as an Australian basketball team of 50-something women who wore matching thigh-hugging minidresses sparkling with sequins and Aussie flags draped over their bared shoulders. Crowds lining the parade route soaked up the uniforms and the spectacle. One 50-something female soccer player who had rented a villa with her teammates told me that the attention was almost overwhelming. "No one's ever cheered for me like this, *in my life.*" As for competing here rather than at a masters soccer tournament, she laughed: "Hey, this is our Olympics." And the athletes celebrated it as such at the opening ceremony, singing, chanting, and chugging beers late into the evening.

Throughout the week, we took in a number of events, always

with an eye toward seeing which athletes aged most youthfully. I admired the shoulders of kayakers, the legs of cyclists, the strong cores and muscles of sprinters, the low body fat of distance runners. Which sport is best for healthy aging? The research has yet to be done on that, but the track events were a brilliant showcase of human performance across the adult life span. For each distance, the oldest runners competed first, with each heat going off in 5-year increments from 95 down to 30, so it was possible for us to see how runners perform and also age over a lifetime. A couple of things stood out: The difference between the front and back of the pack tends to widen in older age groups, and often the vastly superior winners of older age-group heats ran fast enough to be competitive in age groups younger than their own, clearly able to maintain their incredible speed through training, talent, or some other means of resistance to aging. As thrilling as it was to see a super-fast 76-year-old like Christa Bortignon break a world record in the 200 meters, I found it equally inspiring to see the 85-year-olds at the back of the pack doggedly pushing—sometimes even limping—to the finish long after the front-runners had crossed the line. They often waved and pumped a fist in the air to fans, for they insisted on having their moment in the World Masters spotlight to celebrate all the training they had put into striving for their personal best. And that sparked huge applause from fans, who filled the stands.

Then, just 2 nights before my big race, Nancy and I went to see her high-school best friend play in a deciding soccer match, which June's team dominated, yet lost in penalty kicks. Team members still took away a gold medal for their age group, as the age 50-plus women had dropped down to play against 40-somethings for better competition. The loss made it difficult for team members to celebrate their medal, however. But an important lesson I have learned from my running career: While we can't control the outcome of a race, we can control the effort we put into it, and it's important to celebrate that effort, and to celebrate ourselves. I reminded them all that they had put in a terrific effort on the field, mostly outplaying women a decade younger, and that they should feel pretty fantastic about that. Then Nancy and I pulled out our cameras and convinced them to put on their gold medals and pose for pictures, and, in that way, we finally got them celebrating their amazing journey. That, however, kept me up longer than I would have liked, because we were catching a ride on their team bus, and the wine and beer flowed for hours before the bus driver retrieved us from the bar.

○　●　○　●　○　●　○

SO ON THIS FIRST 5-kilometer loop of my big race, while I am channeling that word "fun," I am more than a little worried that I have had *too much fun* at these Games. Yet, I feel strong. Mary and I are running well. I am trying to hold us to our target pace by feel, but when Mary checks the pace on her watch, she says we are going too fast. It's a struggle to slow down. We blaze past our first cheering section on the front side of the course, with Nancy, Ed, and little Anna screaming, "Go, go, go!" And 1.5 kilometers later, we pass our second cheering section, with Tim, Alan, and Bruce on the back side of the course cheering us on. I failed to heed Bruce's strategy of going out below target pace and even my own strategy of racing right on target pace, but Bruce shouts out that we're looking strong. And that buoys me on. A former Olympian cheering us on! What a gas! What *fun*!

As we hit the massive hill toward the end of our first loop, I think of my running soul mother, BJ McHugh, the 85-year-old world-record marathoner who finished the Vancouver half-marathon with a huge smile on her face. I conjure up BJ's smile as I charge up that hill, in a good place, I think.

○　　●　　○　　●　　○　　●　　○

ON THE SECOND LOOP, Mary sets the pace. I can tell she's already feeling the effects of the heat and starting out too fast. Even going out a few seconds faster than target pace can devastate a runner by the end of a race. Bruce had warned us to think of this hilly half-marathon more like a distance race on the track and worry less about pace and more about strategy, such as drafting people—tucking in within a meter behind another runner—to cut down wind resistance and conserve energy. We could then use that energy to build speed through subsequent loops. He's a brilliant strategist, having raced many of his 5-K and 10-K international triumphs on the track.

A working watch might have moderated my exuberance through that first loop. As we pass by Bruce's cheering section a second time, I can feel Mary struggling in the heat. Bruce will tell us later that he could see on our faces that we had expended too much energy too soon. To spur Mary on, I point out a woman ahead who looks about a decade older than us but is setting a rock-solid pace. I suggest that we catch her and stick with her, but Mary calls out our pace instead. We have dropped off badly.

The two of us have prepared for this moment in our sessions with sports psychologist Leith Drury. Being left behind can be devastating, but we haven't trained this hard to run at less than full potential on race day. And racing together isn't about keeping each other company; it's about pushing each other to run at peak potential. So this is in our race plan too: If one doesn't have her best race in her that day, the other must press on alone. Several months later, when we make another attempt to race under 1:40, Mary will be the one pressing ahead to attain that goal. But not today.

I leave Mary and chase the 60-something woman, channeling that word "strong" now. I am a little blown away by how strong training has made me over this past year, physically and mentally. I started my super-fit year being afraid of racing, afraid of falling short of goals and facing the wrath of my hypercritical self. But through mental training, I have learned how to become my own best friend and greatest supporter. My coach tells me that I have been gutsy in setting big goals, even inspiring in that regard. But I have also learned not to beat myself up for falling short of them, as I nearly always did—they are *big* goals after all! And why set a goal that is easily within reach? This year of intense training has taught me that I can often achieve far more than I dreamed possible, so why not aim high, see just how far I can get, give myself the opportunity to surprise and even thrill myself? As I scamper across the bridge in pursuit of that very fast 60-year-old, I feel like a young dynamo, and I love it.

When I hit the massive hill for the second time, I am not thinking of the toll the speed and heat are taking on my body. I am telling myself how proud I am for staying strong. And as I do, I think of pacing ultrarunner Pam Reed through the last 20 miles of the Bighorn 100-mile ultra and how she emerged from the mountain trail at mile 95, hit the flat surface of the road, and accelerated from her funny little jog into a full-out run. If Pam can pick up speed in the last 5 miles of a 100-miler, I tell myself, I can hold pace as I push up that monster hill. But I struggle on hills, and that wiry little 60-year-old clearly does not. She skedaddles ahead and disappears into the thicket of runners.

Still, I push on as hard as I can as other lessons from Pam come back to me, like never give up on a race and never, ever give up on myself. I remind myself that I am a good downhill runner and when I hit that slope, I target runners ahead of me to reel in and pass, and in this way, I move up several places.

○   ●   ○   ●   ○   ●   ○

STARTING THE THIRD LOOP, I am in a tie for a podium place in my age group, though I only find this out from analyzing Nancy's photos after. One shows me running side by side with the Italian Gigliola Capuzzo. It's an amazing snapshot of our effort. We are both wearing sports-bra-style racing tops, both leading with our cores. Capuzzo's abs are astonishing, like a 25-year-old Olympian's. Mine are less astonishing, but a whole lot more impressive than when I started this super-fit year. But what's most incredible is our drive, our spirit. We're both smiling, both clearly having a blast pushing ourselves right to the cliff's edge of aerobic capacity, just under that second threshold. Press too hard and go over it, and lactic acid can shoot up dramatically and stall a runner.

But this, to me, is the beauty of the half-marathon: It's an exhilarating combination of speed and endurance, one of the many reasons why the women's running boom has made this distance the favorite. What the half demands of mere mortal runners—mental focus over an extended period, physical effort, speed, the sheer amount of time on the feet—more closely approximates the experience that the top elites have running full marathons. The average finish time for the half for most recreational runners is about 2 hours. That's closer to the 2:03 to 2:30 times the world's best finish the full, compared with the 3 to 5 hours that most take to complete a full. And compared to recreational runners' pace in the full marathon, the pace in the half is certainly more thrilling—closer to 10-K race pace. And the reduced distance leaves more mental and physical energy at the end to throw in race tactics such as speed changes to shake off opponents, much as elite marathoners would do.

Marilyn Arsenault, an opera singer who became a top masters runner and running coach, loves the half and encourages her runners to focus on it rather than the marathon, at least until their marathon time drops below 3 hours. "Once you're over 3 hours in the marathon, it really becomes an ultramarathon," she told me. "Health-wise, your body starts to break down a little faster than the first 2 or 3 hours, and things can snowball badly. There's a greater risk of injury, and many who get injured can't make running part of their lifestyle and end up giving up running." She also pointed out that training mileage for the half is less onerous, allowing more time for cross-training, making for a healthier balance than marathoners often have in their training. As well, physical recovery from a half is far faster, as little as 6 weeks, which allows a runner to race many more halves in a year compared to the one or two high-quality marathons one can do in a year.

Clearly, many are getting the message that a half can be the full experience. Running USA reports that since the year 2000, finishers in the half have increased by a whopping 284 percent, making it easily the most popular race distance in the United States. Of the 1.85 million finishers in 2012, 60 percent were women. Indeed, the women's running boom is making this distance its own, with all-women half-marathon races and racing series exploding. These single-sex events give women yet another experience of racing like elite runners do, with the chance to set the pace, lead the race, and win the thing outright.

In this masters half, as I'm racing head-to-head with Gigliola Capuzzo, she manages to pull in front of me. I would not have let her out of my sight if we had had our age groups printed on our bibs, I'm sure of that. Then on the flat backstretch of the third loop, as I pass Bruce's cheering section, I find myself running alone. It's easy to lose heart and slow down when that happens. Instead, I pull up the strategy I wrote out the night before the race and find what I need to tell myself exactly now, as fatigue is setting in. And I start channeling that word "faster." Without my race watch, with no electronic calculation of my pace to spur me on, I think, *Faster, faster, faster.* I think of my running pal, Jean Marmoreo, who won her age group at Boston three times between ages 65 and 69, with a faster finish time in each. She told me that when she tires in a race, when she longs to change pace, her default thinking is this: *Go faster.* Sports psychologist Kim Dawson says we can train our minds to, as she says, *Go.* Whether it's contemplating getting out of bed to run, doing another hill in training, or picking up the pace in a race, the response should always be *Go.* Thinking of going faster conjures in my mind an image of 76-year-old Christa Bortignon powering far ahead of her competition to set a world record in the 200 meters. And that imagery unleashes such energy that I manage to catch the runners ahead of me, catch Capuzzo at the bridge crossing the Po. She's running alongside two others now. This time, I size her up and determine that she is very likely my age-group rival. Though I still have no idea what place we're in, let alone what pace we're running, I know the smart thing to do would be to tuck in behind the trio, draft them, and, as Bruce counseled, conserve my energy for a sprinting duel in the fourth and final loop. I do that smart thing for, oh, about 2 minutes. Until another thought enters my mind: *Pass them.*

Who throws in a sprint at 17 kilometers (10 miles), the half's equivalent of the 20-mile mark in the marathon, when so many runners hit the wall? I am thinking—okay, maybe not that clearly at this point—that my sudden spurt of speed will open distance and even break the Italian's will to give chase, at least at this stage of the race. But I would be wrong. I power ahead across the bridge and open a lead through a twisty downhill section leading up to that massive hill, then she catches me halfway up the hill and passes me, while I struggle yet again.

○   ●   ○   ●   ○   ●   ○

AT THE START OF THE FOURTH and final loop, I must run past the finish line, where the top racers have already finished and are celebrating. This is not easy. Tougher still, on the flat backstretch, I find myself in yet another dreaded pocket, without any runners around, which is especially lonely without my watch to help me maintain pace.

When I pass by Bruce's cheering section, Tim hands me a sports drink, and Bruce shouts out that I'm looking strong, that I'm running a fabulous race. I choose to believe him and pull up that final word, "fearless," the word so many women runners think of when they think of Kathrine Switzer in that famous Boston Marathon photo in which race director Jock Semple, his face twisted with anger, is physically attacking her. Switzer breaks free, of course, and fearlessly guts it out to the end, knowing she has to finish to prove to the world that women can run marathons. Inspiring as that run was, Switzer has become a hero to me for what she did after Boston: fearlessly challenging the male sports hierarchy to establish women's races around the world. In Italy, on my final 5-kilometer loop, I think about what Kathrine told me when she joined me on a run through my home city: that women must fearlessly push beyond any limits we perceive in ourselves because we can always achieve more, more than we ever thought possible.

Running has shown me that. In my 20s, I believed that my flat feet would never allow me to run. When I started shuffle jogging in my 30s with the help of orthotics, I thought I was too slow to ever keep up with a running club. When I finally joined a club at age 42 to get coaching for a half-marathon, I was one of the slowest, and yet I eventually qualified for the Boston Marathon. Just a few years ago, all four of my pals here in Italy ran faster than I, yet here I am at the World Masters Games leading our pack.

No one has ever told me that my stride is a thing of beauty or that I run effortlessly, as if on wings. So I do not attribute my success to talent, but to determination, discipline, goal setting, years of consistent training, and, yes, to a sense of fearlessness I have developed through running. And that fearlessness has infused the rest of my life with bright, burning possibility, with a sense that I can achieve whatever I set my mind to. Since I started training for marathons at age 48, I ran off 25 excess pounds and out of a crushing midlife depression and into an exhilarating second act to my life. I stopped putting off dream projects and started doing them. I stopped talking about volunteering and started doing it. I cowrote the screenplay for a feature that played at film festivals around the world. I researched, lived, and wrote this book, which I had dreamed of doing since I started running. I also started writing a running column for a national newspaper. In this super-fit year, I gave myself what I had thought was an impossible gift—the wisdom and experience of a 51-year-old inside a body with the fitness and energy level of a 20-year-old athlete. I feel unstoppable.

With that word "fearless" coursing through me, I break out of that dreaded pocket and catch up to another Italian, a man. I learn later that he is in my 50-plus age group. In the heat of the race, I don't think about his age or that he is a man. I think about trying to pass him. I throw in a spurt of speed, but he responds and will not let me get ahead. He tries to pass me, but I will not let him. I don't know if our cat-and-mouse game is about being fearless or being fearful of being left behind to run alone in that dreaded pocket. So we push and respond and in doing so we push each other ever faster, chase each other across the bridge and through the twisty downhill section, then up that massive hill.

For once I have an advantage on the hill, because he is taller and heavier than I. Not that I can get far ahead of him. As hard as I am pushing, he pushes just as hard and will not let me get beyond his reach. I suspect pride is at stake. In a head-to-head race, what man wants to be beaten by a woman? I have experienced it many times at the end of a race—my presence seems to spur every man around me to sprint hard to the finish, if only, it seems, to beat me. Women rarely fear losing to a man; more often, we expect to lose, as I find myself thinking now. At the top of the hill, I am a step ahead, which gives me the inside on the turn. As I pass by a water station on that turn, I scoop up a water bottle. The Italian is on the outside, too far to reach for a bottle without conceding ground. After I take a sip and pour some cooling water over my head, I hand the bottle over to my opponent. Surprised, he takes it and thanks me. It never occurs to me not to share that water, for I am not trying to beat my opponent so much as I am using him, using his strength and speed to make me stronger and faster. And I am grateful for his competition.

On the downhill, his size gives him the advantage, and he pulls ahead. I chase after him, but weight and gravity pull him ever farther ahead. I pound as hard as I can down that monster hill. My quads cramp with the pounding my legs are taking. But the race will be over soon enough, and so I persist. Still, the gap between us widens.

At the bottom of the hill, the course cuts left and slopes up over another grade and then the finish line appears, just 500 meters off. The Italian has gotten a good 100 meters ahead, too far to catch, I think. I try to sprint, but I have no more energy to push the pace, I think.

And then out of nowhere, the gold-medal women's soccer team we had cheered on 2 days before suddenly appears. Its members stream down the hill, are now running alongside the course and running beside me! How I cursed myself for the fun I had helping them celebrate their triumph. And now they are here, a sisterhood of women runners pushing me on, cheering me into the finish.

I feel a wicked release of adrenaline and it pours into my legs like rocket fuel, launching me into another gear, into a speed that I did not know I had in me. I push faster and faster, closing the gap on the Italian until I catch him with about 30 meters to go to the finish line. And then I power past him. He has no answer for my speed (he has no soccer team cheering him on!), and I cross the finish line ahead, beating him by 9 seconds.

I have hardly caught my breath when the Italian I blew past rushes toward me. He wraps me in a giant hug and congratulates me on my finish. He is not upset that I poured on that sprint to power past him at the finish. He is not upset to be beaten by a woman. Rather, he thanks me for pushing him so hard through that final loop so he could achieve his best. *He thanks me.* And I thank him, tell him that I could not have run as hard without him pushing me.

As I stagger away from the finish line, a race official stops me to tell me that I have finished fourth in my age group. It doesn't register. My time is a massive disappointment, 1:45, 7 minutes slower than I had hoped to run here, though all the top runners finished 5 and even 10 minutes off their best times, too. Then it slowly sinks in. I started the year hoping for a top 10 finish in the women's 50-plus age group. Then I hoped for a top 5, and I managed a fourth. And I finished just a minute out of third, and just 2 minutes out of second.

In another minute, sixth in woman's 50-plus, Mary crosses the line. Hard on her heels, Phyllis finishes with a 40-second personal best, which is mind-blowing on this brutally hilly course and in this heat. But at the World Masters, older often is stronger and faster, as the women's 60-plus age category proves one of the toughest—Phyllis's time leaves her in fifth place. Had I been competing in that age group, my time would have placed me no higher than fourth.

Then, in another minute or so, Katherine crosses the line, for fourth in her 30-to-34 age group and just a few seconds out of third. And then Danielle comes in, gritting her teeth against the searing pain in her feet, to finish fourth in her 55-to-59 age group.

Days before the race, my hedonistic side had scouted out the perfect place to celebrate our race, a café that serves organic pizza, beer, and wine on an outdoor patio, just a 2-minute walk from the finish line and on the banks of the Po River, where the marathon kayaking race is taking place. The five of us, our families, and the women's soccer team commandeer several picnic tables. With draft beer flowing, we talk over the details of the race and our year, breaking into raucous hoots and cheering every time a kayak team passes by.

While none of us got on the podium, an outcome we could not control, we assure each other that we gave our best efforts in training and the race, and we are thrilled that we all came oh so scintillatingly close to claiming a medal. We are near euphoric with the endorphins, excitement, and beer coursing through us.

Then, after another pint, I will admit it: I start to wonder about the minute that separated me from third place and a bronze finish at the World Masters, the 2 minutes that kept me from a silver. If I had trained harder. . . . If I had set my sights even higher. . . . Had my watch been working so I could have paced myself better. . . . If the start of the race had been fair. . . . If I had listened to Bruce and gone out slower and finished faster. . . . If I hadn't had quite so much fun at these Games before the race. . . . If I had pushed myself even harder. . . .

Really, I ask myself, how could I feel so fantastic, so joyous, so energized at the end of a half-marathon? I should feel worse, shouldn't I? I should feel physically wrecked. I should have dug deeper, run harder to leave my all on the course.

And there is a nagging, vague feeling of . . . what? Of emptiness? Of *What next?*

My super-fit year has come to an end. But in the next instant, as I look around the patio at my friends, laughing and looking a decade younger than their years, I know that it is far better to run by feel and finish feeling good and smiling—if I want to be still racing at 85, like my running soul mother. And I know my running journey is far from over. I love these friends I am running with. I love the runner and person that I have become. All year long, I exceeded my wildest expectations as I ran my way into the best shape of my life. And in that journey, there is no finish line. There are no competitors, no winning or losing. There is only the striving, the continual striving to find the joy, the thrill, and the love in it.

ACKNOWLEDGMENTS

I gratefully acknowledge funding from the Canadian Institutes of Health Research, Canada Council for the Arts, and Access Copyright. Their generous support made this book possible, underwriting much of the research, extensive travel, and writing time.

This book simply would not exist without editor Lucy Kenward, who first contacted me with the idea of writing about the women's running boom and then offered critical support and feedback as I shaped the proposal. I am deeply grateful.

The brilliant Samantha Haywood of Transatlantic Literary Agency championed that proposal (to the extent of taking up running!) and brought it to my dream publisher, Rodale Books, and into the expert hands of executive editor Mark Weinstein. My handling editor, Julia Johnson, and copy editor, Nancy Elgin, were simply awesome to work with—everything they suggested made the book better. And thank you, Amy King, for the inspiring cover design.

When I needed teachers, they appeared everywhere: Kirsten Bedard, who provided excellent nutritional counseling and personal training and has become a dear friend; running sister and research guru Sooin Kim, who dug studies out of thin suggestions; Muscle Activation Techniques specialist Brad Thorpe, who showed me that stronger, balanced muscles are the way forward; and Dr. Leith Drury, who is such a phenomenal sports psychologist that she taught me how to be my own best supporter.

I deeply appreciate the help of researchers who lent me their expertise and led me to a greater understanding of the science of running, in particular Dr. Jason Vescovi, Dr. Greg Wells,

Dr. Mark Tarnopolsky, Dr. Bruce Urch, Dr. Kim Dawson, Dr. Cathy Sabiston, and Dr. Tanja Taivassalo.

I am indebted to the trailblazers who gave so generously of their time, wisdom, and hearts: the indomitable Linda Somers Smith; ultramarathon legend Pam Reed; the unstoppable Dr. Jean Marmoreo; yoga pioneer Ida Herbert; Iron Nun Sister Madonna Buder; Vancouver world-record holders BJ McHugh, Gwen McFarlan, Christa Bortignon, and Diane Palmason, as well as Olga Kotelko, who passsed at publication; the bighearted Sylvia Ruegger; and the trailblazing heart and soul of this women's running boom, Kathrine Switzer.

Many close friends listened to my stories and offered wise counsel and enthusiastic support when I needed it most: Dominique Cardona and Laurie Colbert; Anne Perdue; Karen Hanley; Peter Mansour; and Richard Almonte and Peter Schneider.

A big shout of thanks to our supporters at the World Masters and in life: head cheerleader Anna Speck, Ed Speck, Alan Shapiro, Tim Reibetanz, and running legend Bruce Kidd, who also pitched in with race strategy and much support for this book.

A writer and athlete could not ask for any greater inspiration than my mom, Isabel Webb, who has also given me her rock-solid support in everything I have taken on; ditto for my Ironman sister, Carol MacDonald, who hooked me on this running journey, which has made both my life and our relationship richer than I could ever have imagined.

Deepest thanks to my running pals who have suffered my company through thousands of miles, pushing me to achieve my personal best not only on the road, but also in life: my coach, Elaine McCrea; Mary Speck; Phyllis Berck; Danielle Beausoleil; Katherine Landell; Janet Wilson and the Tuesday morning running gang; and Barbara Lawrence and all my running pals at the Runners Shop.

And finally, to Nancy Lyons—you are in my heart, every step of the way.

INDEX

ABOUT THE AUTHOR

Margaret Webb is an avid runner, volunteer running coach for underprivileged kids, screenwriter, author, and journalist. Her features have been published in magazines and newspapers such as *Sports Illustrated Women* and the *Globe and Mail*. This is her second nonfiction book. She lives in Toronto, where she teaches magazine writing at Ryerson University.